# ROCKY ELSOM

# ROCKY ELSOM
## LEADER OF THE WALLABIES
### BRET HARRIS

HarperCollins*Publishers*

**HarperCollins***Publishers*

First published in Australia in 2011
by HarperCollins*Publishers* Australia Pty Limited
ABN 36 009 913 517
harpercollins.com.au

Copyright © Rocky Elsom and Bret Harris 2011

The right of Bret Harris to be identified as the author of this work
has been asserted by him under the *Copyright Amendment
(Moral Rights) Act 2000*.

This work is copyright. Apart from any use as permitted under the
*Copyright Act 1968*, no part may be reproduced, copied, scanned, stored
in a retrieval system, recorded, or transmitted, in any form or by any
means, without the prior written permission of the publisher.

**HarperCollins***Publishers*
Level 13, 201 Elizabeth Street, Sydney, NSW 2000, Australia
31 View Road, Glenfield, Auckland 0627, New Zealand
A 53, Sector 57, Noida, UP, India
77–85 Fulham Palace Road, London, W6 8JB, United Kingdom
2 Bloor Street East, 20th floor, Toronto, Ontario M4W 1A8, Canada
10 East 53rd Street, New York NY 10022, USA

ISBN 978 0 7322 9247 8

Cover design by Matt Stanton
Cover photograph of Rocky Elsom by Adam Knott
Back cover image by AFP/Getty Images
Picture section design by Alicia Freile, Tango Media
Typeset in 11/20pt Sabon by Kirby Jones

*To Vicki*
*Matriarch, muse*

# Contents

| | |
|---|---|
| AUTHOR'S NOTE | ix |
| FOREWORD | xiii |
| PREFACE | 1 |
| ONE OF A KIND | 5 |
| OF GREAT AND GOOD MEN | 28 |
| ROCK DOG | 54 |
| BOB DWYER'S EYES | 76 |
| MAN OF GOLD | 112 |
| THE TALISMAN | 154 |
| A BIT OF CRAIC | 184 |
| COME TOGETHER | 229 |
| ROCK OF AGES | 283 |
| ACKNOWLEDGEMENTS | 287 |

# AUTHOR'S NOTE

Just before the Wallabies embarked on their tour of Japan, Britain and Ireland at the end of 2009, I approached Rocky about writing his authorised biography. The first question Rocky asked me was whether I was sure he had done enough in his career to date to justify a book. I was convinced he had done more than enough, particularly after he had inspired Irish province Leinster to its maiden victory in the Holy Grail of European rugby, the Heineken Cup. Rocky is one of the greatest Wallabies of all time and he is now the Australian captain. And he is a winner. It seemed like a no-brainer to me.

Rocky seemed interested, but he asked me if he could think about it, which was a reasonable enough request. I then learned something quite revealing about Rocky. If you give Rocky a day to make a decision, he will make a decision in a day. If you give him six months to make a decision, he'll make a decision in six months. Rocky investigates an issue from every conceivable angle and researches the hell out of it. While engaged in this exhaustive process, his mind is open, but once he has made a decision he is firm, comfortable in the knowledge he has examined the question as thoroughly as humanly possible.

You could imagine, then, my deep sense of disappointment when nine months later Rocky told me the idea of a book interested him, but not now. Rocky knew he had a unique story to tell and that one day he would tell it. He gave me the impression that he wanted to wait until he retired or was close to retiring before going to print. He also indicated he would consider collaborating with me if he ever decided to do a biography, which was all well and good, but I knew there was a another kind of book which could be written now.

The morning after the Wallabies defeated Fiji in Canberra to open the 2010 international season, I took Rocky aside and asked him if he had any objections to me writing a book about him, not an unauthorised biography, but a portrait. I would not even interview Rocky for the book. I would just write it. Like Clint Eastwood in the movie *Dirty Harry*, Rocky looked down at me from his 197cm height and said: 'Go ahead, knock yourself out.'

I knocked myself out for the next eight months, creating a portrait of Rocky as seen through the eyes of those who knew him best — a select number of family, friends, coaches and teammates. Originally, I intended to write a kind of tribute to Rocky and I make no apologies for saying I came to praise Rocky, not to bury him. But as Rocky's portrait was drawn even I was surprised by what I saw. This is not just the story of a great Australian sportsman, but an idealistic young man who refuses to compromise his beliefs, whatever the cost, and like some mythic hero has had to overcome hardship and obstacles to achieve his goals.

## AUTHOR'S NOTE

It occurred to me that Rocky Elsom is the quintessential Australian hero. He has never sought the limelight, preferring instead to concentrate on his game. Self-effacing and unassuming, he is reluctant to be seen as a hero. Nonetheless, others within the rugby world have recognised his innate abilities and encouraged him to be a leader and role model.

As a courtesy I gave Rocky a copy of the manuscript for his perusal. I do not know whether it was a conscious or subconscious decision, but Rocky asked me to meet him for breakfast in the Book Kitchen Café in Surry Hills, an inner-city suburb of Sydney. It was certainly an appropriately named venue. As we devoured our scrambled eggs on sourdough toast the Beatles song 'Across The Universe' started playing in the background. It made me think about Rocky and his world and how nothing's going to change it.

Bret Harris, April 2011

# FOREWORD

## ROCKY ELSOM:
## WHY IS HE SO GENUINELY INTRIGUING?

I asked Robbie Deans why he had chosen Rocky Elsom as captain of the Wallabies. Without blinking, he answered: 'Because he is a true warrior and he lives it! And he is seriously smart.'

That assessment of Rocky was spot on. Rocky is soft and sensitive on the surface – but he has a titanium core. Much more suprising is that his physical power and presence is equalled by his smartness.

The first time I met Rocky, I presumed that his impact as a person would be totally dominated by his physical presence and 'Viking warrior' mindset, and that he would be a bit of a loner.

I can still remember the shock I felt the first time it hit me that Rocky's smartness genuinely equalled his physical power and presence.

Initially the extent of his intelligence was not obvious. It is a bit buried in his quiet scepticism and tendency to deeply examine the many sides of any issue. But once you see his intelligence it is unmistakeable and distinctive in everything he does.

He also buries how smart he is in nudging quiet questions: he asks, 'Tell me what you think of this possibility mate?' rather than make charismatic pronouncements. He always seeks to empower others and he has the patient humility to wait until others feel like they can 'own the solution' that he is nudging them towards. But when an urgent new solution or direction is needed, like during in-game time, he will bring it on and affect it with a sledgehammer!

A big part of Rocky's uniqueness is that he has a brain that can identify and act on the behaviours that really make a difference — for himself and for the team.

Rocky is also very attuned to personal and social connections. He profoundly understands that off-field *authentic quality of connections* between the players will be highly linked to their in-game performance.

Bret Harris has done something truly fascinating in this book — he has crafted together insights from those closest to Rocky. Each insight is a pointer to what it takes to be a great rugby captain and inspire an entire team to always do better. They all show Rocky's uniqueness across diverse parts — and stages — of his life, from the rugged individualist teenager to the sensitive family man and powerful leader. The interviews come together in a clear and complementary way, to show how the whole of Rocky is so much bigger than the sum of his parts.

But this book is not just about a unique rugby captain. It is about what it takes to be a great leader. And it is inspirational to anyone seeking to be the best they can be: the best of Rocky reflects the best of what we all could aspire to be.

I end this foreword with a fascinating glimpse from inside the 'Rock'.

I emailed Rocky and asked him what is his essence beyond the idealistic image.

He answered with reluctance. Rocky is a private man whose actions speak louder than his words and his answer reflects the self-belief and vulnerability of true greatness:

'I work hard on my habits to affect how I act. I have a strong idea of what is right, the person I want to be, and being that is my first priority. I also believe that if I am fully and truly immersed, then that is the best way for me to affect the group. I think that is very powerful in many senses — whether it's popular or not I'd say I have to act in a way that is true to what I believe and become what I idolise. And that is also my biggest struggle.'

Dr Evian Gordon
Founding Director, The Brain Dynamics Centre, Westmead Hospital
Director, BRAINnet.net Foundation
CEO, Brain Resource Company

# PREFACE
## SATORI IN BRISBANE

> A man's ego is the fountainhead of human progress.
>
> Ayn Rand

I was having coffee in an Italian café in Brisbane with Ireland's Australian defence coach, Les Kiss, when I received a 'kick in the eye', the literal translation of the Japanese word *satori*, which means 'sudden illumination, sudden awakening', as American beat writer Jack Kerouac described it in the opening passage of his 1966 novel *Satori in Paris*. Kiss, a former Test rugby league winger who coached defence at the NSW Waratahs for several years, was nicknamed 'Lighthouse Les' because of his tendency to blink a lot. In an enlightening interview, Kiss certainly shone a light on the elusive subject of this portrait, Rocky Elsom, which allowed me to see him clearly for the very first time.

'Have you ever read *The Fountainhead* by Ayn Rand?' Kiss asked me. 'She had a philosophy called objectivism. There's a guy in *Fountainhead* called Howard Roark. He is the quintessential character in this book. He represented her ideal man.

'I see Howard Roark in Rocky. Not totally, but I see this man who says, "I'm not going to be determined by other people's views of me. My existence is for me, but that is not at the expense of being a team man. My worth will be to make sure I'm right to do what I have to do. If I don't fulfil that first, how can I help the team?" He was a man who just knew himself and understood himself. He was comfortable with himself, totally. He didn't need the acceptance of everyone to stand tall himself.

'Read that book and you'll understand what I mean. He is the closest thing I've come to it. When I read that book and I read the first paragraph or page, I loved it. It talks about this person, Ellsworth Toohey. He would subjugate himself for the good of everything. Is that a virtue, or is Howard Roark virtuous? There is selfishness there, but is it a bad thing?'

Listening to Kiss describe Rocky's personality, I had a *satori* in Brisbane. After our interview I rushed to the nearest bookstore and bought a copy of *The Fountainhead*. In the novel, Rand espouses her philosophy of objectivism, which portrays selfishness as a virtue. The hero of the book, Howard Roark, is Rand's ideal man of independent-mindedness and integrity: the embodiment of the human spirit.

The Ellsworth Toohey character whom Kiss referred to is Roark's main adversary. The manipulative Toohey is Rand's personification of evil, representing the oppressive forces of collectivism. A newspaper columnist, Toohey promotes altruism as the ideal social goal, but his ulterior motive is power. His mission is to destroy the spirit of individualism, encapsulated by Roark. For Roark, independence is the only measure of virtue and the standard of personal dignity.

A young architect, Roark, at first struggles to make a living without compromising his ideals. Railing against convention, Roark eventually designs many landmark buildings in a modernistic style in the face of opposition from a conservative establishment that favours tradition. But Roark is arrested for dynamiting a building he designed, which was modified by other architects brought in to water down his vision. The climax of the novel is Roark's trial, which represents the triumph of individualism over collectivism.

As Wallabies captain, Rocky is one of the best known football players of any code in Australia and, after his heroic deeds for Irish province Leinster, he is also a household name in Europe. From Dublin to Durban every rugby supporter on the planet knows of Rocky, but how many actually know who he *really* is? Intensely private, Rocky has been described as an enigma by rugby journalists. He is the most misunderstood of Wallabies.

*The Fountainhead* provided me with a prism through which to view Rocky. Like Howard Roark, Rocky is a young man of independent-mindedness and integrity, not that that was any particular kind of revelation to me or to anyone who knew him reasonably well. It was more the concept of selfishness as a virtue that I found so enlightening. Rand's definition of selfish is to remain true to one's ideals against the influence of others. That's Rocky. You can see this defining characteristic recurring throughout his career, particularly in all the big decisions he has made about where he has played. In other interviews for this portrait with some of the key figures in Rocky's life — family members, coaches and players — this view of him as a man of immense independent-mindedness and integrity is reinforced time and again.

Yet it occurred to me that some people in the Australian rugby community had the wrong perception of Rocky. They see his individuality — or selfishness — as a negative. When Rocky was appointed Wallabies captain in 2009, a former Australian Test player, and analyst of the game, told me he thought Rocky was the 'totally wrong personality' for the job. Sure, Rocky is a rugged individualist. He often reminds me of American actor Clint Eastwood in a spaghetti western — the strong, silent type. You can almost hear the theme music to *The Good, the Bad and the Ugly* playing in the background whenever Rocky walks into a room.

What a lot of rugby followers failed to appreciate about Rocky is that his individualism is a force for the greater good. No one has ever explained this apparent contradiction better than Les Kiss in that Brisbane café, making the comparison between Rocky and Howard Roark. Once you see Rocky reflected in the prism of *The Fountainhead* it becomes clear how at once he is an individual and a team player and how his individualism benefits the team. Rather than being the totally wrong personality to captain the Wallabies, Rocky was the totally right man to lead the team.

# 1
## ONE OF A KIND

*You'll be the colours of a rainbow and we'll watch you glow.*

**Kelly and Sam Elsom**

There is more to Rocky than Howard Roark, much more. After covering Rocky's career for eight years as a journalist, I thought I had a fair idea of him, but when I came to write this book I realised I hardly knew him at all. Not really. Sure, everyone in rugby circles knows Rocky as a laconic, even mildly eccentric, character, who is maybe a little bit different from the average rugby player. A smart guy, no doubt. But I was surprised not only by the depth and complexity of his personality, but by the richness of his interests and talents. Rocky is a modern-day Renaissance man, a Leonardo da Vinci in studs. Apart from being one of the greatest Wallabies of his generation, Rocky is a musician, a philosopher, an entrepreneur and a pilot, just to list a few of his pastimes. But it is part of Rocky's taciturn nature that he does not readily reveal these things — or much else — about himself. Most people enjoy speaking about, or even boasting about, their interests — especially if that is landing a rickety two-seater T-Bird sideways on a slippery runway — not Rocky. He rarely talks about it, he just does it.

But there is something more again, something at the very core of Rocky's being that distinguishes him from most. Unexpectedly, Rocky is empathetic. Okay, maybe he is not a textbook case, or maybe he is. But Rocky has the ability to enter the feeling or spirit of another person, and gain an appreciative perception or understanding, as the *Macquarie Dictionary* definition states. On the rugby field, Rocky leads by example, his 'follow me' approach. And he has a great knowledge of the strategies and tactics of the game. But it is this feeling for others that really makes him an exceptional leader, not just of a rugby team, but in life in general.

With such a unique person, I did not think I could paint an accurate portrait of Rocky without knowing the forces that had shaped him. Rocky has always jealously guarded his background, particularly his family, of whom he is highly protective. While researching this book I scoured 4000 newspaper clippings on Rocky and found few references to his family; over 10 years of press coverage and just a couple of vague references to what Rocky would consider the most important element in his life — remarkable. No mention of his mother or the support of his numerous brothers and sisters or his time growing up. Sports pages are filled with odes to family, dedications and heartfelt thankyous, but not from Rocky. Despite this obvious reluctance, I knew that Rocky's family was the place to start this book.

Rocky's mother, Vicki, was flying down to Sydney from Noosa on Queensland's Sunshine Coast to watch him play for the Wallabies against England. I rang Vicki to arrange an interview and we agreed to meet at Rocky's younger brother Rory's terrace house in an inner-city Sydney suburb. I guess I was expecting a tall, blonde Amazon. Vicki was blonde, to be sure, but she was petite. I am the size of a third-grade club halfback and she was shorter than me. I soon discovered, however, she had a larger-than-life personality. As quiet and reserved as Rocky is, Vicki is vivacious and, luckily for me, talkative.

Vicki wore a long purple sweater with a purple and black scarf, faded blue denim jeans and black suede boots. Her dark outfit was set off by an antique turquoise necklace inscribed with the Chinese characters for the Year of the Horse, which Rocky had bought her in Bellagio on Lake Como in Italy. You could see where Rocky got his good looks, the resemblance between mother and son being quite strong, albeit without the battle scars and broken nose. We sat down at a wooden table in the kitchen to do our interview, drinking coffee. At times I could hear the inflection of Rocky's voice in Vicki's. Then, disaster struck. After talking for over an hour the tape in my cassette player unravelled somehow and looked like a strip of fusilli pasta. I had lost everything. Sheepishly, I suggested we might have to start over. 'That's alright,' Vicki beamed. 'I could talk about Rocky all day.' And we very nearly did.

Rocky inherited his height from the Elsom side of the family, who, according to legend, were descended from Vikings. I was not looking to do a genealogy of the Elsom ancestral line — Rocky can do that himself — but I was intrigued about his Viking heritage, as unverified as it was, although the Norse origin of the name Elson, later spelt Elsom, supported the claim to Scandinavian ancestry. With his dark blond hair, blue eyes and powerful physique, Rocky could easily be cast as a Viking warrior. It is not hard to imagine Rocky, sword in hand, pillaging a medieval village with the same ferocity and raw aggression with which he attacks opposing rugby teams.

Vicki related some of her own family background to me. Her maiden name was Wood, but there were also Stuarts in the family tree — as in Mary, Queen of Scots — on her paternal grandmother's side. 'Dad said we should have been on the throne,' Vicki said. 'We are very solid stock.' Rocky was very much like his grandfather, Jack Wood, who passed away at 90 years of age while the Wallabies were touring South Africa in 2010. 'Dad had this high moral standard for everything,' Vicki said. 'His catch phrase was "he ain't heavy". He always used to say that. I had to give a speech at Dad's 80th. I said there is one thing Dad has taught us and that is to love hard. He taught us how to care and to have a moral code that runs through your veins that you live by.'

Vicki vividly remembers the day Rocky was born: Valentine's Day 1983, two days before the Ash Wednesday bushfires, at the Jesse McPherson Hospital in Melbourne. A big boy, he weighed 10 pound 4 ounces (4.6 kilograms). 'I had him fifteen minutes after I arrived at the hospital,' Vicki said. 'My husband was driving. I was going through contractions and Dusty [Rocky's older brother] was pulling my hair. We went the wrong way to get to the hospital. We ended up going across the street and up the other side of the road because of the trams.

'I was really concerned before he was born because I had all the babies close together and I was worried he would be a little weakling. When he was born he didn't cry. He was like, okay, this is where I am. I thought, oh my god! Look at him. He is so perfect. I was so relieved. We had just seen the *Superman* movie in which they wrap the baby Superman in foil to send him to earth. Because Rocky was a big baby they put him in a thermal blanket to keep his temperature from dropping. They had him all wrapped up. When we went up to the ward all the other kids were with me on the bed and Sam [older brother] kept saying, "Superman! Superman!"'

I could not interview Rocky's mother and not ask her why she gave him such an unusual name. There has been so much conjecture about Rocky's given name. Most people assume he was named after the Rocky Balboa character in the Sylvester Stallone movies or they think Rocky is a nickname that he goes by, or is short for Rockford or Rochester or something like that. Vicki told me she named him Rocky Dan after the 'two heroes' in her favourite song, 'Rocky Raccoon'.

In a way, Rocky's name has helped to define him. Because of its connotation with pugilism and toughness, he has had to live up to it. If Rocky was not strong, physically and mentally, his name would have been ironic, a parody, and a subject of ridicule. It is a little bit like the inverse of the Johnny Cash song 'A Boy Named Sue', in which a father names his boy Sue to ensure he grows up tough and strong because with a name like that he will surely have to learn to defend himself. But because Rocky is who he is, the name seems to fit him perfectly. You really cannot imagine him as a Peter, Paul or Bill. He's a Rocky.

As I listened to Vicki it became evident there was a powerful bond between her and Rocky. 'It would be impossible to have a better son or brother,' Vicki said. 'He is generous of spirit. I wouldn't say generous financially, even though he is to me. He's got your back. He's that kind of person. People do not know that Rocky is all about loyalty and solidarity. He is for the greater good.'

The other Elsom kids teased Vicki about Rocky being her favourite. 'Rocky is very close to Mum,' his sister Kelly said. 'Their relationship is so strong. As a baby he didn't want anyone else but Mum. I was a little bit older so I would help Mum look after the boys. They were always quite happy to come to me, but Rocky never would. Rocky never really wanted to go to my grandmother or me. All I wanted to do was squeeze his cheeks. He had such big chubby cheeks. And he had such a rugby bum. Even at that age. None of the other boys had it — a huge bum that stuck out. I was always running around after him. He hated it.'

Kelly is a songwriter and she collaborated with her brother Sam on a song called 'One of a Kind', which was inspired by Rocky. 'The first line of "One of a Kind" is "you'll be the colours of a rainbow and we'll watch you glow",' Kelly said. 'That was a reference to the fact that as a family we get so much enjoyment out of Rocky. I feel so blessed to have him as a brother. He loves hard. And with everything that is going on in his life and how busy he is, he's always got time for us. It was always family first.'

Vicki had told me that Rocky was very protective towards his sister. I could see why. With short, blonde hair, Kelly looked beautiful in a black turtleneck sweater, black leggings and over-the-knee brown leather boots. 'God help any guy who wanted to come and take me out,' Kelly said. 'Rock always had that death-stare thing going on where he wouldn't say anything. Very protective; he has calmed down a little bit now.'

I am wondering if my description of Kelly looking beautiful will result in a Rocky death-stare or worse. Gulp!

I was keen to gain an Elsom male perspective of Rocky and arranged to interview his brother Sam, who became a fashion designer after deferring medical studies to travel overseas for two years. Sam heads up the Elsom Co-op, which is a unique production house that creates sustainable textiles by collaborating with every link in the supply chain from organic cotton farmers in Punjab, natural silk farms in Guanga to corn starch packaging in Waterloo, Sydney.

'While the garments are very eco friendly, the core of the business is built on the principle of efficiency — sustainable and organic farming procedures, being the most efficient way of doing things, if done well,' Sam said.

My interview with Sam was delayed a few weeks following the birth of his daughter, Sugar — a very Elsom name. We met at the Elsom Holdings office in a converted warehouse in inner-city Sydney. Coincidentally, I lived in the building for ten years, but I did not cross paths with the Elsoms, having moved out before they moved in. There were some writers and artists living in the building, which I think appealed to the bohemian Elsom spirit.

Sitting at a wooden bench top in the downstairs kitchen of the ground-floor warehouse office, Sam reminded me of a folk rocker with his bushy blond beard and straggly blond hair. He was wearing a brown fedora, Levi shorts, moccasins and a T-shirt, which he designed. On the front of the T-shirt was the iconic picture of the Beatles walking across Abbey Road, but the artwork had been altered so that John Lennon and George Harrison appeared to be ascending into Heaven.

'Boisterous; he always liked to fight,' Sam said of Rocky. 'Fighting was a daily occurrence. Us boys would fight every single day. In fact, I remember one time when I was young thinking how strange it was for a day to go by without us having a brawl. We used to fight a lot, but we are best mates. Even now my brothers are my best friends, for sure. We have our friends and then we have each other. We were brothers in arms, but we were no kind of gang. I think we looked out for each other, but at the same time we had our own lives. When we were young I felt like the eldest in the family, like the eldest of the boys anyway. As they grew bigger than me, particularly Rocky, we all just became more or less a team.

'Rock always surprised me. I've got this memory of him being three years old, maybe even two. We were living in Frankston on the Mornington Peninsula. I was in this ute. I had done something wrong. I don't know what I had done, but I was in trouble. We just found refuge in the ute. Rocky had been somewhere and he had blood coming out of his head. We were kind of chatting I guess, but predominantly we were sitting in silence. The next thing an ambulance came for him and he left. He had been hit by a car, but he never mentioned it. He never dramatised the fact he was injured or had been hit by a car. He just came and hung out as if nothing had happened.

'He has always been a little bit the same. Sometimes I feel like we find things out in the newspaper before he has told us. Sometimes he likes it to be that way. It's kind of good in a way because he does it for the best, as opposed to any other, reason. He doesn't do it for theatrics or to make a point or for any other reason other than because he thinks it's best. I kind of admire that about him.

'[He was] always unconventional in the way he would do things. There might be a way that things were always done and Rocky would want to do things a little bit different. He always had his way. Rocky can be objective in certain environments, but he has pretty firm points of view on things. He is well educated and I think he researches a lot of things. It's good to have a conversation with him, but he is pretty firm in his position on certain things.'

According to Kelly, Rocky could never be a politician. 'He couldn't be persuaded to do something. If he thinks it's right, he's going to do it, if they don't like it, tough. If you want to sack me, sack me. I'm not going to do something I don't feel is the right thing. He has always been this kind of kid. And because he hasn't gone with the flow sometimes he has been ridiculed for it, but I think that's where you can see leadership in someone – where they are not just a yes man. The players look at him and they know he's not a yes man. He is going to be fighting for them behind the scenes and that's a really big thing.'

Many regard Rocky as an enigma, but he is actually fairly predictable because as Shakespeare would have described him, he is as constant as the northern star. 'The one thing that stands true to the way he has been all his life is that he has always remained his own person,' Sam said. 'He has just done things the way he has done things from the very beginning.'

Kelly recalled Rocky's fearlessness even as a baby. The Elsoms' grandpa Bob was a gruff farmer and all the kids were frightened of him, except Rocky, who Bob called Valentine Dan. 'When we used to go to visit him in Stawell in the Grampians we were all scared of him because he used to yell and carry on. He would never be friendly,' Kelly said. 'And Rocky would laugh. He was only a baby. Nine months old. He would laugh hysterically every time Grandpa yelled. Grandpa was like what is wrong with that child, laughing at me? But it got to the point where Rocky was his favourite because Rocky was always happy with him.'

Vicki recalled another story. When Rocky was five years old he broke his wrist trying to skateboard down a hill at the request of his then girlfriend Kate. Maybe embarrassed, he did not show he was hurt so no one realised he was seriously injured. 'When I got home with the shopping, Sam said Rocky fell and hurt himself,' Vicki said. 'Sam told me he put him to bed because he hurt his arm. When I went up to his bedroom Sam had put a bandage on him. I said have you hurt yourself, darling? He said yes, it's broken. I said darling if it was broken, you would really know. You'd be crying like anything. He said oh, okay, so it's not broken. I said just rest it. About an hour later I had a look at it again. I said does it hurt a lot? He said yeah. I took him to the hospital. A guy came in with a spear through his leg and Rocky was like wow! This is so cool! And his wrist was broken. They put it in plaster. We had to have three lots of plaster because he'd get sick of it and break the plaster so he could wrestle and do all the things he wanted to do. We had to keep re-setting it.'

Growing up in Melbourne, Rocky's first sporting love was not rugby, not even Australian football, but wrestling. Rocky was fanatical about wrestling and watched it on television all the time. His hero was Hulk Hogan. His brother Robert gave him a Hulk Hogan figurine, which became his most treasured possession. 'He still loves wrestling,' Vicki said. 'They used to tag wrestle in their undies. Freezing cold in winter and they would be tag wrestling. He didn't have footballers. He had wrestlers.'

Rocky was about ten years old when his parents split up after moving to Noosa to make a fresh start. Rocky and his brothers and sister stayed with Vicki. 'It felt like she always was [a single parent] really, because our dad wasn't home much even when they were together,' Kelly said. 'He was always off working. It always tended to be Mum and us.

'Mum is a bit of a gypsy at heart. We had a kind of bohemian upbringing. I remember being a child; everyone would fall in love with her, even my friends. Your mum is so nice. I wish I was in your family. The way she related to us ... no matter how old we were it was never like separation because she was the mum. She was like my friend and then my mum. For the boys she was young at heart. Life was to be lived.

'By the time I was 17 we had moved 14 times. We were constantly moving. I remember when [my parents] broke up we moved into a dive of a place. Mum hated it, but she never let on to us that she did. She turned it into this amazing little pad. She put all her heart and energy into the garden. She's got such a green thumb. She made this little rental home come to life.'

It became obvious to me while talking to members of the Elsom family that much of Rocky's strength of character came from Vicki, as did all of the family's. 'She made everything seem like an adventure even when it was really tough,' Kelly said. 'I remember one time she had a really big fight with Dad. I would have been 16. In the middle of the night we packed up the car and drove. Mum was okay, we're off on a holiday. The boys were excited. They didn't know she had just broken up and left him.'

As you could imagine for a single parent raising five children, making ends meet in the Elsom household was at times pretty tricky, reminiscent of the Beatles song 'Lady Madonna'. Vicki remembers Rocky asking her if they were poor. 'I said, oh my god, Rocky, no! We're not poor. Why are you asking that question? He said someone at school said we were poor. I said, do you think we are poor? He goes I don't feel poor. I said, if you don't feel poor, then we are not poor.

'There were times when we just didn't have enough. We weren't the only ones, but without going into it we had our challenges as a family. We always set the table. It was a ritual for the table to be set with a tablecloth and each one would take pride in it. Maybe the boys would bring in some flowers from outside or put special glasses on the table. It was always a special time. It's how you live whether you are poor or not.'

Interestingly, Vicki recalls Rocky never corrected people in later years, even if they were being critical of him, when they assumed he had always enjoyed a comfortable life.

Rocky never wanted his mother to feel ashamed about not being able to provide everything he wanted or even needed. 'I think it was his 10th birthday,' Vicki said. 'I was really broke and his shoes fell apart. He came home from school and the sole had come off his shoe. I thought, god, he can't go to school with the sole off his shoe. I had only 20 dollars for his birthday present and now he needed shoes. I didn't have any money for the shoes. I said to him do you want shoes for your birthday? He said, yeah, I do. I really want them, Mum. It's not just because my shoes are broken. I really do want them.

'We went to a shoe shop and he picked up these sneakers and said what about these? I said, no, I think they are too expensive. He said okay and put them down. He goes to another pair. What about these ones? I'm like no. We go through all of the shoes and finally he comes down to a pair of Converse. What about these? I looked at the price: 18 dollars, terrific. He said I don't know why I didn't see them first off. I like these ones the best anyway. And that's what he was like. Never ever made you feel bad.'

While talking to Vicki about Rocky's childhood you get a sense of what really makes her proud of him. 'He has empathy,' Vicki said. 'He can feel what other people are going through. Some people do it naturally and some people have to be taught it. He always understood it. He could see what it must be like.'

At Tewantin State School, Rocky made friends with a boy named Shane, who had Down's syndrome. Some of the other kids picked on Shane, but they soon stopped when Rocky started looking after him.

'One time at school there was an almighty thunderstorm just as the lunchtime bell rang. Shane hadn't run back to class with everyone else and their teacher sent Rocky to find him. He was under a tree at the bottom of the playground, petrified of the lightning. They ran across the oval together in the torrential rain. Back in the classroom, a crack of lightning sent Shane running to Rocky. The teacher wasn't having any of it. She wouldn't let them sit together and Shane started to cry. When Rocky came home from school that day he told me the story and how he was so upset with his teacher. A week later I received a call from her asking me if I knew what was troubling Rocky. He wasn't answering any questions or participating in class discussions, something that he normally loved. [When I told her,] she said, oh my god, I feel terrible. I just wanted Shane to learn that in the real world Rocky wasn't always going to be there to watch out for him. She explained this to Rocky, but he didn't buy it. He said the real world is never going to be like that for Shane, is it? What difference does it make? She let Rocky have his way.'

But Rocky was not perfect. It may seem incongruous, but the same sensitive boy who would befriend a kid with Down's syndrome and look after him was the same one who would be fighting at lunch time and spending a lot of time in the principal's office. 'Rocky was very prone to fighting and would often get into fights at school, particularly in primary school,' Vicki said. 'I was concerned because I knew he could be easily angered. It was very worrying. I knew he wasn't the type of boy to pick on people, but he did have a temper and couldn't step away from a fight and it didn't always work out for him.'

Old school friend Sam McGregor remembered an incident on Rocky's first day at Noosa High. While most kids were finding their feet and were excited about meeting new people, Rocky was initiating himself into school life in his own way. 'I knew Rocky's cousin Tom from Yeppoon and was keen to meet up with [Rocky] 'cos I'd just moved to Noosa and was starting at a new school,' Sam said. 'When I saw him he was in a fight with a senior and I wondered what he was thinking.'

No doubt, Rocky paid for his error of judgement, but he could not back down. I guessed that sort of incident gave you an insight into Rocky's natural aggressiveness on the field, but Vicki disagreed, arguing that he had learnt to control his temper. 'I really noticed when Rocky matured because he didn't react any more, and you see it all the time on the field,' Vicki said. 'When he was younger anything would make him angry and he would start fighting in spite of what was good for him. He would react to any kind of provocation. What I see now is someone who is the exact opposite, someone who virtually never reacts without thinking. Sure, he is aggressive on the field, but he is being proactive and doing it on his terms, showing discipline. He has benefitted greatly from controlling that part of his temperament.'

Vicki was right. If you look closely at Rocky's career, there have been numerous occasions where he has ignored provocation as if it had never even occurred. In Rocky's Super 12 debut for NSW Waratahs against arch-rivals Queensland Reds, he received a clear blow to the head from Wallabies number 8 Toutai Kefu — for which Kefu was penalised — but did not react at all. Perhaps you could argue there would be other reasons why a 20-year-old rookie would disregard intimidation from a powerful international forward, but this has become a pattern of Rocky's behaviour, which suggests otherwise. Fast-forward seven years: Rocky came to the aid of Brumbies captain and number 8 Stephen Hoiles in Pretoria and was hit from behind by Bulls skipper and second-rower Victor Matfield in what could easily have been a suspensible offence. Again no reaction, just an evasive roll and back into the defensive line.

For a player of such high intensity, Rocky's career has been clean on and off the field, with not even a whisper of scandal or wrongdoing, which unfortunately cannot be said for some of his ex-teammates, who have had their multi-million-dollar contracts torn up for one reason or another. It may have been Rocky's relationship with his stepfather, Russell Clarke, that helped him to learn self-control and shape his life. Russell had, by his own admission, an awful temper and penchant for fighting as a young boy and still bears the scars today. 'I got cleaned up as a kid and lost my front teeth,' Russell told me.

As the story goes, Russell had copped some sledging from older kids while riding his bike in 1940s Melbourne suburbia. Showing a little more circumspection than Rocky at the same age, Russell rode to a safe distance before returning fire with some sledging of his own. Unfortunately for Russell, another group of kids appeared on the other side of the road, blocking his escape. Needless to say, it did not end well for Russell. According to Vicki, the Elsom boys found this story hilarious. I would guess it would have endeared Rocky to Russell, knowing they had to deal with the same demons growing up, albeit 40 years apart.

Russell had to win the approval of the Elsom boys, who were very protective of their mother. 'They were the men of the family,' Vicki said. 'They took that very seriously. When Russell came to pick me up they shook his hand. He couldn't just pick me up at the door. He had to come in. They had to talk to him, just like a father might do if he was checking out the date. They were always little men. To me they were never like toddlers. They were always like little grown-ups.'

Russell grew very fond of the family and they of him, to the point where he obtained a kind of cult status within the family circle. 'Russell could always relate to the boys,' Kelly said. 'When they moved in he said listen, there are two things I won't tolerate.

Fighting and swearing. Everything else we'll get through. The boys weren't wild. They were good boys, but they were boisterous. And all of a sudden here is this man who is very old school. He grew up in a very good family. Manners, shaking hands and looking people in the eye when you spoke to them and being honest and true was very, very important to him. He taught that to the boys. He instilled it into them.'

When I had the idea of flying up to the Sunshine Coast to see for myself where Rocky had grown up, Russell offered to chauffeur me around. I arranged to meet him in a bar in Noosa. As I approached him he was reading a copy of *The Australian*, the newspaper I worked for, and, grinning, held it for me to see. Around 70 years of age, Russell was short and stocky, but he looked fitter than me, 20 years his junior. He was wearing a T-shirt and shorts, which is like a uniform on the Sunshine Coast, and quite conservative for Russell, who once attended a formal function at Nudgee College in a Hawaiian shirt, khaki shorts, sandals and an aqua tie with orange pineapples on it.

Russell is partially deaf as a result of a fall on a building site, but he can make out what you are saying if you speak loudly and clearly. We had a pasta lunch in a restaurant on Hastings Street and then he gave me a guided tour of the landmarks of Rocky's life in Noosa. It was like a Rocky version of 'Penny Lane' or 'Strawberry Fields Forever'. We drove over to Tewantin, a working-class suburb neighbouring Noosa, where the Elsoms had moved from house to house. Vicki could never afford removalists and I pictured Rocky and his brothers carrying furniture through the suburban streets. We pulled up in front of Tewantin State School and Russell pointed out a signboard at the entrance. He then showed me a photograph on his mobile phone of that same signboard taken the day Rocky was appointed Wallabies captain. It read: 'Rocky Elsom, Past Student, Aust – Captain, Rugby Union.' I could see the pride in Russell's eyes as he showed me the picture.

Back in Noosa we went past Le Monde Café where Rocky and his brothers had worked, often after a swim at the secluded Little Cove Beach at the southern end of the town. 'The boys had a lot of fun,' Russell told me as we passed the full brick house on the Noosa riverfront where Rocky spent his teenage years. The boys would swim across the river and play football in a park on the other side, go water-skiing or race each other around the neighbourhood on skateboards, which is still a mode of transport for the Elsoms to this day.

'They would fly down the stairs, bounce off the deck onto the boat and into the water,' Russell continued. 'They had some wonderful times coming up the Noosa River. There is a ski run there. I thought it was a great way to keep young kids out of trouble. It kept them active, fit and competitive. Competition was always on. They were always trying to outdo each other and every one of them thought they were better than the others.'

Russell attempted to teach the boys how to drive, but they all ended up having driving lessons. 'That was nothing short of hair-raising,' Russell said. 'I started teaching Rocky to drive. We went down one street and went around a curve at the bottom in a Toyota 4Runner. He had it going around to the left on two wheels. I started screaming at him. It was driving school after that. I couldn't hack it. It was the safest way. It's false economy trying to teach them yourself.'

Russell built a gymnasium in the garage where he introduced Rocky and his brothers to weightlifting. Russell started lifting weights while he was a boy growing up in Melbourne after that day he misplaced his front teeth. He once held an Australian bench-press record, albeit briefly. 'That was in '62,' Russell said. 'I made it to 460 pounds and I got cleaned up by this Polish or Yugoslav guy. My record lasted as long as it took to put more weight on the bar.'

Russell accepted that Vicki was the matriarch of the family and never tried to become an authority figure to Rocky and the boys. 'I always admired Vicki for her strength,' Russell said. 'She is very resolute. Vicki was the authority person. She has always been the matriarch of the family. She had a very, very strong survival instinct and she wasn't going to let anything get in between the family and herself. They were prime. She still carries that.

'They were good lads. They weren't cheeky or anything like that. Slowly I got to know them all. It's been a wonderful experience. We've had a lot of lovely times. The overall family effect has been very fulfilling.'

As the boys grew older, even though he was not the eldest child, Rocky matured and emerged as the natural leader of the family. 'Rocky is the third eldest boy, but it feels like he is the eldest,' Kelly said. 'Everyone feels that way, even Sam, who is the eldest.

'Rocky is like the don of the family. If we looked at it in *Godfather* terms, if you've got a problem, you go to Rock and he'll sit down with you and look at it from all different angles, like a psychologist maybe. And he can be tough. He tells it to you the way it is. He knows how to get the best out of you, even Mum and our stepdad. If they've got something that's worrying them, it will always be Rocky who they will go to first.'

Sam agreed with Kelly's description of Rocky as the pillar of the family. 'I would say that's true,' Sam said. 'People do go to him with their issues. No one really talks to him too much about emotional things, but everything else. For instance, he is a director in this company and helped me build this business. That's been a big part of our adult relationship. Fashion is a very difficult business. I've worked in it for a long time. Rocky knew nothing about it and we've tried to do it together. It's been a real journey. The global financial crisis, managing cash flow, balance sheets, profits and losses, everything that comes with running a business, not only designing a product and making sales.

'With the business we are in there is a kind of left side and right side of the brain kind of thing going on. Obviously, Rocky's primary interest is his rugby, but he has been a very useful resource along the way. I think we have educated each other. It's been a great relationship. I think it's important to him to look after everyone in the family and make sure they are doing well. He has a true and honest interest in what everybody is up to and whether it's going well and ways he thinks it could go better.'

A godfather always has a consigliere or counsellor. So who does Rocky go to for advice? 'Because Rocky holds his cards so close to his chest he is never really vulnerable,' Sam said. 'In a sense, to play that role I feel like you need to have no insecurities yourself, do you know what I mean? He has no need really to go to somebody else, I don't think. I think he works stuff out for himself. He just doesn't talk about things. He keeps his private affairs private. I don't know if he consciously sees it as a weakness or he figures things out for himself somehow. I have no idea what's going on in his head.'

Interestingly, in the original *Godfather* movie, Don Vito Corleone, played by Marlon Brando, tells another character at his daughter's wedding that 'a man who does not spend time with his family is not a man'. I guess that that would be Rocky's sentiments exactly.

Kelly believes her brothers would have all become professional musicians if the family had remained in Melbourne. All the Elsom boys are musical in some way. Rocky plays drums and piano, Sam the guitar, banjo and harmonica, Dusty the guitar and Rory the didgeridoo. Vicki could not afford music lessons so they were all self-taught.

'They are all musicians now, but they've all got something else as their main thing,' Kelly said. 'When we moved to Queensland it changed the dynamic. Rocky has pretty much taught himself. A friend of mine taught him how to play drums. Toia [Kelly's daughter] has been playing piano since she was eight. I remember Toia came home one day from an exam. She played this amazing, incredible song and Rocky was like I want to learn that. He just sat there and she taught him. He would hear things and play them rather than sheet music. With that he could just pick up an instrument and start playing. It was the same with my other brothers. They just taught themselves.

'I used to have band practice at the house. I was about 15, Rocky was six. He used to come in and watch the band rehearse and he'd always want to get up and play. We would have a break and he would always want to go to the drums, like he was Animal. Rocky didn't want anyone to hear him. It's very hard to play drums if you don't want to be heard. I could see his frustration because he didn't want to do it unless he was good. He had that whole thing. I won't do it until I'm really good. I'll practise by myself and then I'll come back and blow everyone away. He'll practise in private and then one day he'll bring it out and you think where the hell did that come from? That's the kind of kid he was and that's how he is even now, a very private person. He doesn't like to talk about it. He just does it.'

Howard Roark's got nothing on Rocky.

# 2

## OF GREAT AND GOOD MEN

*I likened him to being an adult in a khaki uniform.*

Former Nudgee boarding master Robbie Martin

On a hot, humid Brisbane afternoon, Peter Gledhill, coach of the St Joseph's Nudgee College First XV, noticed a tall, athletic boy with dark blond hair running hard at pre-season training. The boy ran and ran and ran until he could run no more. 'I didn't know anything about Rocky until pre-season training in Grade 11,' Gledhill said. 'In six weeks we do our aerobic work and we do it very seriously. This tall, blond fella came down and just ran until he vomited. Seriously, he ran as hard as he could until he was physically sick. I remember quite clearly one day we were doing 10 repetition two hundreds and he won the first six. I said to the fitness trainer, who is this guy? This guy will do me. He just wants to go until there is nothing in his tank. In pre-season training guys will step back a bit to make sure they get through the 10. He just went as hard as he humanly could until his body physically couldn't do it any more. He was probably already six-three and obviously showed he was athletic. After I saw him I said, mate, I think we can really do something with you.'

Gledhill was a legendary coach in schoolboy rugby, taking Nudgee to four premierships. Like many winners, Gledhill polarised opinion with his gruelling training sessions, meticulous technical analysis and Vince Lombardi philosophy that winning isn't everything: it's the *only* thing. Ten years after guiding the Rocky-led Nudgee side to an undefeated GPS premiership-winning season, he was coaching the school's Fifteen As. I wondered what that said about Gledhill, and then after I met him I knew. Peter Gledhill was a lifer.

I interviewed Gledhill at Bede's Café, situated between a gymnasium and an Olympic-size swimming pool in the magnificent grounds of Nudgee College in Brisbane's northern suburbs. Gledhill was a talented openside flanker for Brisbane club Brothers from the late 1970s to the early 1990s and still looked very fit. An intense character, Gledhill was wearing glasses and a Western Force T-shirt, for whom he does some consultancy work.

'The good thing about Rocky was he didn't have any bad habits,' Gledhill told me as torrential rain poured down in an unseasonal spring thunderstorm, which I did not realise at the time would contribute to the catastrophic flood in Brisbane that summer. 'He was pretty much a blank canvas. He's no dill either, Rocky. He was just a big sponge. We did quite comprehensive video analysis and gave the kids individual feedback after every game. He was always very open to that. All through the term we held lineout clinics. He was very enthusiastic to come and learn. He still sets up exactly the same way in the lineout to how we taught him. He still holds his hands exactly the same way.

'He was a kid who needed encouragement. You are doing well, you are doing well. But he just had this drive. I think in Grade 10 he sat back and saw how big [rugby] was at this school. How the school would turn out in the grandstand. We were very successful in those years. The whole school is about the First Fifteen, rightly or wrongly, and I think Rocky said, I want to have a crack at that.

'Rocky was a real bolter, he really was. There are hundreds of kids here who go through Thirteen As, Fourteen As, Fifteen As, Sixteen As. They go through the whole thing and he's done none of that and picked it up in one pre-season with the ability to play in a Nudgee First Fifteen, which is quite spectacular really. I can't remember it happening before or since to be honest. Rocky was picked on his attitude in pre-season and just his ethic. I had a very strong gut feeling about Rocky.'

It was Russell's idea for Rocky and his brothers to board at Nudgee. The Elsoms were nominally Church of England, but the family was not religious. It was irrelevant that Nudgee was a Catholic school. The quality of the education was important, but had Peter Gledhill not guided Rocky in the rugby program, things might have been very different for him. It was fortunate Gledhill followed his gut instinct because when he said Rocky was a blank canvas he was not exaggerating. Much of the pre-season was spent showing Rocky — and sometimes even physically moving him into — positions that were foreign to him. Pre-season training was something of an institution at Nudgee with 50 or so boys displaying their skills to the First XV coach, yet Gledhill spent much of his time showing Rocky the basics of the game that every other player already knew, which was a very rare occurrence. A sympathetic Gledhill put it more diplomatically: 'Let's say his feel for the game was very low.' But Gledhill backed himself and more importantly, he backed Rocky.

Nudgee is justifiably proud of its reputation as the cradle of Queensland rugby. Over 120 years Nudgee has won more GPS premierships than any other Queensland school and has produced the most players to represent their state and country, from their first Wallaby, Voy Oxenham, to Test captains Mark Loane and Paul McLean to their 22nd and most recent international, James O'Connor. The first time Rocky watched Nudgee's First XV play he was determined to wear the famous blue and white butcher stripes of the school's 'Great and Good Men'.

'We went down to watch a game of rugby at Nudgee,' Vicki said. 'There were at least 6000 people at the game. Rocky loved it straight off.'

Rocky did not play rugby in his first year at Nudgee. He suffered from a virus, lost 17 kilograms, and did not play any sport at all. Once he recovered he threw himself into sport. It was on the athletics track that Rocky first attracted the attention of Nudgee sports master Greg Hose. I interviewed Hose at the same café at Nudgee where I talked to Gledhill. Hose played breakaway for the Nudgee First XV in 1962, but was forced into premature retirement following a succession of knee injuries. Retired from teaching now too, Hose is tall, slim and still kind of boyish. He reminded me of a Hollywood cowboy like Gary Cooper or James Stewart: tough, but a gentleman.

'I came across Rocky in a track-and-field carnival,' Hose said. 'He ran in the one hundred and he ran in the low elevens. I think it was around eleven-three, eleven-four. For a big lad I couldn't believe it. When I saw the time I was just staggered. We had a very good track-and-field team at that time and there is no doubt if time was available he would have made the team. But of course he devoted his time to rugby. He certainly was right up there and we had a lot of good sprinters. He was very impressive. He was just naturally quick. He was the quickest forward I saw.'

In a photograph of the 1999 Nudgee First XV Rocky is standing in the middle of the third row, towering over his teammates. Rocky's height suited the second row, but Gledhill also thought it would be a better position for him to learn the game. 'We didn't have enough time to go through the running lines of a back-rower,' Gledhill said. 'We put a lot of work into his scrummaging and lineout work. He ran around like a back-rower anyway so he was a real bonus. He still didn't have that arrival knowledge of first man, second man. He didn't have those little subtleties. That's why I put him in the second row. It was a good place for a young kid to learn the game. He could lock out a scrum very well. He had modern age second-rower written all over him.'

Gledhill's decision to play Rocky in the second row had one unfortunate consequence, which was to deny his brother Dusty a spot in the First XV. Only 14 months older than Rocky, Dusty was a handy second-rower and had the potential to play club, perhaps even Super rugby, but maybe not the desire, although he later represented NSW and the Australian Police at blindside flanker and inside centre. You could imagine a fierce sibling rivalry developing from such a competitive situation, but Dusty supported his younger brother fully. With Rocky on the field, Dusty leading the war cry and youngest brother Rory in the bell tower videoing games, it was a real joint effort by Team Elsom.

Rocky improved with every game and earned selection in the Queensland under-16 squad midway through the season. After only a handful of games of rugby, Rocky, playing number 8, captained the Queensland side to an undefeated Australian championship. The leading try-scorer in the tournament, Rocky was a walk-in selection for the Australian under-16 team to tour New Zealand. His first taste of the back row was successful, but he still had plenty of work to do in the second row back at Nudgee. 'In '99 he was just making his way,' Hose said. 'He forced his way into the second-row spot and he was very much the new boy on the block. Nudgee being the rugby powerhouse that it is, he was just finding his feet. But it didn't take him long because he acquitted himself in that First Fifteen. He showed a lot of potential.

'He was raw. He dead set was raw with regards to knowing rugby. He is a very intelligent young man and he just worked at it. Every game in '99 he just got better and better and better. His whole approach to things, he is just so determined. He absorbs everything. The coaching here was first class. He made outstanding progress in '99.'

Watching Rocky play for Nudgee became a Saturday afternoon ritual for the Elsom family, who would drive down to Brisbane from Noosa. Nudgee's home games were played on the hallowed Jack Ross Oval and thousands of spectators filled the grandstand, more than some Brisbane club games. 'Rocky went into the First Fifteen and from that day on every weekend it was an event,' Kelly said. 'Mum would get up early on Saturday morning, pack the coffee, pack the scones and the cakes. We would drive down. Mum, Russell, Toia and me. The boys were already there. There would be two or three thousand people at these games. They were big games and very different for us.'

Kelly was also relieved that Rocky had found an outlet for his restless energy. 'I remember saying to Mum, thank god he plays rugby because when he started playing he was less ... he must have had so much testosterone as a kid that he was just buzzing around the house. It was like he was a bull in a china shop. Once he started playing rugby he settled down a lot. I think it helped him to calm himself. I know that when he has been injured and he hasn't played that he gets really antsy and needs to get out there and release this energy that he must have. Maybe they are all like that. I don't know. I think he needs rugby. Once he retires he is going to need something else.'

Nudgee finished third in the 1999 GPS competition, which was not a satisfactory result for a Peter Gledhill-coached side, but both Rocky and the team showed signs of greater things to come. In a prophetic comment, the rugby report in the 1999 Nudgee Year Book said of Rocky: 'From very humble beginnings to Australian under-16 rep football in a year is a testament to a well-ingrained, intrinsic motivation and determination. Rocky developed fine hand skills and scrummaging ability. With another year in 2000 to further develop his phase and defensive skills, there is no reason [why] Rocky can't have an enormous impact on the competition.'

A bolter the year before, Rocky was an automatic selection for Nudgee's First XV in 2000. Rocky was one of eight players who backed up from the 1999 team, including flanker Herman Hunt, a future Queensland Reds prop. In the 2000 team photograph, Rocky stood in the centre of the middle row. He was still the tallest player in the team, although not by as much, but he had filled out considerably.

In a key positional change, Rocky was switched from lock to number 8, which suited his intelligence, physicality and mobility. Rocky revelled in playing at the back of the big Nudgee pack, with seven of the eight forwards weighing around 100 kilograms. 'Rocky had a year of experience under his belt,' Gledhill said. 'In '99 we had a good back row. He saw how they played. He grew a little bit more. Put on a little bit more meat. He was a perfect number 8 to get us going forward. It's a good place to lead a side from too; 6, 7, 8, 9 and 10, people who are right there all the time. Just the fit of that team too, it was a very good fit.

'When I saw his development I said there is no reason why he can't be an international back-rower because he's got speed. He's got genuine speed. He had a lot of foot-speed. You know how he has got that little bit of a shimmy. He can go the dominant role, but he's a smart kid. That's not always going to be the way because there are big kids and good teams. He can go off either foot if he has to. He's got a very strong palm. For a young boy he had a very, very strong palm. He was scoring tries in games that only Rocky could score.'

And score he did. Rocky scored 17 tries in 2000, setting a record for the most number of tries by a forward in the eight-game GPS competition. One of Rocky's most memorable tries was a last-minute game-clincher against arch-rivals the Anglican Grammar School, known as Churchie. As former boarding master Robbie Martin described it, Nudgee 'came out of the blocks in reverse'. With their strong-running Polynesian centres creating havoc, Churchie got out to a 23-point lead early in the first half. Nudgee had prepared for a great season, but this was looking like a disaster. Slowly, but surely, Nudgee came back. Time was running out. With 10 seconds to go the ball was shifted to Rocky out wide. He sped past Churchie's winger and pinned his ears back for the corner as the whole of the opposition seemed to be coming across in cover. As the defence converged on him, Rocky dived for the line, disappearing beneath the rubble of bodies. The try was awarded, giving Nudgee a 24–23 win. The grandstand erupted and Nudgee boys spewed onto the field to congratulate their hero. Rocky's younger brother Rory was in the bell tower, filming the whole thing for posterity.

Tony McGahan, a physical education teacher, was Nudgee's backs and defence coach in 2000. McGahan played outside centre for Queensland Schoolboys, but switched to rugby league when he left school. Known as 'Dumper', he played for the Brisbane Broncos in the Queensland Cup for a few years before returning to rugby union, playing halfback with Brisbane club Eastern Districts. After retiring as a player, McGahan took up coaching. He was assistant coach of Irish province Munster when they won the Heineken Cup and then became head coach. He could not have imagined then that one of the young players he was coaching at Nudgee would one day be his nemesis.

I learnt that McGahan was holidaying in Maroochydore on the Sunshine Coast during the European off-season. I asked Rocky how I could contact McGahan and he told me to get in touch with Robbie Martin, the former Nudgee boarding master, who gave me the coach's mobile phone number. I rang McGahan to arrange an interview and flew up to the Sunshine Coast. In brilliant winter sunshine we sat in the courtyard of an apartment building across the road from Maroochydore Beach, a stark contrast to cold weather that was awaiting McGahan, and eventually Rocky, in Ireland.

'Physically, Rocky had wonderful attributes to play number 8 at schoolboy level,' said McGahan, who would fly back to Ireland the following day. 'He had a wonderful ability to get off the back of the scrum. He was fearless in that regard. At schoolboy level, or any level really, but particularly at schoolboy level, if you've got a number 8 who can come off the back of the scrum and put fear into the opposition, you are going to be well over the gain line.

'With any good player at any level you are looking to get the ball into their hands as much as possible and number 8 certainly provided the platform, especially at schoolboy level where there is a neutral aspect to the scrum. Any ball won was going to provide a great platform to release him into the game.

'One of his outstanding traits was his ability to change momentum with a large hit. He was so physically capable at a schoolboy level. With raw aggression and a competitive nature it was always going to be a no-win situation for the opposition. He dominated opposition sides in that capacity. It was fantastic to have a player like that who could stop momentum and turn a game with a turnover. It was certainly a wonderful attribute and it was a strong point in his final year.'

McGahan observed Rocky's strong determination to succeed from the very start. 'At that young age he had that single-mindedness and drive to know what he wanted,' McGahan said. 'He really knew what he wanted to achieve and where he needed to go. He is very comfortable with himself as an individual. He didn't need to be mollycoddled at a schoolboy age and be told how good he was. He was certainly very forthright in his approach and forthright in critiquing himself. He had a very driven personality. He really knew where he was going and what he wanted to do. I don't think anything was going to step in his way. It needed to be moved, if there was anything in his way.'

McGahan would usually refer me to Robbie Martin, the former boarding master who had given me his number, when he could not answer any of my questions. 'I think you should ask Robbie Martin that question,' McGahan would say, or 'Robbie Martin would probably know the answer to that.' As I was driving down to

Brisbane to interview Les Kiss before the Wallabies played Ireland, I thought it might be worthwhile to look up this Robbie Martin fellow and see what he had to say for himself.

I met Robbie in a classic Queenslander high on top of a hill in the northern Brisbane suburb of Hamilton, which had spectacular views. Sitting at the dining table, Robbie offered me a slice of lemon pie, which he admitted he had a weakness for. I asked him a little bit about his own background and how he knew Rocky. Robbie played in the St Joseph's Gregory Terrace First XV for three years as a halfback, representing Queensland Schools, and later played for Queensland University Colts and Southern Districts. A solicitor with Martin Law, a boutique Brisbane law firm, Robbie had worked as a boarding master at Nudgee while he was a post-graduate law student.

'I met Rocky through his older brothers, Sam and Dusty,' Robbie said. 'I met him in the dining room one time, had a bit of a chat. I was quite impressed. Rocky was a mature young man for his age. I likened him to being an adult in a khaki uniform. He was a man among boys.'

Robbie realised Rocky was different from the average schoolboy when he started giving him successful tips for investing in the stock market, which was one of Rocky's sidelines for making pocket money. Rocky's initial share tip was biotech stock Peptech, which from 1999 to 2001 was a darling of the market, rising spectacularly. Obviously, Rocky did not know the inner workings of the company and was simply passing on information he had heard, but his apparent acumen certainly captured Robbie's attention.

'We must have been in conversation in the boarding house or having a meal in the dining room and we started talking about shares and he provided me with a couple of tips that I purchased and made some money,' Robbie said. 'I was always happy to perk my ears up when I was around Rocky to see if he could deliver any more good mail.

'It's an interesting question, how you would describe Rocky's personality. He's an interesting character. He can be reserved. He can be outgoing. I wouldn't call him arrogant, but he is a bit eccentric. He keeps a bit to himself. It takes a while to get to know him. You don't meet him once and walk away and say, I know Rocky. He can be many things, outgoing, eccentric, quiet, reserved, arrogant; he is a great, decent person.

'He delves into different things. He's got a music interest. He's got a fashion interest. He's got his sporting interest. People wouldn't know those sides to him unless they spent a bit of time with him. He keeps things close to his chest. He doesn't give too much away. When he says something, it is worth listening to. He's not full of bullshit.'

Rocky, like his brothers, was a talented basketballer and played for Nudgee's First V. He also helped Robbie coach a team. 'My role was the coach, but I became the manager and Rocky was the coach because I didn't even know the rules,' Robbie said. 'Rocky was good enough to give me a helping hand and we won three premierships. He was outstanding in his input in running the drills, tactics and substitutions.'

Robbie coached Rocky in Nudgee's Fifth XI and remembers him as a lusty batsman. 'Rocky was the captain in his senior year,' Robbie said. 'A few of his mates were in the side. He showed a little bit of cricketing prowess. He scored three centuries and was quite happy with himself. He could certainly hit a cricket ball. He hit it out of the park a few times and held the game up while we got a replacement ball. He threw the arm over, but his batting was better than his bowling.'

Rocky also enjoyed boxing and would let off steam hitting the punching bags in Terny Hall. One day, Rocky and Robbie got into a disagreement and decided to resolve the issue in the ring. 'I had a key to the boxing area,' Robbie said. 'Rocky borrowed the key and organised to meet me at a designated time. I thought he turned up late, which annoyed me, and he said I hadn't given him the right key. I said let's settle this the old-fashioned way. We'll have a fight. It didn't happen, thankfully. I thought, Rob, you're the adult, Rocky is the schoolboy. How are you going to explain knocking out the First Fifteen captain or him knocking you out?'

Rocky could certainly look after himself, but he also had three brothers to back him up. 'They were pretty tight,' Robbie said. 'They would run amok together. It stood out that they were close knit. The boys did lots of things together. Like any brothers, they would fight, but they were pretty close and they still are today. They supported each other. They were different in years, but they were as thick as thieves. If one got in trouble, he had three brothers to back him up.'

Rocky's 'unique' style of leadership was recognised when he was appointed captain of the Nudgee First XV in 2000. 'Rocky has always had some natural leadership in him,' Peter Gledhill said. 'The good thing about Rocky is he has never been afraid to question. He will question in a polite manner. He always wanted to know why. That's really good. I'm a big one in coaching to get across why you are running that line or why you are doing this play or whatever, and every time you knew you had Rocky's ear. When I talk, I have a look at who is really listening and Rocky really listened. And he was driven. And he had a bit of an aura about him. And what happens in a good environment, people are sucked up by that.

'That 2000 side was a very strong side. There were a lot of very good footballers in that side. He was the perfect fit for that team. You know a team is a good team when the captain can stop a session — not the coach — and say this isn't up to our level. We don't want to train how other teams train. We want to train at our pace. He would say Nudgee pace. We used to try to do all our skills faster than at game pace. Rocky was all for that. He took a lot of pride in his performance.

'He was quite a manly type of young lad. He was his own man. That's why I liked him, too. He wasn't pretending to be anyone else. He wasn't pretending to be like the captain the year before or like John Eales, or anyone around the place. He was just going to be Rocky Elsom and it sat very easily with him. If there was nothing to say, he wouldn't say anything. But if there was something to say, he would say it. We probably had a no dickhead policy before [Sydney

Swans coach] Paul Roos. If Rocky needed to go up to someone and say hey, you're being a dickhead, he would do that. He had his own unique style of leadership, which I fully encouraged.

'He knew the honour of being a Nudgee First Fifteen captain. He was a good captain. If you've got a good captain, the season is very enjoyable because it's not your voice all the time. Rocky spoke up. And he was very well respected by the team. Fear is not the right word, but the players wanted to perform. Rocky really appreciates firm, but fair. As a captain he can be very firm, but fair. I've always had a massive soft spot for Rocky. We have a great mutual respect. We bump into each other and always have a chat. I just sit there quietly with great satisfaction that I might have been a very small contributor to his career.'

Gledhill consulted Hose on the captaincy, and the sports master was in full agreement to give the role to Rocky. 'There was always discussion about that sort of thing,' Hose said. 'Peter discussed it with me. We were very impressed with the way he went about things in '99. He was a true leader. He led the team exceptionally well. His physique, the way he held himself — he just had tremendous respect from the boys.

'He wasn't one of these over-the-top guys. He was fairly level-headed in the way he addressed the kids. The old story, he led by example. They responded accordingly. He wasn't a ranting and raving type captain. He had concern for the players too. You put all those things together and it's a great response. It's a bit hard to comprehend. He was so well thought of and so well respected. If he was going to address the grandstand, you could have 1300 kids. He would walk in front of the grandstand and you could hear a pin drop.'

Rocky led Nudgee to the GPS premiership in an undefeated season, the school's 35th since the start of GPS rugby in 1918, and took his own game to a higher level, his powerful running delighting the spectators in the grandstand at Ross Oval. Rocky was nicknamed 'Rock Dog' at Nudgee and whenever he made one of his characteristic bursts the boys cheering on the sideline would deviate from the school war cry and yell, 'Rock Dog!'

The 2000 Nudgee rugby report said of Rocky: 'The team responded well to Rocky's unique style of captaincy, especially when the chips were down. As a ball-runner there was no peer in Queensland.' According to Greg Hose, Rocky compared favourably with Nudgee's best ever players, including Mark Loane, arguably Australia's greatest number 8. 'I went through Nudgee myself,' Hose said. 'I was here with Dallas O'Neill [former Wallabies number 8]. He was up there with the best Nudgee has produced and I've seen them all come through since then. Rocky in 2000 had all the hallmarks of going all the way. Peter and I said on a number of occasions that nothing was going to stop him getting to the Wallabies. He was totally dominant in the GPS competition in 2000. He compared extremely well [to Loane]. As a matter of fact, I'd rate them comparable. Mark Loane was an outstanding schoolboy player. Rocky is right up there with the very best.

'That was an outstanding year. The results they achieved that year were just ... I can recall the game against Gregory Terrace; 66-nil. Boy! It was unheard of. Rocky scored three tries in that match.'

Nudgee rugby was very ceremonial. The night before a game the Nudgee players would attend a First XV dinner in the school's dining hall. After dinner the kindly elderly Brother Wal — who had an affinity with Rocky because he was 80 years old and Rocky wore number 8 — would place jelly beans in a bowl, the flavours representing the colours of the opposing team, which in the case of Gregory Terrace were red and black. 'Eat 'em alive!' Brother Wal exhorted the boys, who symbolically devoured their opponents.

Nudgee's incredible 66–0 victory against Gregory Terrace, their traditional rivals, was televised live on Optus. Robbie Martin sent me a copy of the game on DVD, managing to get to a post office in Brisbane as floodwaters deluged the city. As a fresh-faced Rocky led Nudgee onto the Internationals Oval in the Brisbane suburb of Tennyson on a beautiful Saturday afternoon, commentator David Fordham described him as 'a likely looking lad'. In front of their supporters, the Nudgee players formed a circle and said a prayer as they did before every game. Rocky then led the team onto the centre of the field where they shook hands with their opponents, who included goal-kicking outside-centre Michael Buchanan, the son of former Australia cricket coach John Buchanan. Gregory Terrace had been led out by a Year 7 student, Andrew Denby, who had had two operations to remove brain tumours and was now undergoing chemotherapy treatment. 'It brings a lump to your throat,' co-

commentator and then Queensland Reds coach Mark McBain said. Rocky shook hands with Gregory Terrace skipper, Graeme Legh, and then reached out to shake the hand of the young cancer patient.

In a pre-game interview, a very composed Rocky predicted Nudgee would be too skilful for Gregory Terrace, but he could have added too powerful and too fast as well. The Nudgee forwards outweighed the Gregory Terrace pack 789 kilograms to 700, which was just over 10 kilos a man, or boy. The Nudgee side, which trained 12 times, or 25 hours, each week, was very well organised, playing with the sophistication of a club – or even a Super rugby – team, as it constantly changed the point of attack and employed a host of rehearsed moves.

Rocky was such a superior physical specimen compared to most of the other boys on the field, he looked like a ring-in from a senior rugby team. In his first involvement in the game he picked up a Gregory Terrace forward in a ruck and pile-drove him into the turf. Interestingly, when Nudgee received its first penalty it was in the Gregory Terrace 22, but Rocky passed up the easy three points to kick for touch and an attacking lineout. It turned out to be the correct decision. Nudgee secured the ball at the front of the lineout and from the ensuing phase Rocky crashed his way across the advantage line. Three phases later centre Neil Hunt scored. 'It looks a bit ominous,' McBain said to Fordham in the commentary box.

Nudgee led 19–0 at halftime after scoring three tries and while Rocky did not have a lot of involvements in the first half, he made an impact when he did. Towards the end of the first half, Rocky picked up a ball that had been dropped by another player in the Nudgee 22 near the left-hand touchline and charged downfield, beating one defender cold and then flicking the ball inside one-handed to a support while he was being tackled. 'What about the big number 8 when he strides out!' Fordham enthused.

Nudgee old boy Mark Loane was interviewed during the halftime break. 'It has certainly changed from the time I was here 29 years ago,' Loane said. 'These young lads are very, very well coached. I think superb rugby, could be a little bit better at the finish, Nudgee has scored three tries already, but they could have scored more if they had finished them off well. There is an enormous amount of possession coming Nudgee's way, they are a big side, they are dominating the set-play and also the loose-play, so it's going to be hard for Terrace to turn it around, I think.

'When I was here 29 years ago to the day we had 25 Terrace supporters and 25 Nudgee supporters and a dog. And a cross-field wind. There's more trees around now. It's a much more refined area. We certainly didn't have television coverage. There was actually no coverage at all. It was like a black hole. There was no information at all, no record.'

At the end of Loane's interview, Fordham made a tribute to the great number 8. 'No wonder there were only 50 supporters, Mark probably scared them all away in those days. He was a wonderful player, wasn't he? One of the awesome sights I remember at Ballymore was in '82 in the centenary year when he scored that magnificent try against Scotland where he just destroyed ... we hadn't seen Mark run like that for a number of years, the try had to be scored and he scored it.'

McBain chimed in. 'Yeah, he was unbelievable that day. He was very hard to stop, maybe like this number 8 who is playing today.'

Rocky scored the first of his three tries early in the second half after taking a pass out wide from Neil Hunt and skirting the defence with a surprising turn of speed. 'He's a good prospect, isn't he?' McBain said, possibly anticipating he would coach Rocky at the Reds one day. Rocky's second try started with a break 10 metres on Nudgee's side of halfway, busting through two defenders and outpacing the fullback. 'He is an awesome specimen, this number 8 for Nudgee College,' Fordham said. 'Leading by example with his second try ... the talent scouts will be marking down the name Rocky Elsom.' Rocky scored Nudgee's 10th and final try after taking the ball first off the ruck from five metres out and crashing through three defenders. When he got up, Rocky had a sombre expression as if he had just scored a consolation try in a thrashing, but he did break into a smile as the Nudgee players clapped the shell-shocked Terrace boys off the field.

An interested TV viewer of the Nudgee–Gregory Terrace game was former Queensland and Wallabies hooker Michael Foley, who would later coach Rocky at the Wallabies. I interviewed Foley, now forwards coach with the NSW Waratahs, at the poolside café at the Sydney Football Stadium. Foley was casual in T-shirt and shorts, but his dark beard, perfectly trimmed as always, gave him the look of a Zen master.

'I can remember it vividly,' Foley said. 'I was in Test camp in Sydney. It was the day of the game. We were playing that night at Aussie Stadium. I flicked on the television and there was a schoolboy game on in Brisbane being played between Nudgee and I'm pretty sure it was Gregory Terrace. I remember the number 8 on the day for Nudgee. It was Rocky. I thought he was just a standout. He really looked like a man among boys, which is a clichéd saying, but certainly has real relevance in this context.

'Every involvement he had in the game was dominant and, physically, he was particularly impressive. He had a presence in the game. Nudgee dominated the game very, very strongly, but even in a side that was dominant, he was the dominant player. You thought to yourself, that guy one day will play for Australia. We used to have a joke in the change room after Wallabies games that the game he just played was the second-best game he ever played because you couldn't go past the game he played for Nudgee that day.'

Wallabies number 8 Richard Brown was a year below Rocky at Nudgee, but he played a couple of games in the First XV as a replacement second-rower. 'Rocky was never much of a kid at school,' Brown said in the courtyard of the Wallabies' hotel in Coogee in Sydney in the lead up to a Test. 'He was pretty much a fully grown man. When the rest of us were hitting puberty he was shaving twice a day. Rocky, he was a big kid on campus. The boys had a lot of respect for him. He was definitely a favourite son of Nudgee College.

'One day I was watching the First Fifteen play and his brother, I think it was Dusty, was leading the war cry. I wasn't cheering loudly enough for Rocky so he kicked me up the bum. I started cheering.

'I was 15 when I had my first game off the bench. It was against Ipswich Grammar. It's fairly similar to your Australian debut. It's a very nerve-racking experience. I have a photo at home that my dad took. I was walking behind Rocky. I think he was 105 kilos and I was 84 kilos. I'm walking behind him after the game, a special moment.

'I think I was a substitute second-rower. That's where they could fit me. Rocky would never play second row. He was very good at seagulling [roaming out wide on the field]. He had it down to a fine art. He was a pretty exceptional athlete. He was playing with an aggressive streak back then. I think everyone believed he would be going on to bigger and better things. We've talked about Nudgee once or twice. We know the same coaches, we know the same people. Rocky is pretty genuine when he talks about those days.'

Eleven years after first playing alongside Rocky at Nudgee, Brown still gains confidence from having him on the field. 'It feels sort of natural because you have been training and playing with Rocky since you were 15,' Brown said. 'It gives you confidence. I would say he still has this ability to pop up at the right time. We've seen that a few times where he has scored tries, an opportunistic moment that he has seen and gone for. That's what you want out of your blindside flanker — to really impact when the opportunity is there whereas your 7 and 8 can really be just workers.'

One of Rocky's schoolboy opponents was future Wallabies

hooker Stephen Moore, who played for Brisbane Grammar. If I had to choose only one player to talk to about Rocky, it would be Moore, who became one of his closest friends at the Wallabies. I spoke to Moore in the lobby of the Crowne Plaza Hotel in Coogee, a long, in-depth conversation which spanned Rocky's schoolboy days to the present. At the end of the exhaustive interview Moore slumped back in his chair, held his head in his hands and exclaimed: 'God! I feel like I'm his wife!'

Rocky scored two tries in Nudgee's 52-15 win against Brisbane Grammar in the third round of the 2000 season. 'They had a very good team,' Moore said. 'We didn't have as good a team. They put 40 points or something on us. I've got pretty strong recollections of him running over some of our little inside backs.'

Even though they went to different schools, Rocky and Moore hung out in the same social circles and became good mates. 'My schoolmates were good mates with a lot of the Nudgee guys,' Moore said. 'We used to hang around a fair bit together and we ended up becoming close mates. I guess when we were that age we just used to hang around together. We didn't have the same depth as we do now. It was more just casual mates. Maybe not see each other during the week, but see him once a week on a Saturday night.

'I never found it difficult to get to know him, but he doesn't really open up to many people or any people. He has always been reasonably guarded about his personal life. I've never had any issues with that. I've always felt I could go to him with anything and get an honest opinion about something or get his thoughts on things.

'He always did things his way even at school. He had a way he thought things would go and he had a very good reason for all those. That's the way he lived his life. It's always worked out to be whatever works out for him always helps the group. He knows what he needs to do to get the best out of himself and in turn that helps the group. From day one he was very aware of what he needed to do to get things done.

'At Nudgee he used to have a few classes off to get a couple of extra sleeps. Just to prepare for games or training. He is no different now. He always likes to have a rest whenever he can. If that makes him play well and do the best for the team, that's what's got to happen.'

I asked Moore why he thought his friendship with Rocky had lasted to this day. 'I suppose we have similar ideas about a lot of things,' Moore said. 'We agree on a lot of different things whether it be rugby or off the field as well. We both have an interest in business and that side of things as well. We are always bouncing things off each other. I guess that's a big part of it.

'He is a guy I can talk to on the same level. I can really ask him his opinion on just about anything and I know I'll get a well-thought-out, calculated response. If I ask him something, he might take a few days to get back to me, but he will always come back with an honest, well-thought-out answer. That's what makes a good friend. He won't just say something for the sake of it. I really respect that. Hopefully, we can continue our friendship.'

Rocky played for the Australian Schoolboys against Irish Schools at Ballymore in August 2000. The Australian team was captained by future Wallabies centre Morgan Turinui and included Will Caldwell, Luke Doherty, Mark Gerrard, Peter Hynes, Lachlan Mackay, Jone Tawake and Lei Tomiki. Rocky was forced off with a shoulder injury in Australia's 34–22 loss in the 'Test'. Gledhill, who coached the Australian team, said: 'Rocky banged his shoulder up playing for Queensland in the Australian titles. He wasn't on the field for a long time. I think he got hurt maybe halfway through the first half. He might have lasted to halftime. He played with a brace. He was very courageous.

'When he came back to Nudgee we had to do a lot of maintenance work to get him through the season. We got it checked out. The damage was done. The physio said you are not going to make the shoulder any worse, but you are going to need surgery. He had a reconstruction at the end of the year.'

It was assumed that he would follow the traditional Nudgee rugby pathway to the Queensland Reds, but in the lead-up to the Australian Schoolboys' match with Ireland, *The Courier-Mail* reported Rocky was 'open-minded' about his football future.

# 3
## ROCK DOG

*He was a tough nut, Rock.*

**Bulldogs trainer Gary Carden**

Just as Rocky was being primed for a fast track onto the Australian rugby pathway, he signed with the Canterbury Bulldogs club in the National Rugby League (NRL). The Bulldogs are one of the proudest clubs in the country and are renowned for their hard edge and mental toughness. The club boasted numerous legends of the game, including Les Johns, Johnny Greaves, Johnny Rhodes, George Peponis, Chris Anderson, Braith Anasta, Peter Tunks, Steve Price and Steve Mortimer, and has a reputation for having the finest development program in the NRL. All the signs seemed bright for the next step in Rocky's career, but instead he descended into a dark period.

Bulldogs' talent scout Mark Hughes believed Rocky was going to be the Next Big Thing in rugby league; maybe in his wildest dreams he thought Rocky was another Sonny Bill Williams, the Samoan kid he had spotted in Auckland as a 14-year-old, who was on the verge of superstardom. It would not work out that way for Rocky at the Bulldogs, but the two years he spent with the NRL club, in the toughest culture in the game, forged him into a hardened professional footballer while he was still just a teenager.

Along with his brothers Garry and Graeme, Mark Hughes played for the Bulldogs in the 1970s and early 1980s, helping to create the 'family club' image. A talented five-eighth, lock or centre, Hughes was nominated for the Berries to Bulldogs 70 Year Team of Champions. Thirteen years after retiring as a player, Hughes returned to the club in 1996 as development manager, a role which involved scouting for talent. It was Hughes who signed Rocky to play for the Bulldogs' Jersey Flegg, or under-20, team straight out of Nudgee.

I met Hughes in a coffee shop in Bondi Junction in Sydney's eastern suburbs one Friday morning. Now with actor Russell Crowe's South Sydney Rabbitohs, Hughes was looking comfortable in a black Converse T-shirt, shorts and sandals. 'Mufti Friday at the Bunnies, mate, a nice relaxed way to finish the week,' Hughes said.

The Bulldogs became aware of Rocky through a connection between Justin Hagan, the son of the club's former chief executive Bob Hagan, and Tony McGahan. 'The contact through the Hagan family was a young coach at Nudgee,' said Hughes, who had a habit of making a wry smile whenever he emphasised a point. 'Bob Hagan was the CEO at the time and young Justin had trialled for the club. He actually played second grade for one season, young Justin, a very good athlete himself and a very good judge. He knew the coach at

Nudgee. I don't think he was the head coach. I think he was an assistant. Tony McGahan? Yes, that rings a bell.

'I only saw [Rocky] once to confirm his athletic potential and then met with his mum and manager. I always contact the parents first and introduce myself and how we do things as a club, and obviously what I thought would be a good transition for Rocky to league and how we might go about it. His mum it was. They knew a fair bit about the Dogs. The Bulldogs at the time were very well credentialed, financially strong, always a good development system. It wasn't a hard sell. The roster we had at that time and the kids coming through, we were right up there if you like. You were competing against the Broncos and maybe some other Sydney clubs. We would be in the top four clubs all the time.

'I can only remember being consistently impressed by Rocky – confident kid, very mature for his age. I've only met him the once since he left the club, but I've seen him plenty of times on telly. He has always carried himself well, hasn't he? He seemed destined for success and he craved it. Some kids are better trainers, more coachable. He was a very intelligent kid. Rocky was very impressive at 17-turning-18 for his clear goals, you know, and just how he carried himself.'

It was a momentous decision for Rocky to switch to rugby league after leaving school. Rocky was the most lauded schoolboy rugby player in Queensland and Nudgee's star players were almost honour bound to go to the Reds. But Rocky never did anything just because other people expected him to. Rocky was on a Reds scholarship while he was at Nudgee and certainly considered following the pathway to Ballymore, but as always, he would only do it on his terms. Even as a high school kid, Rocky had a good idea of his worth as a player. Player agent Anthony Picone tried to negotiate a deal with the Reds, who offered him a place in their academy, or college, as it was called in those days, for considerably less than he was seeking.

'Rocky wanted to go to the Reds,' Vicki said. 'When the time came he got a manager. It was interesting because the manager had a meeting with us and he was talking to me like I was going to decide. I had to say to him, look, I'm sorry, but this is really Rocky's decision. I'm just here because he is underage, not because of anything else. He was a bit taken aback. He thought I would influence Rocky, which is not possible. Maybe it is, but certainly not with something that I don't know anything about.'

Former Wallabies flanker Jeff Miller, fresh from a victorious 1999 World Cup campaign as Rod Macqueen's assistant coach, was working as the Australian Rugby Union's (ARU) high performance manager. Miller put together a full package for a contract with the ARU and the Reds, which included tertiary studies and attractive remuneration, but friction developed between Miller and Picone and the deal turned sour.

Michael Foley, who was keen for Rocky to join Queensland, believed the Reds misjudged him, a recurring source of frustration. 'I remember people who were dealing at the academy level of things at that time, their attitude was it was a bit of a foregone conclusion that he was going to go to rugby league and maybe he wouldn't be good for rugby anyway,' Foley said. 'There was some inference that he was a bit of a big head. When I eventually came to meet Rocky I realised that was completely opposite to what he is, but I also could understand why people might take that view even though it wasn't true.

'I remember thinking to myself he would be fantastic for rugby. I suppose when you watch a schoolboy play it is going to take a few years for them to convert to an international. In my mind it was pretty certain that if this guy had the desire to do so, that's what would happen. At the time he was a Queensland schoolboy and I was playing for Queensland and thinking Queensland should be getting this sort of guy. He is exactly what we need.'

It would not be the last time the Reds let Rocky slip through their buttery fingers.

The Bulldogs flew Rocky and Vicki to Sydney, wining and dining them at a restaurant on the harbour with head coach, Steve Folkes, and the coach of the Jersey Flegg team, Ricky Stuart. 'They flew us down and looked after us pretty well,' Vicki said. 'They took us to lunch at one of those beautiful restaurants on the harbour. They took us to the house where the players lived. They had done everything to show us why he should come to the Bulldogs. And then we went to the meeting. They were saying stuff to me. What do you think? And I said look, I think this is totally what Rocky wants to do. I have no opinion about it. When you get to know Rocky you'll know Rocky will decide what's best for him, not me. They were a bit taken aback by that.

'Then they said, okay Rocky, we've got a contract and we'd like you to sign it. He said, I'll take that contract, if it's okay, and I'll think about it. They said we'd like you to sign it now. If you don't sign it now, the offer may not be on the table. He said okay, I'll leave the contract with you and I'll go away and think about it. They were not happy. I thought, that's good, Rocky.

'Then he went back [home] and everyone said big mistake. You should never go to league. They were saying things like it's a poor man's sport. You are going to live in Belmore. They are not your type of people.' But Rocky had grown up watching and playing rugby league and he loved the NRL competition.

The boys at Nudgee were surprised to learn that Rocky had switched to rugby league. 'I remember hearing about it,' Richard Brown said. 'At Nudgee you watch the Reds. You want to play for the Reds. That was definitely in my case and the other boys around me. When we found out Rocky had signed with the Bulldogs everyone was pretty surprised. In the same instance he was good enough to pick and choose where he wanted to go. So that's where he went.'

Peter Gledhill believed Rocky's close family ties influenced him to accept the Bulldogs' offer, which included university tuition. 'What influenced Rocky was he was very close to his sister and brothers,' Gledhill said. 'I've never had this conversation with Rocky about why he did it because that's his business and we would support whatever he did. They put him halfway up the totem pole and paid for his tuition. And like a lot of league clubs they put him in Bulldog house or whatever. Apparently it was a pretty flash type of place.

'And his brothers were living in Sydney. That would have been huge. He is very close to his family. They were brought up by his mum, lovely lady. Adversity sometimes brings people closer. I think he wanted to live with his brothers anyway. And the Doggies came up with a very good whole package. Ricky Stuart was the Colts coach. Set him up in a career in high finance, accelerated growth. We'll pay for your way through. We'll bring in a lady to cook meals and clean up. I think that won him over rather than going into a big shed at Ballymore and doing a few weights.'

But Gledhill was confident Rocky would come back to rugby, mainly because he did not think the monotony of league would suit him. 'I didn't think the meat market — I'm not saying this in a derogatory way — but just the up and get hit, the up and get hit, would suit Rocky, whereas as a back-rower [in rugby union] he could pick his times. I didn't think the weekly grind of league would suit Rocky. I was hoping he would do well, but I just thought it wouldn't suit him.

'I did think it would help his defence. Out of his whole profile probably his defence wasn't as high as his other attributes. He could tackle, but league would do no harm to his defensive capabilities and he would come back the full package. It certainly didn't do him any harm. It brought him up to speed. In league 50 per cent of the training time is done on defence. They don't have to do scrums and lineouts, rucks and mauls. It's just tackle and be tackled.'

Conversely, Greg Hose was deeply concerned Rocky would be lost to rugby for good and was one of the few people who tried to talk him out of making the switch. 'I remember he came to me and told me he was going to the Bulldogs,' Hose said. 'Of course I tried to talk him out of it. I can remember saying to him, Rocky, you'll play for Australia in rugby. You don't want to miss that opportunity, do you? He just said, Hosey, it could be good for me.

'As it turned out, there were a couple of things in his game which did need improvement and there is no doubt his defence improved by his stint with Canterbury. That 2000 side, it was such a dominant pack of forwards. He could virtually roam wide. He didn't have to do a great deal of defence because there were plenty of others there. There were a couple of absolutely ferocious defenders in that side.

'What worried me too was that he hadn't had a lot of rugby. He'd gone to rugby league and then he'd have to come back again. He missed out on those couple of years of rugby, which might make it difficult for him to get to the top. It's been great to see. Rocky and I always got along extremely well and it has been really satisfying to see him get to where he has got. But gee, he has worked hard. He has put in. Rocky, he is dedicated. He thoroughly deserves it. It's just great satisfaction to see him achieve what he has achieved.'

Tony McGahan supported Rocky's decision because he thought he would develop more as a footballer in a hard-nosed rugby league environment than in the Reds' college. 'For someone to sit back at that age and assess where rugby was at with pathways to professional rugby ... for a young player to stand back and view the situation and think this is a pathway that will improve me professionally: to be a member of a Jersey Flegg Bulldogs side where you trained closely with the senior side — exposed to top class, professional methods in a really hard, competitive environment — nothing was going to come out of it that wasn't positive,' McGahan said.

Stephen Moore was not at all surprised by Rocky's decision. 'Rocky would have been the most well-known schoolboy player of that year,' Moore said. 'That undefeated Nudgee side put big scores on a lot of teams. At the end of the year there was speculation he might play league. To be signed by an NRL club was a big thing for a schoolboy. That created a lot of publicity and away he went.'

Rocky lived in the 'Dog House', a cottage owned by the Bulldogs in Belmore, a working-class suburb in the clamouring heart of Canterbury territory in the south-west of Sydney. Other young, project players living in the house included future NRL stars Sonny Bill Williams, Jonathan Thurston, Nate Myles, Jason Williams and Roy Asotasi. In the highly competitive Bulldogs culture, it was dog eat dog, so to speak. 'Rocky settled in good, but he was independent,' Hughes said. 'He was strongly independent. You might want to ask some of the boys who were there at the time, but I'd say they would have said Rocky ran his own race.'

The unforgiving training at the Bulldogs was harder than anything Rocky had experienced before and possibly since. It was designed to condition raw young athletes into hardened professional footballers. Tough and uncompromising, it is reminiscent of the American marines where recruits are broken down and built back up again.

It was all part of the famous — or infamous, depending on your point of view — Bulldogs culture. 'The Bulldogs culture forever — and that goes back to me getting graded as an 18-year-old in 1972 — was a tough, relentless, disciplined approach,' Hughes said. 'There have been eras, the Ted Glossop era, where we got the Entertainers tag. We were only a small side, but we had massive mental toughness and had discipline drilled into us.

'The Dogs have never changed that culture. I've only experienced the two rugby league cultures — my current club the Rabbitohs and the Dogs — who have vastly different cultures. At the time that Rocky came, the head trainer was Billy Johnstone and he is still renowned as the toughest trainer in rugby league. And Steve Folkes, of course: for a small man, pound for pound, the best defensive player of his time and he took that into his coaching philosophy.

'Rocky experienced all of that, mate. If you weren't tough or disciplined, or pretty hard-nosed about things, you didn't come through the junior ranks at the Dogs. You didn't make it to the next level.'

I asked Hughes who created the Bulldogs culture. The answer, ironically enough, was a former Wallaby, Kevin Ryan. Nicknamed 'Kandos' after the New South Wales cement-producing town because of his toughness, Ryan is still considered to be the hardest man ever to play rugby league. Ryan played five Tests for the Wallabies in 1958 before changing codes, and becoming a front-rower or second-rower with the St George Dragons in the latter half of their 11-year consecutive premiership-winning run from 1956 to 1966, playing in seven winning grand finals. In 1967 as captain-coach of Canterbury, Ryan led the Bulldogs, known as the Berries at that time, to a 12–11 win against St George in the preliminary final, bringing the Dragons' world-record run to an end.

Like Rocky, Kevin Ryan was tough, but he was also a Renaissance man. Apart from being a dual international and a Queensland amateur boxing champion, Ryan was a barrister, a mayor of the City of Hurstville in Sydney and a NSW state parliamentarian. And which school did Ryan attend? You guessed it — Nudgee. I wondered if Rocky was some kind of a lineal descendant of Kevin Ryan, bringing the 'hard as cement' culture that 'Kandos' instilled into the Bulldogs back to the Wallabies.

'Kevin Ryan is arguably the toughest front-rower the game has seen through that St George 11-premierships reign and he brought that culture to Canterbury,' Hughes said. 'That's the history. Mate, when I got there it was like ... I remember they made fun of me in my first first-grade session. I was still 18. It was just a come and mix with the big boys because hopefully you can get there one day. I had to climb one of the big ropes they used to have in gyms. You had to go to like a 30-foot ceiling. They sent me up in a pair of shorts and a singlet and of course I've grazed every bit of the inside of me thighs and all the old dudes were just pissing themselves laughing at me, trying to get up this rope, you know.

'There was a trainer there and he is still there — Gary Carden. He started during the Warren Ryan era, which was, if you like, the real tough era. He took what I explained about the Bulldogs culture to the nth degree. Everyone who graduated at Canterbury passed through the gym with Gary Carden from 1984, I think, when he started with Warren Ryan. Not the most scientific of trainers, mate, just the old-fashioned gym in his backyard. The kids would do extras with him on top of what they would do at the Canterbury gym.

'I've had some criticism levelled at that kind of training too because some kids can't handle it. My view on it was I didn't think it made you any worse off. If you came through it, you certainly were ready for the next level.'

Gary Carden was one of only two people Rocky suggested I interview for this book and is the only person he regularly mentions when asked about his time at the Bulldogs. When I tracked him down, Carden asked me to meet him at the café at the Flower Power nursery in Enfield in Canterbury territory, which I thought was an incongruous setting for a talk with a hard-as-nails rugby league trainer. Then when I thought about it a little bit more it seemed like the perfect place because a nursery was where something was bred, nourished and fostered. And that is what a bloke like Gary Carden, a lifer, was all about.

Carden, who everyone called Gaz, was already seated at a table in the courtyard when I arrived. In his late fifties, Carden was short and stocky with dark hair and the bluest blue eyes, which glinted cheekily. He did not look anything like an ogre who would whip young boys into shape, but he obviously had a sense of humour. He wore a white T-shirt with a cartoon drawing showing the back of a fat, naked woman. Squeezed between the woman's big buttocks was a skinny, little man. The woman was saying: 'Jim, where are you?'

Describing himself as a 'pretty average' footballer, Carden played centre, wing and back row for the St George Dragons, a strange name for a local club in the Canterbury district. 'I only played up to B-grade level you know,' Carden said. 'It would have been under 21s back then. If I had been any good, I would have been playing grade. I think I found me niche in training though. That's what I'm good at.

'I was doing a couple of local sides, who won the comp. I was training David Gillespie, Andrew Farrar, Paul Langmack and Michael Hagan. A bloke said to me one day, have you ever thought about coming down and doing the grade? I said it would be nice. They took me in to meet Peter Moore, and Peter Moore put me on. As you know the Bullfrog — you were always in awe of him because of who he was, but he left you alone if you were doing your job okay. I started with them in 1984. I've been there ever since.

'Train hard and don't ever disappoint your good athletes. If you've got blokes who are good, you train 'em hard and you turn up with something that's constructive so when they walk away they say I got something out of that, you know. Train hard at the top and train hard at the bottom, that's been my philosophy.'

For new Bulldogs recruits hell was a gymnasium. Despite the torturous training, the Bulldogs culture was more about mental strength than physical fitness. 'Everyone is physically strong,' Carden said. 'I think everyone does the same type of weight training. Everyone gets themselves big and strong, but it's the mental side of things, you know, where you can just try that little bit extra, and that's how we train. We train to find that bit extra, you know. A lot of clubs don't do that. We put them under the pump.

'A normal day's training back in [Rocky's] day would be the same as what we do now, probably. I haven't changed too much; an hour in the gym followed by an hour on the paddock. One of my standard fitness regimes I do is four laps in five minutes and most blokes find it extremely hard. I used to do those every night of the week until everyone made it. If we had two blokes who didn't make it, we'd all go back and do it again.

'And if I had the shits, we'd start with a four and five and do a four and five at the end, you know. I'd be looking at me kids. Half of them would be blowing up and telling me to get knicked, you know. I'd be looking at the kids who would be saying yeah, I want to have a go at this, you know, and test themselves out mentally, which is what footy is all about. That's what would have instilled some mental toughness in Rocky. I guess he took a bit of that with him to union.'

Carden recalled being hard on Rocky. That, however, was a perverse mark of respect, perhaps even affection, more than anything. A mate of mine — Matt Green, who worked as a physiotherapist at the Bulldogs while Rocky was there — remembered Carden always being the hardest on players he liked the most, which, in a strange way, made sense if Carden believed what he was doing was beneficial, which he clearly did.

'Mark Hughes was excited about signing Rock,' Carden said. 'He struggled to get him, but he finally got him. He was excited about getting him because he thought he was going to be the next big thing, you know. He was a standout schoolboy. When he turned up he said I've got this big, gangly kid. He started training. I've got two types of blokes. I have me good trainers and I have me blokes that I call me sponge cakes. Unfortunately, Rocky was a blancmange, which is softer than a sponge cake. I'm thinking when you tell him that he'll start laughing. Whenever we did a hard training session it was always Rocky I was getting into.

'Rocky was a goer, he was a real goer, you know. What you've got to realise is that when you come to a place like Canterbury and you come out of schoolboys stock ... every schoolboy says yeah, I've done weights and I'm fit. And they go to this level, they've done nothing, you know what I mean? It's just a different ball game. He was a trier. He wasn't a naturally gifted athlete, running wise. He was big and gangly. He was just starting to develop a motor, you know. As you know, to be a forward in league you've got to have a fair motor on you. You've got to keep doing the same thing, the same thing over and over, whacking the ball up, whacking the ball up, tackling, tackling. As a back-rower that's what you've got to be doing.'

Rocky had a shoulder reconstruction after he left Nudgee and it put him in a difficult position at the Bulldogs. 'I guess if he had turned up without having had a shoulder recon, it could have been a whole different ball game,' Carden said. 'When you have a shoulder recon it more or less wipes out a whole off-season for you, you know.'

Carden was just as frustrated at not being able to coin a nickname for Rocky. He just could not come up with anything better than Rocky. 'When Mark Hughes said we've signed this kid called Rocky

Elsom I said, what's the background to his name, Mark? He said that's his name. I'm big on giving blokes nicknames and making sure they stick. I love it. The Hughes boys, Steven and Glen, were named the Dodgy Brothers because they used to dodge training all the time. Everyone has called them Dodgy all their lives. Jarrod Hickey, his name was Lovva — love a hickey. To this day everyone calls him Lovva.

'I was trying to come up with some type of name [for Rocky]. The first thing that came into my head was Rocky and Bullwinkle. I didn't come up with anything for Rocky, which disappoints me now. I came up with nothing. I came up dead. It's turned out alright. He has climbed the tree and his name is Rocky. How good is that? Geez, what was that song? "My Name Is Sue". That's a great song. I must Google it and listen to it again. Now I've got a bloke called Diamond Charlie. He leaves Rocky for dead.'

It was clear the hard man of the Bulldogs had a soft spot for Rocky. 'Do you see Rock much yourself?' Carden asked me. I told Carden I had fairly regular contact with Rocky in my role as a rugby writer for *The Australian*. 'I bumped into Corey Payne, who is playing for Canterbury at the moment, and he said he bumped into Rock,' Carden said. 'He said, Rock wants to catch up with you and have a beer. I said, sweet, I'm happy to do that. He was a good bloke and he was good to have around.

'One thing I do remember about Rocky: he very rarely raised his voice. Whenever he spoke, he always stopped and thought about what he was talking about, you know. He doesn't rattle on and on.

He thinks about what he is talking about, you know. He fitted in good, you know. He was a knockabout. He liked having a good time like all 19-year-old kids do, you know. He was a social bee. I used to be into him all the time about the elbow patches, coming from union, coming from the upper echelon background of growing up with the leather patches on your elbow. Who do you think you are type of thing, all that crap, you know. He got a bit snarly sometimes, but that's what it was meant to do, get him up on his toes. That was the reaction I was looking for. I always found him a gentleman, Rock. I admire what he has done in union. It's just nice to be part of his career, I guess, whatever little part I played.'

In private I've heard Rocky tell a story about the last training session before the 2000 Jersey Flegg grand final between the Bulldogs and the Cronulla Sharks. Carden had been riding Rocky hard all year, but now the 'blancmange' got his chance for revenge. At training, Ricky Stuart would sometimes use the coaching staff and leftover players as opposition to run through some plays. Stuart, a dual international, was still a slick ball-player, but the players wore sandshoes and went through the manoeuvres at a slow pace. Stuart got out from dummy-half and lobbed a long, floating pass to Carden, who simulated a hit-up in slow motion. Rocky shot out of the defensive line like he was making the first hit in a State of Origin match, burying his shoulder into Carden, driving him into the ground. Carden did not see it coming. He lay on his back, looking up at the sky, and started laughing. 'You got me, princess!' Carden knew Rocky had been busting to do that all year and he did not seem to mind one bit. Gaz was much loved by the players and that was just Rocky's way of showing his affection.

Rocky only played in a handful of games for the Bulldogs in his first year, one of which was the Jersey Flegg grand final with the Bulldogs beating the Sharks in the curtain-raiser to the NRL grand final at Stadium Australia in Homebush Bay. There is a photograph of the Bulldogs' premiership-winning team taken on the field after the grand final. All of the players are smiling, except Rocky. Tall and thin, he is standing at the back with his head tilting towards Jonathan Thurston, who is standing next to him, as if he is not sure whether the cameraman has captured him in the frame or not. In stark contrast to his jubilant teammates, Rocky is wearing a sombre expression. Maybe the camera caught him at the wrong moment and a split second later he was carrying on with the rest of the players, or perhaps he had a sense of foreboding about where his rugby league career was headed.

There were doubts about whether Rocky would make a successful transition to rugby league and carve out a career in the NRL. Tony McGahan keenly followed Rocky's progress at the Bulldogs and sensed he was having some difficulty. 'He didn't do it easy down there,' McGahan said. 'There were question marks about his ability that were raised. He moved out of the back row into the front row because they didn't deem him fast enough or aerobically good enough at that stage to play there. That's where they saw his future. It's a tough environment in the league world. He went through some tough times.'

I was interested to know what Ricky Stuart thought of Rocky. A Wallaby tourist to Argentina in 1987, Stuart switched codes and became a wonderful halfback, playing for the Canberra Raiders during their threepeat in the 1990s. Stuart was certainly impressed with Rocky's intelligence and maturity. 'Rocky was a kid who came down from Brisbane and took himself out of his comfort zone,' Stuart said. 'It was a big decision. He was mature beyond his years. He was a very confident kid. He had the aggressive attitude and commitment for hard work for rugby league. He was a kid who wanted to make a career out of his football.'

Perhaps euphemistically, Stuart believed Rocky's body shape was better suited to rugby union. 'Rocky's agility and height were always going to be difficult for him in regard to making it in rugby league,' Stuart said. 'I always thought it was going to be hard for him. He was always going to be suited for a rugby union career. Knowing he had that background, I just felt as though it was always going to be a little bit harder for him to make it across.

'It was a transitional year. It was basically a season where he had to find his feet, adapting to rugby league. As I said, he came from rugby union. He had a rugby union shape. He had no problems in regard to his attitude and commitment, but his body shape was more suited to rugby union. Even with the line speed of the game today, it was definitely at a stage where the game was getting quicker and quicker and it was always going to be a struggle for him. But his commitment and aggression were never going to be a problem in either rugby league or rugby union.'

But Stuart still thought the hard grind at the Bulldogs benefitted Rocky when he returned to rugby union. 'Canterbury had a tough work environment. It would have been a lot better than spending two years in rugby union,' Stuart said. 'I believe rugby union lacks that tough work ethic. It's something that is still missing, to be honest: that little bit of grunt and grinding your way through fatigue. It was no negotiation at Canterbury; a very tough environment.'

Not surprisingly, given that he was the one who recruited him, Mark Hughes did not regard Rocky's height as a disadvantage in rugby league. In fact, he saw it as a potential advantage. 'It's not a disadvantage if you can play,' Hughes said. 'You look at all of the back-rowers who are succeeding — and front-rowers, I guess — there's not too many under six foot any more. If you are taller than someone and you've got the equal athletic stats, strength and so on, offloading, the ability to get the ball away, nudge your way through the line, it's an advantage. Ask all the short blokes.

'I guess we never had Rocky long enough to determine how good a rugby league player he might have been. He was certainly showing great promise for a boy, who I think — I'm not sure he had that many years in rugby either, had he? He tested very well for his strength and agility. I've read all the American recruitment books. The basketball books, the baseball books, and character assessments and everything they go through, and I guess you learn that that's just as important as their physical attributes.'

Rocky's rugby league career was a stop-start affair at best. While his first season started with him recovering from a shoulder reconstruction, it ended on a positive note with the Jersey Flegg grand final win, but his second was marred by injury and inconsistency. 'He was a tough nut, Rock. I thought he was just starting to come good,' Carden said. But others at the Bulldogs were not so sure.

'With Sonny Bill we were certain, but with Rocky there wasn't that certainty,' Hughes said. 'There was the potential and the hope. But the competition to get into the [Bulldogs'] NRL squad and pack at that time was incredibly strong. The Bulldogs' philosophy was when you think you've got enough forwards buy two more. My recollection was if he wanted to stay, he was going to stay with us. When there was high interest from rugby I could see why. I know enough about rugby; this kid could be very good for them.'

Now that Sonny Bill Williams is playing for the All Blacks, you can guarantee Hughes will be watching if his two discoveries come up against each other in the event Australia and New Zealand should meet in the 2011 World Cup final. 'That's unbelievable, isn't it, the way it has fallen,' Hughes said. 'Are they going to come in contact with one another? I guess they will. I reckon Sonny might get an offload on him, but I reckon Rocky might hurt him too.'

Stephen Moore always thought, perhaps hoped, Rocky would come back. 'I think he would have enjoyed being in that environment initially,' Moore said. 'It would have been good fun. He would have enjoyed that. But I got the feeling he would always end up back in rugby. Deep down, I always thought he would come back. He was very suited to rugby both in his thinking, and physically. He was suited pretty much perfectly to play in the back row in rugby.'

As the second season of his three-year deal with the Bulldogs drew to a close, Rocky began to look at his options. Robbie Martin thought Rocky had got rugby league out of his system and 'realised his heart was in rugby'. When Robbie became aware of Rocky's decision to return to rugby union, he contacted Jeff Miller, who was now the chief executive of the Queensland Rugby Union, to let him know. Miller was interested in bringing Rocky back to Queensland, but the Reds' back-row stocks were already filled with Toutai Kefu, Matt Cockbain, Daniel Heenan and Luke Doherty. There was little room for an untested rookie like Rocky. Miller's old Wallabies coach Bob Dwyer, however, loved nothing better than finding a diamond in the rough.

# 4

## BOB DWYER'S EYES

*He's got a very strong mind. Very strong will. He was very
determined and he wanted to go somewhere.*

Former World Cup-winning Wallabies and NSW Waratahs coach Bob Dwyer

Bob Dwyer's eyes see what others do not. As a talent spotter, Dwyer has no peer in Australian rugby. He has the ability to see qualities in players that others are blind to. As Wallabies coach, he plucked Phil Kearns out of Sydney club Randwick's reserve grade in 1989 and started him against the All Blacks, beginning the Test career of one of Australia's greatest hookers. Even though Rocky had only played schoolboy rugby and had been out of the game for two years, the keen-eyed Dwyer did not miss his potential.

Dwyer took the train from his home in the Southern Highlands of NSW to Sydney and asked me to meet him under the clock at the country terminal at Central Station. While I was waiting for Dwyer, I read a plaque dedicated to John Whitton, father of the NSW Railways. A brilliant engineer, Whitton was an Englishman who migrated to Sydney in 1856 and was engineer-in-chief of NSW Railways from 1857 to 1890. 'His foresight and uncompromising will overcame opponents, who proposed narrow gauge, horse-drawn trains on wooden rails,' the dedication reads. 'Whitton insisted on adopting the standard rail gauge of four foot, eight and a half inches [1435mm] using steam trains on heavy steel rails. This set a high standard of construction, which formed the basis of our present railways.'

Funnily enough, the dedication to Whitton reminded me of Dwyer, who, incidentally, was also an engineer. In many ways, Dwyer was the father of modern Australian rugby. With 'foresight' and 'uncompromising will', Dwyer revolutionised Australian rugby in the 1980s, introducing a new style of attack, which helped the Wallabies win the 1991 World Cup, and still reverberates in the play of Australian teams today. As I was reading the end of the dedication to Whitton, I heard the unmistakable sound of Dwyer's voice behind me. I turned around and saw him standing there in a long brown overcoat, bundled up against the winter chill. Nearing his 70th birthday, the old coach's curly, once-brown hair had turned grey, but his eyes, those all-seeing eyes, were still as bright as ever.

Rocky's manager, Anthony Picone, rang Dwyer and told him he had a young player Dwyer might be interested in. Picone told Dwyer the story of how Rocky went straight from Nudgee's First XV to the Bulldogs' Jersey Flegg squad, but he now wanted to come back to rugby and he had a future in the game. Picone was managing Wallabies forwards Toutai Kefu and Nathan Sharpe at the time and Dwyer valued his opinion. Dwyer asked Picone for a video tape of

Rocky in action for the Bulldogs and he was sufficiently impressed to send former Wallabies number 8 and Waratahs forwards coach Steve Tuynman to watch Rocky play and confirm his assessment.

'Steve Tuynman is one of the great rugby brains in Australia,' Dwyer told me over black coffee and mineral water at the Grand Central Bar and Bistro. 'He understands the game really well and he was a super player. Anyway, he went to have a look at Rocky and he came back with some glowing reports, and not only glowing reports, but clearly defined reasons why his report was glowing.

'One of the important things was that he had a very high work rate. We were of the opinion that rugby league forwards don't have a high work rate. They go in and out of the game in succession whereas rugby forwards tend to need to be in the game most of the time. Added to that was his athleticism and his height — not many blokes Rocky's height succeed in league.'

Dwyer arranged a meeting with Rocky at a café in Queens Park in Sydney's eastern suburbs, which was a world away from Bulldogs territory. Dwyer brought along Tuynman and Waratahs backs coach Gary Ella. 'Our next step was to interview him and try to see what made him tick,' Dwyer said. 'He interviews impressively. He's got a very strong mind. Very strong will. He was very determined and he wanted to go somewhere. We were happy with what we learned, what we saw and we did the deal.

'I remember ringing Steve Folkes about him because he was still under contract. I said, you've got a guy in your academy that we are interested in. He said, well, we don't normally let players go, but we've got three players in our academy, all back-row forwards, and the three of them are pretty good, but there's no way we can take three of them into our senior squad. We can take one. We might at a pinch be able to take two. But there's no way we could take three.

'One was Sonny Bill Williams. The other one I'm not sure — he was an Islander kid — and Rocky. I said, you don't have many lineouts in rugby league so you might as well let Rocky go. He said, yeah, you're right. Maybe he thought the others measure up better or alternatively maybe he thought we want Sonny Bill and someone wants to take one so we might as well get rid of the one that someone wants to take. I don't know what his thought process was, but he agreed anyway.'

What Steve Folkes did not say to Dwyer was that when you are deciding on a player to let go of the one who, in the previous two years, has had a shoulder reconstruction, a facial reconstruction, two broken jaws, and was developing a nasty case of hamstring tendonitis, would no doubt stand out. Also, if the player they let go was playing rugby union, not rugby league, he could not come back to bite them.

However, Rocky was only on a six-month training contract with the Waratahs and he still had to prove himself if he was to secure a fulltime position in the Super rugby squad. He dropped everything so he could focus on achieving his goal, deferring his university studies and giving up every other pursuit. He had never been so single-minded about anything, and for Rocky that was saying something. Troubled by hamstring tendonitis, Rocky worried he would not have enough time to be able to impress Dwyer, but the coach reassured him. Dwyer said, 'Don't worry, Rocky, the Melbourne Cup winner isn't running its fastest in April.' And Rocky hung onto those words.

Dwyer was sympathetic towards Rocky's particular way of managing his fitness and health. 'We only train so we can play better,' Dwyer said. 'If we could play better by not training at all, we wouldn't train at all. We only practise so we can become better players. I'm totally clear on the fact that if a player is going to suffer with a training regime, then we need to modify it. Now the only other thing we need to consider is what parts of the week impact on the rest of the team? We have to fit in those sections which impact on the players around him, and the players around him have to understand what he has to go through to get himself right — this is any player, not just Rocky — in terms of his physical condition and in terms of his readiness to play and his understanding of the game plan, et cetera, by game day.

'Players are sensible too. They understand that if that's what he has to do, then that's what he has to do. And generally speaking, they see the pain and torture he has to go through to get right so they are more than sympathetic. They are only too glad that they don't have to do the same.'

Dwyer was confident Rocky had the ability to make it in Super rugby, but he was concerned about his weight — or lack of it. Rocky was still a string bean and Dwyer told him he had to put on nine kilograms to be able to compete in the physical contests. Rocky has a high metabolism and wondered how on earth he was going to gain nine kilos before the start of the season.

There was only one way to do it. He went on a super-size, but healthy, diet. Rocky and his brother Sam would go to the Flemington markets each week to buy meat, fruit and vegetables in bulk. In a matter of weeks, Rocky turned himself into the Incredible Bulk.

'An old guy I used to work with told us about these markets where you could buy wholesale produce straight from the grower but you have to buy a fair bit of it,' Sam said. 'We said great, we eat a lot of food. That will be perfect. We would go and buy meat at a fraction of the cost that you get it at the supermarket. We would buy boxes of apples, 15 lettuces or whatever. We would have to buy a whole bunch of everything.

'I would cook things like osso bucco and big casserole sort of dishes. They were really enough for a family. I'd have a standard portion and Rocky would eat the rest. He would be full at the end of dinner, but then he would have a roast chicken that he would pull out afterwards. He would slowly eat this whole chicken after his full meal. He had probably eaten kilos of food and then he'd eat this chicken. He wouldn't want to. He was full. But he would eat and eat and eat. He would do that every other day and he put on weight. If there were any leftovers, they would all go in the lunchbox, which was more like an Esky or a garbage bin that he would take to training.

'I really enjoy cooking. We had cookbooks and things like that. Our food wasn't boring. We tried to mix it up. It was pretty good, actually. I don't have any memories of it being a pain in the neck, which I think I would have if there were any problems. Because we didn't have a dishwasher there were heaps of dishes at the end of every meal. We would pitch in and just get it done. But the food bills were astronomical. I remember on the wage I was on at the time it was pretty hectic.'

The Waratahs found it amusing to watch Rocky arrive at training every day with an Esky full of food. 'Rocky was a lot smaller then,' Dwyer said. 'When we brought him in he was about 96 kilos. He might have hit 100 kilos by the time we started playing. He is a big eater. The blokes used to laugh. He would bring his food for the day in a full-size Esky, the kind you would take on a family picnic. That was Rocky's morning tea, lunch, afternoon tea and pre-dinner snack on his way home.'

Even Dwyer underestimated the extent of Rocky's stomach-stretching diet. I remember having a brief chat to Rocky in which he told me he was embarrassed to weigh in at only 92 kilos in front of Waratahs strength and conditioning coach Peter McDonald in September 2002. Then, stepping on the scales again a week before his Super 12 debut the following February, he had increased his weight to 104 kilos.

It is easy to underestimate the enormity of the task that confronted Rocky when he first arrived at the Waratahs. Still raw-boned, Rocky only had two years of rugby experience under his belt and that was at schoolboy level. After a stint in rugby league he was now competing with Wallabies for a place in the Waratahs back row. He was not going to displace number 8 David Lyons or openside flanker Phil Waugh at this stage of his career, anyway. The blindside flanker's spot was up for grabs, but he had never played the position.

So, having not played rugby for two years, Rocky had to try out for a spot on a professional team while learning a new role.

Of all 15 positions on a rugby team, blindside flanker suited Rocky best, not just physically, but also personality wise. Like Rocky himself, the role of blindside flanker was not easily defined. From wing-forward to breakaway to flanker, it has never been entirely clear exactly what the number 6 position entailed. There is no doubt some players have revolutionised certain positions, such as Mark Ella, who reinvented five-eighth play. But as innovative as Ella was, it was always obvious he was playing five-eighth. The perception of blindside flanker as a distinct position from openside flanker is only a comparatively recent development. It was not so long ago that teams, including the Wallabies, played left and right flanker similar to left and right winger. You were a flanker, just as you were a winger, regardless of what side you were on. In some countries, such as France, they still play left and right, while in South Africa the blindside flanker, who wears number 7, is often indistinguishable from the openside flanker, particularly in terms of physique.

While specialist positions such as hooker, halfback and five-eighth have clear responsibilities, blindside flanker offered a player the opportunity to make of it what he could. Ideally, coaches look for a blindside flanker who can run with the ball, execute a dominant tackle, play hard on the ball at the breakdown, jump in the lineout, scrummage and link with the backs in attack. Quite often a number 6 will only excel in perhaps one or two of those areas, but it will be sufficient to hold down the position, depending on the make-up of the rest of the back row and even back five. If the back-rowers complement each other, you can carry a blindside flanker who jumps in the lineout, but does not carry the ball, if the number 8 is a ball-runner. I had a conversation with Rocky about this once and he suggested blindside flanker should be the last position filled in a team – wait and see what you need. Back in 2003, Rocky was learning the role of blindside flanker, whatever that was, but eventually he would master every art of the position and in the process reinvent what it meant to play number 6.

While starting out, Rocky was lucky he had a coach like Bob Dwyer, who had no qualms about picking players on potential. 'We always thought he would be a 6 or an 8,' Dwyer said. 'We had Dave Lyons, but we had lost Stu Pinkerton. The idea was to have him as a lineout forward back-rower. We actually even thought he had enough pace to play 7, but he was a bit tall to play 7 because it's a bit hard to get down on the ground.

'He was extremely impressive. His first trial was up at Bathurst. We played NSW Country. Both Gary Ella and Steve Tuynman said after that first trial let's not buggerise around anymore, let's put him in the senior squad straight away. We knew he had the determination. We knew he had the pace. He just had to spend more time in the game. And the more time he spent there the better he was going to get.'

Dwyer noticed that Rocky had an unusual, upright running style, similar to Sonny Bill Williams, which was devastatingly effective, although it left him vulnerable to big hits in defence. 'Rocky runs the ball differently,' Dwyer said. 'He runs a lot higher. He uses his lower-body strength to break tackles and his upper-body strength to drag players off him whereas a lot of players in that position ... I know he is playing number 8, but [All Black] Kieran Read uses a low body position and uses his leg drive via his upper body to knock players out of the road. Rocky doesn't run that way at all.

'I suppose Jerome Kaino [All Black blindside flanker] is a bit like Rocky, but not as big and not as tall. Yet, he runs more upright and tries to knock people out of the road and get the ball away. Rocky exposes his body so that he can keep his arms free whereas most people will want to use their arms to cover their body, protect their body. He doesn't worry about it. He is tough enough to take it, get his arms over the top and get the ball away.'

Les Kiss had heard of Rocky, but he did not meet him until he joined the Waratahs. 'Being aware of Rocky and knowing him are two different things,' Kiss said. 'All I knew was there was a guy named Rocky Elsom, a guy from Nudgee who didn't quite nail it in league, but was impressive in the quality of his work rate. We used to train a couple of times with the Canterbury Bulldogs. Just the usual comment: good kid, goes well. Probably another year or two he might make it. But he was obviously keen to get back. He was slight. He wasn't underweight. But he wasn't as big as he is now. When he joined us he hit that diet. He was eating five chickens a day, bananas or whatever. And he expanded his body.

'He was quiet and reserved. He was like he is now. He didn't get flustered. If there was hard work to do, he would do it. He was very particular about certain things that he felt had to be done. He got into strength and conditioning and his diet. They were the two things that drove him more than anything. He built up and built up and built up. Size became a big issue.'

As defence coach, Kiss was impressed not only with Rocky's physicality, but also his understanding of the defensive system he had put in place at the Waratahs, which was based on rugby league principles. 'His tackling was fine,' Kiss said. 'He is not a classic legs tackler as such. League doesn't have classic legs tacklers. They have legs, upper body. His strength and aggression in the tackle was the thing. We were always pretty good in defence at the Waratahs, but he definitely lifted the intensity. Once you are in the contact it's not just the tackle, but how you win that whole battle. He brought that mentality.

'If anything, he linked with my way of thinking. It was his understanding of how you worked in twos, threes and fours effectively. In rugby league when you shift forward there is a connection between defenders. That was in rugby, but he had an intuitive understanding of that. He probably just brought a bit more depth of knowledge about what defence meant to the whole package. It wasn't just an add-on. It was an integral part of the game.'

Kiss also thought blindside flanker would be Rocky's best position after having not played rugby for two years. 'He didn't have to be part of the critical linking elements of the set piece, particularly the scrum, but he could become part of the next play,' Kiss said. 'He could get the ball in his hand and take the line on. He didn't offload the ball in his early years, but he was a hard man to stop.

'The other side of the coin in the back row is you are trying to get another jumper at least. Rocky developed into a beautiful lineout option, didn't he? Over a period of two or three years that became rock solid. To be able to go three jumpers confidently and even four really gave you strength. When you had Googy [Justin Harrison], Dan Vickerman and Rocky you had all these options and that was a big plus.'

While Dwyer included Rocky in the senior squad, he did not get much time on the field, missing the trials against Super rugby opposition altogether. Having played only 100 minutes of rugby in the last two years, it looked from the outside like it would take time for Rocky to work his way back into the game. The fact that he was unable to run for most of the pre-season because of his hamstring complaint would not have helped his cause either. Dwyer, however, did not see it that way.

In a major surprise, the unheralded Rocky was named in the Waratahs' 22-man squad for the opening game of the Super 12 season against the Blues at the Sydney Football Stadium. Dwyer announced the team at the Waratahs' season launch at the Australian Stock Exchange in the CBD. The three Rs of investment — risk, reward and return — flashed on an electronic information board as Dwyer read out the players' names. The basic principles of investment could have applied to Dwyer's rugby philosophy, which was never risk averse. While Rocky was a long-term investment, he was about to deliver some short-term dividends.

Rocky's return to rugby coincided with the height of the game's fixation with rugby league following the ARU's poaching of high-profile converts Wendell Sailor, Mat Rogers and Lote Tuqiri. Rocky was one of seven uncapped Super rugby players in the Waratahs squad. Six of the seven new caps — Rocky, Omar Hassanein, Ryan McGoldrick, Tuqiri, Paul Sheedy and Milton Thaiday — came from rugby league backgrounds, while Mat Rogers was at fullback and Nathan Blacklock was in the wider squad. McGoldrick had played on the Sharks team that lost to the Bulldogs in the Jersey Flegg grand final.

In explaining Rocky's stunning selection, Dwyer revealed that his performance in the Sydney trial against NSW Country had convinced him he was ready. 'Rocky's got great speed, great agility and a tremendous work rate,' Dwyer told me at the team announcement. 'He made two triple plays [three successive tackles] in defence last weekend, which I haven't seen anyone in the Waratahs do at all in the two and a bit years I've been here.'

Rocky had only played in two minor trial matches for Sydney against NSW Country and a NSW President's XV against Wellington-Tonga so his selection took most of the Sydney rugby media by surprise. 'When Elsom's name was announced, many at the function looked at each other with looks of bewilderment,' the *Sydney Morning Herald* reported. 'Rocky who? Rocky Balboa. Buddy Ebsen. Buddy who?'

When I think back to Rocky's first major media conference I am struck by how well he handled it, answering questions from veteran reporters intelligently and candidly. Rocky admitted in *The*

*Daily Telegraph* that he was surprised about his call-up. 'I'm not sure why they chose me ahead of some of the other guys,' Rocky said. 'I haven't asked. I probably should.' Asked whether he felt under pressure, Rocky told the *Sydney Morning Herald*: 'I'm not feeling that much pressure yet because when I arrived at NSW I don't think they were expecting that much of me.' Shock selection or not, Rocky was determined to make the most of his unexpected opportunity. 'I'm really excited about it,' Rocky told me and although his laidback body language did not seem convincing, there was something about him, maybe just a look, suggesting you would put your house on it that he was actually jumping out of his skin.

The *Sydney Morning Herald* published a photograph of Rocky at the media conference, which revealed more about him than the photographer probably realised. Rocky is seated next to Tuqiri and McGoldrick on a platform behind Dwyer, who is speaking to the gathering. While Tuqiri is slumped back in his seat, seemingly staring into space and lost in his own thoughts, Rocky's head is tilted slightly forward, listening intently to Dwyer, soaking it all in.

What we did not know at the time was that Rocky was unaware he had been selected in the squad until he arrived at training that Monday morning, an hour after the rest of the players, who had practised earlier than usual so they could attend the team announcement. Waratahs officials had tried to contact Rocky on the Sunday, but his mobile phone was not working. In a mad rush, Sam picked up a suit for Rocky on the way to the Stock Exchange and he arrived just in time to meet the press.

'He was really happy, but Rocky is never over-demonstrative or says this is a dream come true, I can't believe I've made it. I've made this step. Now I have to prove myself. I have to stay on the field longer. It's never as if he arrives anywhere. It's all about what you have to do now,' Vicki said.

Rocky burst onto the Super rugby scene like a human dynamo in the Waratahs' 31-18 loss to the Blues on a rain-soaked evening in Sydney. He replaced Omar Hassanein at blindside flanker for the last 26 minutes, playing at a frantic, almost manic, pace, as the Waratahs surged back from 23-6 down. Australian rugby had not seen anything like him since dual international Ray Price, who was known as 'Mr Perpetual Motion'. I remember sitting in the press box, thinking to myself, if this Elsom kid keeps this up, he is either going to burn out or break down.

'Early on he threw himself into it and that's what we liked about him,' Kiss said. 'He brought that extra edge. It was his scramble that he brought as well. I wouldn't say it was just the domain of rugby league, but you could see him working hard in critical moments. He would come up with critical plays in defence and attack.'

The Waratahs elevated Rocky's training contract to a fulltime three-year deal before they embarked on a two-game tour of South Africa. Dwyer promoted Rocky to the starting line-up at blindside flanker for the game against the Cats in Bloemfontein and was immediately vindicated. The Cats' back row included Springboks Bob Skinstad and Joe van Niekerk, but the Waratahs' loose trio of Rocky, David Lyons and Phil Waugh made their night hell as they would do to numerous teams over the next half-a-dozen years. In an outstanding run-on debut, Rocky shone, scoring a try in traffic, creating turnovers and punching holes in defence in the Waratahs' 48–36 win.

In typically industrious Rocky fashion, he played at a ferocious pace. His try was not spectacular, just sheer power and determination, picking up the ball at the base of a ruck and forcing his way over. 'Rocky was phenomenal,' Dwyer told me after the game. 'But he doesn't need to get too excited. It was his first run-on game and he has to back it up week after week.' Rocky was already being touted as a 'left field' candidate for the Wallabies, which was quite remarkable given he had played only a game and a half of professional rugby.

Stephen Moore, who made his Super rugby debut for the Reds that same year, was not surprised to see Rocky make an immediate impact for the Waratahs. 'As a schoolboy, Rocky was extremely dominant,' Moore said. 'He used to basically run over people. He was quick, physical. He still maintained those attributes. That's what I remember about him first coming back to rugby. He came bursting onto a few balls and made some great carries and made some good yards and all of a sudden people were going who is this bloke? He had just come from rugby league and a lot of people wouldn't have been aware of his background in rugby. He came onto the scene with a bang. I wasn't really playing regularly then. He came on and held his spot. It was a good feat for a guy who was only twenty.'

The Elsom family attended the Waratahs' next home game against the Bulls on a Saturday night. Vicki and Russell flew down from the Sunshine Coast on the Friday to join the other players' parents in a group that was known as the 'propagators'.

'We got in on Friday night,' Vicki said. 'We were running so late. The plane was delayed. We got off the plane and rang to say we were running late. Pip Waugh [Phil Waugh's mother] said, we are all waiting for you. We really want you to come. When we arrived they all started clapping. We thought this is nice. We were a bit taken aback. And then Matt Burke's dad said, I'd just like to say how happy we are to have Rocky here. Everyone had name tags and Russell said, does your son play rugby? They thought it was hysterical that Russell didn't know who Matt Burke was.'

The Waratahs beat the Bulls 26–16 and Rocky produced a man-of-the-match performance, scoring the first try of the game just before halftime after stepping off his right foot to get through the defence. Rocky played with gusto for the full 80 minutes, inspiring the headline in the next day's newspaper, 'Hungry Elsom Devours Bulls'.

'There were people yelling out his name,' Vicki said. 'I almost started crying. I can't believe it. To me, he was still like a little boy. When he came off the field he's bruised and battered. I go did that hurt? He says no. I said, Rocky, you've got so many stitches. Who did that to you? He said, oh, I just put my head in the wrong place, Mum.'

The sheer joy of watching Rocky play has never diminished for the Elsoms. 'Just to watch him progress,' Kelly said. 'When he was picked up for Super rugby there was a lot of hoo-ha. The fact he hadn't played a club game. He has come from league. We were just so excited. Oh god! Before the game, the nerves, the sickness, it was like we were on the field. Mum's bad. Even now, Mum has to get up and exert some energy. And it doesn't end. You think oh yeah, he's just playing another game. The further he goes the more it is. Now he is the captain. Oh my god! The pressure that is on him, we feel it too. We are sitting there watching it, trying to give out good vibes for him.'

The Waratahs dropped two costly home games to the Stormers (39-29) and the Reds (35-23), but a penalty goal by Shaun Berne after the siren gave them a 34-31 win against the defending champions, Crusaders, in Sydney, which kept them in touch with the finals contenders. Rocky continued to impress although he did hit a speed bump towards the end of the season. On a cold, wet night in Wellington, the Waratahs went down to the Hurricanes 42-26 and their back row was taught a lesson by the Hurricanes' loose trio, which included All Blacks Jerry Collins and Rodney So'oialo, known as the Devil's Henchmen. The Waratahs lost David Lyons early with a head knock and Rocky, while still playing at a frenetic pace, was not as effective as he had been. It seemed the heavy workload was starting to tell on the young flanker. When you think about it, playing Super rugby was an enormous step up for Rocky, who just a month earlier was on a training contract, trying to gain enough weight to be considered for selection.

Looking to bounce back, the Waratahs then headed to Canberra to face an out-of-sorts Brumbies. Rocky, more than anyone, made an impact with some big hits early in the game and a couple of steals at the front of the lineout. Rocky came under fire from some of the senior Wallabies forwards in the Brumbies pack after his enthusiasm led to him being penalised for late tackles on Test halves George Gregan and Stephen Larkham. The late shot on Gregan resulted in a scuffle on the ground, one of the few in the halfback's long career. Despite the Waratahs' passion, it was one-way traffic with the Brumbies handing out a 41-15 thrashing. Tireless, Rocky's work rate was astonishing in a losing team, and he was named player of the round.

Watching the match on television at his home in Sydney, former Wallabies captain and flanker Simon Poidevin was highly impressed with Rocky's play, which was not surprising when you knew how 'Poido' approached the game. I first came across Poidevin while I was playing for St Leo's against St Patrick's Goulburn at our home ground in Wahroonga on Sydney's upper North Shore. It was my first year in the First XV and the coach put me on the wing, a position I did not always enjoy because you did not get your hands on the ball as much as you wanted. But if there was one game when I was happy to be on the wing, it was this one. I was a mere spectator as this red-haired terror in the St Pat's pack smashed our forwards, including his own cousin Matt Troy, who was one of my best friends. I'm sorry 'Troy Boy', I thought, but you are on your own today, mate.

After that frightening experience it did not surprise me at all to see Poidevin become one of Australia's greatest flankers and the first Wallaby to play 50 Tests. Retiring after playing an important role in the Wallabies' 1991 World Cup victory, Poidevin entered the highly competitive world of stock-broking. He was managing director of Equity Sales at Citigroup in Australia before becoming the executive director of Pengana Capital in 2009.

I interviewed Poidevin in the boardroom of Pengana — an Aboriginal word meaning hawk — on the 12th floor of an office tower in Sydney's Big End of Town, with spectacular views of the Botanical Gardens and the harbour. I was expecting Poidevin to be dressed in a power suit befitting a master of the universe, but he wore a plain, light blue business shirt and dark blue trousers, the colours of his old team NSW Waratahs, and no tie. After 25 years working in the cut-throat world of stock-broking and investment banking as part of a global commercial empire, Poidevin was enjoying the comparatively slower pace of life in a boutique company at the other end of the financial market, funds management, which allowed him to spend more time with his three young sons, act as co-president of the Classic Wallabies and pursue his new sporting passion, cycling. Sipping a skinny latte, Poidevin looked as fit as he did when he first took on the All Blacks, and beat them, in 1980.

I asked Poidevin what it was about Rocky that first impressed him. 'I think my first major impression of Rocky was watching him in a Super 12 game when he was playing for NSW Waratahs against the Brumbies in Canberra,' said Poidevin, who peppers sentences with the words 'out there' as if in his imagination all the real action in life was still 'out there' on the playing field. 'It was a night where clearly there was a lot of emotion between the two teams out there, but Rocky just stood out as that warrior, classic back-rower, who for 80 minutes of the game was just going hammer and tongs. I thought, this guy has really got it. He's really got that warrior spirit. He really took the Brumbies on and put his body on the line and caused a lot of damage to the Brumbies. I thought at the time, how did Queensland let this bloke slip through the cracks?'

Poidevin, who was coached by Bob Dwyer at Randwick and the Wallabies, could certainly see what Dwyer saw in Rocky. 'Bob would really like the way Rocky plays the game from a Bob Dwyer view of how rugby should be played,' Poidevin said. 'Rocky's ability to offload a ball in a tackle and keep continuity going is something that Bob Dwyer salivates about.'

Perhaps surprisingly, Poidevin did not really get to know Rocky until later in his career. 'He is hard to get to know, Rocky, because he is a guy who ... there's no flowery talk about the way he looks at the world,' Poidevin said. 'It's pretty black and white. Once you get him going he is a good conversationalist, but he is not a natural guy to be leading a conversation in a room as such. You probably get more out of Rocky Elsom sitting down having a coffee with him on a beachfront, and getting to know the real Rocky, than in a public venue where he'll be quite guarded in what he says. I've had a lot more to do with Rocky the last couple of years. We text each other all the time, especially coming into Test matches. I'll text him before every Test match.

'Being a combative back-rower out there, people immediately think this guy is all about passion, and maybe brutality. They say that's the bucket he's in. Well, that's not the bucket he's in. He's actually a deep thinker. Putting players in buckets doesn't necessarily tell the real person.'

The discovery of the year, Rocky was looking more and more like a bolter for the Wallabies. There were question marks over the Test blindside flanker position following veteran Wallabies number 6 Owen Finegan undergoing a shoulder reconstruction. But days after his heroics in Canberra, Rocky injured his own shoulder and an MRI scan later revealed a fracture in his left shoulder, sidelining him for six weeks and ending his Super 12 season.

The Waratahs rallied in their remaining games without Rocky and went oh so close to making the top four. In the final game of the regular season, the Waratahs needed to beat the Chiefs in Sydney and gain a bonus point for scoring four tries for entry to the finals. The Waratahs were well ahead and playing for their fourth try when Matt Dunning landed one of the best field goals by a prop in the history of the game. Unfortunately, the Waratahs did not need three points. They needed a try, prompting the newspaper headline the following day, 'Dumb and Dunning'. The Waratahs won 25-14, but missed out on the playoffs. In the end the loss to the Brumbies came back to bite them. The Waratahs and the Brumbies finished in equal fourth on the table with 31 competition points each, but the ACT side advanced on a better for and against.

Rocky recovered from his shoulder injury in time to play for the Australian under-21s in the 2003 World Cup in England. Rocky's worries continued with a further injury to his left shoulder. He played on and Australia eventually went down to New Zealand 21-10 in the final in Oxford.

On return to Australia, Rocky would have picked up the newspaper to read about Poidevin urging Wallabies coach Eddie Jones to consider Rocky for the Bledisloe Cup match with the

All Blacks in Sydney. 'We are struggling at the breakdown at the moment,' Poidevin told *The Daily Telegraph*. 'The question mark is who to bring in at blindside. Owen Finegan would be a starting point, but I wouldn't rule out someone like Rocky Elsom. He has the work rate and the go forward in attack and defence.'

Jones dropped David Lyons, who had started at blindside flanker in the previous four Tests, but he did not bring Rocky into the team. Instead, Jones played two openside flankers, George Smith and Phil Waugh, in tandem. The downsizing of the back row provided the Wallabies with greater mobility and ball-scavenging skills at the breakdown, but it sacrificed their capability in the set pieces, particularly the lineout. The Wallabies lost to New Zealand 50–21, but Jones continued with his two opensides policy right up to the World Cup final against England.

In any event, Rocky was still struggling to regain full function of his shoulder and, after another MRI scan revealed considerable damage, he underwent a reconstruction in August, which sidelined him for six months.

Rocky's start to his professional rugby career went better than he possibly could have imagined. Just think about where he started — struggling to secure a Super rugby contract — to where he finished — on the fringe of Wallabies selection. But if he felt any sense of satisfaction, he did not show it. 'I don't think satisfaction is something Rocky ever feels,' Vicki said. 'After that first season he said he had a headache all of the time and that every inch of him hurt. He could never get rid of the headache.

'You could never say he was elated or he felt it was a great start. Rocky always seems to be like there is more to do. He is always looking forward. He is always a person who wants to have some sort of productivity.'

It seemed almost certain Rocky would earn his first Test cap the following year, but the 2004 season turned out to be the worst of Rocky's career. Former Wallabies prop Ewen McKenzie replaced Bob Dwyer as Waratahs head coach and things began to change for Rocky. While McKenzie – who had been a Wallabies assistant coach under Rod Macqueen and Eddie Jones – had a good knowledge of the game, for a young player such as Rocky it would have been a less than ideal situation to lose his mentor after only one season. After establishing himself under Dwyer, Rocky would have to prove himself all over again.

Rocky started where he left off in the opening game of the season, a rare 43–21 win against the Crusaders in Christchurch. Outstanding against the Crusaders and impressive against the Sharks and Cats, Rocky was again touted as a Test contender. Against the Cats in Sydney, Rocky's ferocious running was on display once again. In one instance, Rocky was handed a turnover and systematically brushed off defenders, skipping out of tackles, shifting the ball from one side to the other, charging up field. The Cats must have been sick of the sight of him.

Jetting off to South Africa on top of the table, the Waratahs seemed to be the team to beat, with Rocky as their new spearhead. The republic, however, was a different story, the Waratahs losing to the Stormers in Cape Town (27–23) and the Bulls in Pretoria (38–27). The Waratahs' season was grinding to a halt and the same fate was in store for Rocky, who received a yellow card in Pretoria and was dropped to the bench for the match with the Chiefs in Hamilton. He was replaced by Simon Kasprowicz, an honest toiler, but without Rocky's dynamism.

Rocky was playing with tremendous vigour, but there were concerns about his error rate, particularly his ball retention at the tackle. In explaining his decision to drop Rocky, McKenzie reasoned that Rocky was still learning the game, which he was, but when does anyone ever stop learning the game? 'Rocky only came to this level 12 months ago,' McKenzie told me in an interview at the time. 'He has come a long way in a short space of time. He hasn't had the advantage of learning the subtleties which other players learn year in and year out. He's still developing. He's a young kid. Coming off the bench will be part of his learning experience.'

Bob Dwyer, who was now running the Waratahs academy, argued with McKenzie about dropping Rocky, but to no avail. 'I think it was influenced by a philosophy that crept in, which measured people in a negative sense by the number of mistakes they made,' Dwyer said. 'I remember in discussions with Ewen McKenzie and Andy Friend [Waratahs assistant coach] that Rocky makes too many mistakes. I said well, that's because he does twice as much as the other guys. Are we going to pick someone who does three things and makes no mistakes or someone who does 20 things and makes four mistakes? I said, I'm for the guy who does 20 things and makes four mistakes. I voiced my opinion about it, but I didn't have a vote or any influence.'

If Rocky's relationship with McKenzie was lukewarm to begin with, it was now ice cold. Both McKenzie and Friend had lost faith in Rocky, and he seemed more than aware of it. In a domino effect, less faith resulted in fewer minutes and less game-time led to a gradual slide in form. From starting every game to receiving five or 10 minutes off the bench, Rocky appeared to grow more and more agitated.

'I think Rocky was a little bit frustrated at that time,' Kiss said. 'I remember running the sideline one game and the message given to me was to tell him not to give any penalties away. I thought, I shouldn't say that. You don't put something like that in a guy's head. I said, Rock, just a message, and he looked at me. There was probably a bit of frustration there because he wasn't nailing it and they were looking at the things he did wrong rather than what he could offer.

'I didn't tell him what he couldn't do. I just believed what he could do and what influence it had. My philosophy on coaching is if I tell you what's wrong with you all the time, that's what I'll get. I want to tell you what you're good at and work on the little things we can work on. I look at what you bring me before I tell you what you can't bring me. Rocky probably appreciated the fact I worked with that and let him be his own man. Why would I interfere with that and try to over-coach him?'

In the final game of the regular season, the Waratahs again needed to win to secure a finals spot, but this time facing the Reds, a side they had never beaten in Super 12 rugby. Rocky played impressively in the five minutes Kasprowicz was in the blood bin, but he had gone from playing a starring role to that of an extra. The Reds, true to form, beat the Waratahs 23–7 and scuttled their post-season plans, leaving them to dream of what might have been. In the aftermath, the Waratahs released Kasprowicz, but that did not necessarily mean the situation was improving for Rocky.

Rocky was still struggling with a persistent hamstring injury that he brought with him from the Bulldogs and his particular way of looking after himself was not always appreciated by everyone at the Waratahs. 'Early on he had a lot of niggles and things that he had to manage,' Kiss said. 'He would say I can't train with that, and that became an issue with some people. This is where he was quite particular, determined. He understood himself better than most people understood themselves. He would say no, I can't train. I'm not ready to train. I need to get this [rehabilitated].

'He even went to the point of getting independent advice on how to work on certain things, which didn't sit well with some people. A lot of people thought: he has to train if he is going to play. Rocky could turn up for the last trial and blitz it because he threw himself into it. You look at him in a game and he would look totally out and then he would just snap on and do something brilliant. That was just his nature. It was just little niggles that he managed differently to most other players. He knew his body. He knew what was going to work for him.

'That sort of particularness – if that's a word – was unique to him. A lot of players are told what to do, but Rocky was very determined.

He understood his body better than the person telling him. And I think he did. He was quite unique in that way. People said he should conform. Why should he conform? He did what he had to do for himself. He wasn't a conformist, but it didn't mean he was an individual at the expense of the team. He did what he had to do.'

Rocky did not regain his starting spot for the Waratahs and was not in Wallabies contention, but he was selected again in the Australian under-21s in the 2004 World Cup in Scotland. Unfortunately, he was restricted to just half a game in the tournament because of his hamstring injury. 'I remember he had a bad hamstring that year, which really hampered him,' said Stephen Moore, who was a member of the under-21s team. 'I don't think he played at all in the tournament. It's not something that he talked about much. I knew it was serious. If you don't play, it's serious.

'It all comes back to him knowing his body really well. He knows exactly what it takes for him to fire and if it's not right, then he'll say it. It took him a while to get it right. Maybe that injury was what sort of really ... he looked at all different avenues to get it right and I think he still uses a lot of that to this day. Yoga, he does a lot of his own stuff in the gym, which he knows gets his body in the right shape.

'If you didn't know the background and he was doing a different program and you didn't know why, I could see how it could cause an issue. I've seen it for a long time. I know he has to do certain things for his body to get it right. That's the approach at this level. You've got to do whatever gets you right physically and he knows what that is.'

Vicki and Russell had flown to Glasgow, but instead of proudly watching Rocky play for Australia, they were told his hamstrings would be the ruin of his career. 'The doctor said Rocky will never be a Wallaby because his hamstrings are too bad for a professional player,' Vicki said. 'He doesn't choose to explain it. Maybe he should. That's a problem [Rocky] deals with on a constant basis. Figuring out how his body is going to work at its best and that's not necessarily running around the oval six times and his legs don't work at all. He gets very tired, extremely tired. When he played in Ireland he could rest as much as he wanted or as little as he wanted. Michael Cheika [former Leinster coach] is a great person. I say that not just because he coached Rocky. He genuinely cares about the person.'

Dr Angus Bathgate, who was the Australian under-21s doctor in England in 2003 and is now the Brumbies' medical officer, provided an insight into Rocky's hamstring problems. 'There were some hamstring issues which went back to his Bulldogs days,' Dr Bathgate said. 'These are bad injuries. Once you have a chronic hamstring tendonosis it is very difficult to treat and tough to keep playing. He has done well to be a professional football player.'

One of Rocky's teammates in the Australian under-21s was future Waratahs and Wallabies second-rower Al Kanaar, who would become a close friend. Kanaar remained in contact with Rocky even after he prematurely retired with a knee injury in 2007. I decided to interview Kanaar after Kelly told me Rocky was the only professional rugby player he invited to his wedding. An environmentalist, Kanaar was trained by Al Gore to be a climate change advocate. He rode a bicycle from his home in inner-city Redfern to my office in Surry Hills to do our interview. With his corkscrew curls and bushy beard, he looked more like an activist for Greenpeace than a burly rugby lock.

'I guess we did [hit it off],' Kanaar said of his friendship with Rocky over a coffee in the News Limited canteen. 'We are both very driven people. He looks after his body extremely well, pushes his body to the limit during the game. He's got that bit of mongrel in him, which I guess is essential. If I was to look at any characteristics that we had similar, it would be that mongrel and that drive.

'We are both very individual-type of characters. We also see that rugby does provide you with a lot of opportunities that people in a normal career wouldn't have. We've both tried to take full advantage of that. He has always got something on the go. I guess that's one of the characteristics, always making the most out of life.

'My upbringing is similar to his. It shows by how well he and I have hit it off, and my parents and Vicki and Russ, and Sarah [Al's wife] and Kelly and all of his family. He is very family orientated. He is driven. He wants to achieve success and he wants to be busy, always doing something, always achieving something. He plans everything extremely well. He is a good manager. He is able to manage his time and relationships well. He is a very moral person and he stands up for what he believes in. He will work to achieve a result, but he's got firm beliefs and he sticks to them. He is a very deep thinker.'

If 2004 was a hard year for Rocky, then 2005 threatened to be much worse. While Simon Kasprowicz headed off to Japan, competition for places in the Waratahs' back row was even fiercer.

McKenzie recruited a powerful ball-running back-rower, Wycliff Palu, who had played rugby league with St George Illawarra Dragons. Also, Stephen Hoiles, a very skilful footballer, returned from the Wallabies' tour of Europe at the end of 2004 as a Test player. And there was still Phil Waugh and David Lyons.

Al Kanaar, a rookie in 2005, remembered it well. 'There were a lot of challenges with Palu and David Lyons and Phil Waugh and those back-rowers at the time. [Rocky] had to fight really hard to get his spot back. He worked hard to get back into the Waratahs and cement his spot.'

Palu impressed in the trials and Rocky did not. After the opening trial there was a new order at the Waratahs and it did not look like Rocky was in it. In the second trial, 28 players were selected to give everyone a chance to impress. Rocky was not one of them. Instead, he had a date with the Wellington Academy XV at TG Milner Field in suburban Eastwood. For a player with more than 20 Super rugby caps to his credit, to be left out of the top 28 players sent a very clear message that his career was like the name of the great 1980s band, Dire Straits.

Al Kanaar remembered butting heads with Rocky in pre-season training as tensions rose over competition for spots. 'We trained quite hard against each other,' Kanaar said. 'There were a few instances in contact and that kind of stuff. We clashed a few times. But it was all in good spirit.'

Reduced to appearances in lower level trials, Rocky, critically, responded to the intense pressure he was under to make the

Waratahs' 22-man squad. He was outstanding at blindside flanker in NSW A's 31–22 win against Auckland A, and took full advantage of playing in the unfamiliar openside flanker role in the reserve team's 31–17 loss to Wellington Academy. He donned the number 7 jersey again in the Waratahs' final pre-season hit-out against the Blues in Whangarei.

McKenzie likened Rocky to versatile South African forward AJ Venter, who could play in every position in the back five. 'Like AJ Venter, Rocky has versatility,' McKenzie told me at the time. 'We've played Rocky at number 6, but we have talked about playing him in the second row. He is big enough to play there. In some ways, Rocky is more suited to openside than blindside. Number 6 is a ball-running position, but Rocky likes to play on the ball. He likes the contest and the physicality of the game. Speed is an issue, but he is determined.'

While Rocky was capable of playing in all five positions in the middle and back rows, blindside flanker did seem to be the role that suited him best. 'Rocky as a blindside flanker: he is a sensational lineout jumper, especially at two, and can jump unaided better than most people, so that's a big tick in the box,' Poidevin said. 'Rocky as a bread-and-butter option at two is an absolute standout and that's a really strong thing for a blindside flanker because you just need to have that choice in your lineout throws.

'Having that combative warrior ability to hurt and move people, he's got all those attributes and he is tremendously physical and doesn't really respect his body. The ability again to offload that ball as a blindside flanker — you might not be the first guy to the breakdown, but you are there to take the next ball and keep the ball going. He has also got fantastic vision where holes are and working with backline distributors to put him through a gap. He is really good in the way he times his run and finding that gap. I think overall just that desperation that he can put on the field for 80 minutes and just empty the tank completely is a huge attribute.'

Adopting a horses for courses approach, McKenzie chose Rocky as the reserve back-rower ahead of Hoiles, believing his aggression would be better suited to the physical Chiefs forwards. 'It was a hard selection,' McKenzie said at the time. 'It was a close thing to be honest. Someone had to miss out and unfortunately this week it was Stephen Hoiles, but we've picked a team for this week. We'll move on and things will change. When you get down to these close decisions it is the little things. We looked at how the Chiefs are going to play. They are probably going to play a little bit closer in. We felt the way Rocky has been playing the last two or three games he has been very strong in that area and we felt that would give us an advantage.'

While Rocky would have been pleased to be back in the 22-man squad, it was unlikely he would be fully satisfied until he had regained his number 6 jersey. The Waratahs beat the Chiefs 25-7 and went on to win their next four games against the Sharks, Cats, Stormers and Bulls before losing to the Crusaders. Even though Rocky started at openside flanker against the Sharks in Durban while Phil Waugh was playing in the tsunami appeal game in London, it looked like he would be a permanent fixture on the bench, at times not getting on the field at all. When Hoiles was preferred as a replacement for the injured Palu for the game against the Hurricanes in Wellington, you could almost feel Rocky's position in the team slipping away.

Many would have assumed Rocky's disappointment would have made him hungrier and more determined to work harder, but he did not need external motivation because he was intrinsically motivated. When interviewed on the *Inside Rugby* television show, Rocky was asked whether competition motivated him to work harder. If viewers were surprised when he flatly answered, 'No, it doesn't', it was because they did not understand that it is part of Rocky's nature to work hard, irrespective of competition. He did not need a competitor to remind himself of his own work ethic.

Rocky replaced Hoiles for the ninth-round match with the Highlanders in Dunedin. It was the only change to the line-up which had started in the historic 10–6 win against the Brumbies in Canberra the previous week. McKenzie explained that Rocky would give the Waratahs extra muscle in what would be a physical encounter. 'If you spent any time watching the way the Highlanders play, you will see that they are a hard-driving, close-in-type forward pack and I think that's one area of the game we've got to get stuck in early,' McKenzie told me at the time. 'Rocky has been giving us a fair bit of abrasive play late in the games when some of the sorting out has been done.'

Interestingly, Rocky was out of contract at the end of the season and the Waratahs had stepped up negotiations to re-sign him. The player market had become highly charged following the admission of Super 14 expansion franchise Western Force, which was aggressively recruiting on the east coast. Wallabies and Waratahs hooker Brendan Cannon was the Force's first signing, while NSW five-eighth Lachlan Mackay and prop Gareth Hardy had also announced they were going west. Rocky had received approaches from the Force and the Reds, but both denied tabling formal offers.

It is common practice for Super rugby teams to promote bench players to the starting line-up when they are trying to re-sign them. Whether the Waratahs adopted this negotiating tactic in Rocky's case is hard to know, but starting was certainly a priority in his considerations. The Waratahs had just offered Rocky a new contract with a Friday deadline, the day before the Highlanders game. Never one to be pressured into making a decision, Rocky let the deadline lapse, something that would become a habit in future negotiations.

With the walls closing in on him, Rocky produced what was arguably his best ever performance for the Waratahs in their emphatic 41-20 win against the Highlanders. In a storming all-round game he was a menace at the breakdown, tackled hard and was a handful in the lineout, but most pleasing of all was that he rediscovered his running game. Rocky's ball-carrying was dynamic. The sight of Rocky galloping in open space demoralised the Highlanders. He also made some big hits on unsuspecting Highlanders runners, including a bone-cruncher on flanker Josh Blackie, which forced a vital turnover. This big defensive play came at a crucial time in the game when the Waratahs were under intense pressure from the Highlanders' attack.

It was the turning point of the game, but it was also as if Rocky's career turned on that one play.

McKenzie conceded it would be almost impossible to drop Rocky after his 'terrific' display against the Highlanders and he retained his place in the starting line-up and played strongly in the Waratahs' 27–8 win against the Reds in Sydney, their first ever against their traditional rivals in Super rugby. Rocky's charge into Queensland fullback Chris Latham, the most dangerous player on the field, was a telling blow. After being knocked out cold while attempting to tackle Rocky, Latham was helped off and the Reds' hopes went with him.

The Waratahs then beat the Blues 25–20 in the final round of the regular season to become the most successful NSW team in Super rugby history, with nine wins, which saw them finish second behind the Crusaders on the table. But after disposing of the Bulls 23–13 in the semifinal in Sydney, the Waratahs were outclassed 35–25 by the Crusaders in the final in Christchurch.

Rocky began the 2005 Super rugby season just scraping onto the Waratahs bench and a little over three months later he was the premier number 6 in the country. Bob Dwyer's vision for Rocky was coming to fruition.

# 5

## MAN OF GOLD

*Waters run deep with Rocky. There is a lot to him.*

**Former Wallabies coach John Connolly**

John Connolly, in a white golf T-shirt and black shorts, looked as easy-going as the vacationers having fun on the golden sands as we sat in the courtyard of the Cracked Pepper Café across the road from Mooloolaba Beach on the Sunshine Coast. It was only October, but it was already warm, at least to a southerner like me. There were swimmers in the surf and sunbakers on the beach. In between bites of a muffin, Connolly pointed to an apartment opposite the beach that he'd bought in the mid-90s on a hunch Mooloolaba would be the next Noosa. It was a wise investment. Similarly, Connolly could see good returns from Rocky.

Known as 'Knuckles', Connolly, the one-time nightclub bouncer, had been coaching first-class rugby for 20 years when he was appointed Wallabies head coach at the end of 2005. Connolly succeeded Bob Templeton as Queensland coach in 1989 and he guided the Reds to the Super Six (1992) and Super 10 titles (1994 and 1995) as well as two Super 12 minor premierships (1996 and 1999). Connolly's supporters believed he should have succeeded Bob Dwyer as Wallabies coach in 1996, but the job went to NSW coach Greg Smith instead. Connolly remained at the Reds until 1999 when he went to Europe where he coached Stade Francais, Swansea and Bath before returning to Australia for his belated, if unlikely, term as Wallabies coach.

A knockabout character, Connolly enjoyed a beer and a bet. He was as relaxed as his predecessor Eddie Jones was intense. Connolly was also as conservative as Jones was innovative. While Connolly could never be accused of trying to reinvent the wheel, he still had an astute rugby mind and an eye for detail. He understood the importance of the fundamentals of the game, particularly the set piece. He gave the scrum and lineout a priority which had been missing in previous years. And he appreciated a big, abrasive flanker like Rocky.

'I thought Rocky was a young guy with a lot of upside to him,' Connolly said. 'Courage was never a problem. I always thought he would grow into a very good player. There was a view from the previous guys, selectors and coaches, that he didn't have the endurance or stamina to take him through a Test match and that he may have peaked as a player. I wouldn't subscribe to that. He had a lot more to show us on the rugby field and, spending time with him, I was convinced of that. His work ethic, his preparation, he had a lot more to give us. I was very willing to persevere with him.

'Rocky had down times in his game. People put it down to endurance. I didn't think it was an endurance issue as much as a game management issue. Rocky, at times, used to get caught out on the wing. He would stay out there instead of work his way back in close to the breakdown. As soon as he got hold of his game management, which he did fairly quickly, we saw the results when he went to Europe and how fantastic he was at Leinster where he was in the middle of everything. When his game management is good his involvements go through the roof. If you went purely off the stats sheet, his stats are low. There are stats and stats.'

Connolly's appointment as Wallabies coach was a major turning point in Rocky's career, which can be measured by the fact that he has never been dropped from the Test team since. 'The second that John Connolly got appointed I said to [former Wallabies second rower] Rod McCall, who is a mate of mine, that's good for Rocky Elsom,' said Peter Gledhill, who had played with Connolly, a former hooker, at Brothers. 'Connolly will love Rocky. He is abrasive. Rocky will stand up in front of the All Blacks and say hey, I'm going nowhere. Connolly would like that.'

Yet, Connolly was never meant to be Wallabies coach, at least not then. When Rocky arrived on the international scene in 2005, Eddie Jones still had two years to run on his ARU contract, which would take him through to the 2007 World Cup in France. Jones had earned a reputation as a brilliant, driven and innovative coach, guiding the Brumbies to their first Super rugby title in 2001 and succeeding Rod Macqueen as Wallabies coach the same year. He took the Wallabies to the final of the 2003 World Cup, losing to England 20–17 after Jonny Wilkinson kicked *that* match-winning field goal in extra time. Jones had not only gone close to winning the World Cup, he had almost revolutionised the game.

A keen student of rugby league, Jones borrowed heavily from the 13-a-side code with his extensive use of decoy runners and the use of an attacking formation from the middle of the field with a playmaker on either side of the ruck, which kept the defence in two minds about which direction the attack would strike. Jones also continued to employ the multi-phase game, which was invented by Greg Smith and perfected by Rod Macqueen, making rugby union resemble a modern version of unlimited tackle rugby league. It was no coincidence that Mark Hughes, the Bulldogs talent scout who discovered Rocky, thought the Wallabies' win against the All Blacks in the semifinal of the 2003 World Cup was the closest thing to a game of rugby league he had seen on a rugby union field. And that became a problem for Jones and the Wallabies, including Rocky.

The one thing that distinguishes rugby union from all other football games is that it is a continual contest for possession in every aspect of play, but the Wallabies' multi-phase game was making the 15-a-side code look more and more like rugby league. The International Rugby Board (IRB), determined to differentiate rugby union from rugby league, began to instruct referees to interpret the laws differently to ensure a contest for possession at the breakdown. As a result, much more leniency was shown to the defending team. By the time Rocky played Test rugby, the Wallabies' rugby league-style game plan was no longer working. They would either incur a penalty or turn the ball over before they had built up their attacking phases and their strategy fell apart. But Jones was determined to persevere with it. I felt sorry for Jones. He reminded me of my political hero, former Australian prime minister Gough Whitlam, the great reformer, who failed to adapt to changing times.

As expected, Rocky was included in the Wallabies squad of 2005, which was laden with back-rowers — George Smith, Phil Waugh, David Lyons, Scott Fava, Stephen Hoiles and John Roe, while second-rowers Hugh McMeniman and Mark Chisholm had the ability to play in the back row. But Rocky appeared to be in the enviable position of being the only specialist blindside flanker. Jones had played two openside flankers, Smith and Waugh, together in the back row since 2003. The presence of two small, mobile flankers who played hard on the ball increased the Wallabies' competitiveness at the breakdown, but compromised their performance in the scrum and lineout. It made the back row unbalanced. Jones indicated he was searching for a tall, ball-running, lineout-jumping blindside flanker, but he would persevere with the two small breakaways until he found what he was looking for.

Simon Poidevin urged Jones to groom Rocky, who fitted the description of a tall, ball-running, lineout-jumping blindside flanker perfectly, for the role for the 2007 World Cup in France. 'It's a huge dilemma with those world class two in Smith and Waugh, but, logically, you try and get a bit of balance in the back row and then let them fight out who starts the game at number 7,' Poidevin told the

*Sydney Morning Herald*. 'And on the other side [of the scrum] I think on form this year Elsom has been the guy hitting hard in attack, running the ball strongly and he's been very prominent. There's no doubt that I think in 2007 we will need an established, traditional number 6.'

Despite Rocky's emergence as Australia's premier number 6 — in the eyes of most critics, at least — Jones did not see it that way. It seemed almost certain Rocky would be omitted from the 22-man squad for the opening Test against Samoa at Stadium Australia, placing him third at best in Jones' pecking order for blindside flanker, but a twist of fate worked in Rocky's favour. Phil Waugh was originally pencilled in to join his old comrade and adversary George Smith in the back row, but after what appeared to be an innocuous mishap at training, he was rushed from the Wallabies camp in Coffs Harbour to Sydney for knee surgery. Enter Stephen Hoiles. Rocky had started ahead of Hoiles at the Waratahs and there was a feeling the Wallabies would need his aggressive and robust style of play against the physical Samoans. But Jones believed Hoiles was more skilful in attack and slightly better in the lineout. Hoiles also had the advantage of having toured Europe with the Wallabies the previous November, coming on as a replacement in two Tests.

Jones told Hoiles he would be starting at blindside flanker the day before the team was announced, but 20 minutes after he received the good news his luck would dramatically change. Inside back Elton Flatley threw a skidding pass which Hoiles and John Roe both attempted to catch. Roe was more aggressive in going for the ball and Hoiles came off second best in their collision, damaging his knee. Hoiles was sent back to Sydney for reconstructive surgery, sidelining him for six months. His season was over. As it turned out, it was a very fortunate series of events for Rocky, who was thrust into the role of starting blindside flanker in his Test debut. Jones gave the distinct impression Rocky was not his first choice for Samoa. 'He's probably been fast-tracked a step ahead of where he needs to be, but that's the opportunity he's now got in front of him,' Jones said of Rocky at the time.

Stephen Moore also made his Test debut against Samoa, coming off the reserves' bench. 'To get our first caps on the same day was great,' Moore said. 'It meant to him what it does to everyone. You are representing your country. You are getting an opportunity and he got the chance to start the game and he did a really good job. I'm sure it meant an enormous amount to him.'

Nathan Sharpe led the Wallabies against Samoa and he certainly appreciated having a third jumper in the lineout. 'It's crucial,' Sharpe said. 'When Rocky hasn't played over the years we have struggled to get that third quality jumper. It's an important thing for number 6s to have and Rocky certainly brings that. He is a big guy. He is athletic. He has really developed well.

'He is a guy you really enjoy playing rugby with because he enjoys his football. He has the ability to cross the white line and play hard rugby. He just plays in the moment and they are always good players to play with. I'd say he is dynamic. Rocky works bloody hard, but when he chooses to involve himself in the game he really makes an impact. It might be with a big run or a big tackle or a big breakdown play, a turnover. That's really inspirational for a lot of guys. Hence, when Rocky's playing well, the team is generally playing well.'

Rocky's start was not what he had hoped for, dropping the first two balls that came his way. Just as things were looking grim he settled in and scored the first of the Wallabies' 12 tries midway through the first half of their record 74-7 win. 'It was fantastic,' Vicki said. 'The whole family was there. Rocky got the first try and Russell got so excited. This is the stepfather who didn't know anything about sport. He doesn't like competitive sports at all. He jumped up and he got so excited. He was jumping up and down. Ron Giteau [Matt Giteau's father] said congratulations and started shaking his hand. He introduced us to everyone and everyone was shaking Russell's hand. They were so nice. They were all rugby heads. We didn't know anything. After the game Rocky looked happy, he would have been happy.'

Samoa coach, legendary All Black flanker Michael Jones, lauded Rocky's performance. 'I thought Rocky played extremely well,' Jones told *The Daily Telegraph*. 'He really brought a physicality to the Aussie pack. It is the Owen Finegan factor that the Wallabies will need going into the Test campaign. I had the privilege of playing Owen and he was a menace, a handful. Rocky is very young and has that raw boneness. He is also very skilful, a good runner and did all the right things.

'When [the Wallabies] got into that zone he was a big part of what they were doing. The big hit-ups, the inside passes, taking the ball and really making yardage and he was obviously a really good option for the lineout. I definitely believe he has got the goods. We are two or three notches down, but having also had a successful Super 12 season with the Waratahs, the step up from there to the Tests is not that much bigger. He has more height than the Kiwi number 6s. I don't know if I could say he is more intimidating than [Sione] Lauaki and [Jerry] Collins, but he certainly would be on par with those guys.

'In Rocky and Lyons and with opensiders like Phil and George in tandem, they will have something. If you have a big, strong, rugged number 6 and a hard-running number 8, with those three or four the balance will be very good.'

An assessment like that from Michael Jones, arguably the greatest flanker of all time, was rare praise indeed, but Rocky would go on to prove him right.

Rocky started in the Wallabies' first five victories of the year, including a dominant display against the Springboks in Sydney. Jones was concerned about the heavy load on the young flanker and rested him for the next two matches with an eye to bringing him back fresh for the return leg against South Africa in Perth. 'Rocky has done very well, but he's feeling the effects of a tough campaign and we just need some fresh legs in the back row,' Jones said at the time. 'John Roe is a very good player, who still gives us lineout jumping, but also plenty of ball-carry.'

I remember hearing at the time that Rocky was only good for 65 minutes of a game before he would fatigue, but that may have had more to do with the way the Wallabies trained, or perhaps overtrained. Jones was a great admirer of rugby league and he thought the Wallabies did not train hard enough compared to players in the 13-a-side code, which in general was probably true. Jones' training sessions were intense, almost as physical as an actual match, which may not have always suited Rocky's particular way of managing his body. It was feasible Rocky would use up valuable reserves of energy during a hell-for-leather training session before a game and then tire three-quarters of the way through it. It was routine for Rocky to be replaced before the 70th minute mark and while Jones' faith in him had increased, he was aware of his limitations.

Rocky was recalled for the Test against the Springboks in Perth after the Wallabies' 30-13 loss to the All Blacks in Sydney, replacing stand-in John Roe. In a further change to the back row, Waugh took over from Smith at openside flanker. 'We just feel that he [Rocky] has had a little bit of a break, has freshened up and gives us a bit of a physical presence around the ruck where certainly against New Zealand we were dominated,' Jones said at the time. 'We just feel Rocky is a bigger, physical player. He will certainly give us a little bit more in the lineout than Roey, but Roey is very unlucky. While we certainly don't use a rotation system, we need to have players who are fresh. This is our seventh Test in 11 weeks. Waughy and Rocky will give us fresh legs into the game.'

The Wallabies slumped to a 22-19 loss to the Springboks, but Rocky again was impressive in his 65 minutes. While Rocky was gaining valuable experience in his debut season, bigger issues were developing in the Wallabies camp. After a good start to the season, the Wallabies had been winless for almost two months and Jones was feeling the heat. A growing injury crisis did not help things with most concern over star playmaker Stephen Larkham. For the final game of the tournament, Jones restored Smith to the back row, but in the new role of number 8 in place of David Lyons, who had a season-ending groin injury. It was the Wallabies' fifth back row combination in as many Tests.

Al Kanaar played his sole Test against the All Blacks in Auckland. Although Rocky was only in his first season with the Wallabies, he took Kanaar under his wing and showed him the ropes. 'It was all happening that year,' Kanaar said. 'First year of Super rugby, I had only played one year of senior rugby before that. Going from Colts to that in the space of two years was amazing.

'[The Wallabies] were still based at Coffs Harbour at that stage. I guess that's where our friendship really started to develop. The training ground was a couple of kilometres from the hotel over the hill. We had this old Defender land cruiser kind of thing. We'd just head to training in that and head out to dinner. It was like something you would see Malcolm Douglas in out in the bush. It suited our personalities. It suited us to a T.

'He was my friend as I started to come into the Wallabies team. I definitely looked to him for support and guidance. There were a lot of senior players around when I came in. George Gregan, Stirling Mortlock. It was awe-inspiring, I guess. Rocky was a good friend during that learning period. He was still new. He was more experienced to a certain degree, but not much.'

With regular playmakers Stephen Larkham, Matt Giteau and Elton Flatley all unavailable, outside back Mat Rogers started at five-eighth, forming a new partnership with George Gregan, who was equalling English prop Jason Leonard's world record of 114 caps for his country. Unfortunately, Gregan celebrated his milestone with a 34–24 loss to the All Blacks. The Wallabies could take some heart from the fact they fought back from 20–0 down and scored four tries apiece, but there was no escaping from the harsh reality that they had crashed to their fifth successive defeat and Australia's first Tri Nations whitewash. An exasperated Jones claimed the players were not good enough and one of the players he seemed to be referring to was Rocky.

In a post-match interview, Jones revealed he was still looking for a big, blindside flanker. 'I also thought George Smith did exceptionally well,' Jones told *The Daily Telegraph*. 'He and Phil Waugh at number 7 and number 8 certainly gave us a glimpse of the future. I'm very keen on that. Now in the back row it's about finding a number 6 that's robust and gives us a third lineout jumper. Rocky and Roey are both doing a good job. But at the moment we've got to get something a little better than that.'

Rocky would have to have been a real rock, or some other kind of inanimate object, if he had not sensed that Jones was not happy. There were several changes to the Wallabies' starting line-up for the opening Test against France in Marseilles with Matt Dunning (loosehead prop), Matt Giteau (five-eighth), Wendell Sailor (wing) and Chris Latham (fullback) coming into the team, while Mat

Rogers was shifted to the left wing. The back row of Rocky, Waugh and Smith remained intact, but the Wallabies' 26-16 loss would be Rocky's last Test under Eddie Jones.

In a disagreement at the team hotel, which was witnessed by players, Rocky questioned Jones' strategy and queried the effectiveness of the team's patterns of play. Jones was not one to be challenged. His 'sprays' are legendary and it was not uncommon for players to be reduced to tears. Jones and Rocky always seemed to have a more respectful relationship, but confronting Jones — who was on a six-game losing streak and had already questioned Rocky's place in the team — was not a good career move. In fact, it was an error of monumental proportions. Just like when he took on the senior on his first day of high school in Noosa, Rocky came off second best in this confrontation. Roe replaced Rocky at blindside flanker for the next Test against England at Twickenham, while the uncapped Scott Fava was preferred on the bench. Rocky did not play again on tour.

Rocky is not the type to hold a grudge, but, like anyone, he does get annoyed. I could just imagine him sitting on the Wallabies bench in his number ones in the freezing cold, while watching the remaining Tests, a quietly rumbling volcano. All players want to play, obviously, but if you appreciate Rocky's powerful, innate need to be productive, you start to understand what kind of hell on earth the remainder of that tour would have been for him. Rocky, I am sure, would have preferred to be doing something else, anything else, than sitting there doing nothing.

At least Rocky was spared the Wallabies' 26-16 loss at Twickenham where the Australian scrum was humiliated by England. It was a watershed in the history of Australian rugby and is still felt today as the Wallabies battle in the scrum. The Wallabies rebounded to beat Ireland 30-14, but lost the final Test of the tour against Wales 24-22. The Wallabies had lost eight of their last nine Tests and Eddie Jones was as good as gone. After a review of the Wallabies' performance, the ARU decided Jones' position as coach had become untenable and his contract was terminated.

Ewen McKenzie and David Nucifora were the front-runners to replace Jones, but they both dropped out of the race, leaving John Connolly, like Steven Bradbury at the winter Olympics, the last man standing. 'Knuckles had a more conventional approach,' Stephen Moore said. 'He had a philosophy where he went with the biggest pack available. Obviously, Rocky was a big part of that. I didn't play much when Phil and George played together, but I know playing in teams with two, possibly three, lineout jumpers, it makes it hard, especially against teams like South Africa. You have to come up with all sorts of ways to win your ball. The more targets you have in the lineout the easier it is for everyone, but you have to make do with what you've got at the time.'

While Rocky was Connolly's kind of player, he still had to prove himself again with the Waratahs in Super rugby. Rocky trialled in the second row against the Blues in the pre-season, fuelling speculation he would be used as a back five reserve. But Rocky was named at blindside flanker for the opening game against the Reds in Brisbane.

If the internal competition at the Waratahs was not motivation for Rocky, maybe coming up against John Roe in his Queensland colours would be. Inking a new three-year deal just days before the game, Rocky and the Waratahs headed to Brisbane, having never beaten the Reds in Super 12 rugby.

In a grafting and brutal match, which was interrupted by frequent brawling, it appeared the Reds would get home on the boot of five-eighth Elton Flatley, who kicked three penalty goals in the second half to edge them in front. But with 10 minutes to go, just as the Waratahs were losing heart, Reds fullback Chris Latham provided them with a ray of hope when he failed to find touch with a clearing kick. Winger Lote Tuqiri ran the ball back at the Reds' defence. The Waratahs shifted the ball wide through long passes from five-eighth Shaun Berne and fullback Peter Hewat, finding Rocky, who ran around a defender before eyeing the line. In a game that produced precious few line-breaks, Rocky found a gap and sprinted, with the added weight of his sopping wet jersey, to the line for the only try of the game. Apart from securing the 16–12 win, what made this try remarkable was that it was scored late in the game, past his supposed use-by 65-minute mark, while Rocky was playing in the second row. Extraordinary stuff!

Rocky continued his outstanding form in a robust display in the Waratahs' 32–26 win against the Stormers in Cape Town, outplaying Springbok flanker Schalk Burger. The last time the two flank men met, Burger was sent off for a reckless high shot on Rocky in a Test against the Springboks in Johannesburg. Burger's cheap shot may have left Rocky groggy at the time, but he had clearly not forgotten it. The Waratahs repeatedly kicked off to Burger, and Rocky was there to meet him every time. It looked like two rams locking horns, going at each other hammer and tongs in modern-day gladiatorial combat. Rocky's job on Burger, as well as his play with the ball in hand, earned high praise from McKenzie, who claimed he had rediscovered the form he first displayed for NSW back in 2003. 'He's probably showing the form he first showed three years ago,' McKenzie told *The Australian*. 'I thought he was outstanding last weekend against the Stormers, even though he didn't get a lot of kudos. All the pre-match talk was of how Schalk Burger was the Stormers' talisman, but Rocky negated him throughout the match and got in some very telling tackles.'

The Waratahs' preparation for their match with the Bulls in Pretoria was disrupted by an incident involving Wendell Sailor, who was sent home in disgrace following alcohol-fuelled misconduct outside a nightclub in Cape Town. Given his own experience at the Bulldogs, I often wondered what Rocky thought of rugby's great experiment in poaching high-profile leaguies such as Sailor, Tuqiri and Rogers. He would certainly appreciate the physical attributes of the league players, but were the cultural differences between the two codes too great?

Whatever, Rocky had his own disciplinary issue to deal with, although it related to an on-field incident. The Waratahs lost 26–17 and Rocky and Matt Dunning were suspended for four and two weeks respectively for fighting. Rocky was punished more harshly because he joined the fracas late. It was a salutary lesson. 'There was a lot of frustration with the whole circumstance, the whole circumstance of how he was penalised for sticking up for Matt Dunning,' Al Kanaar said. 'There was a lot of passion and I guess that's what it resulted in. He has grown a lot over the last few years and he's able to keep a handle on those emotions. To see him during the Tests in the last Tri Nations [2010] you can see that same frustration, but he learnt how to control it.'

Rocky missed the Waratahs' big wins against the Sharks, Cats, Force and Blues before making his comeback in the 26–3 win against the Cheetahs from the reserves' bench. If Rocky worried that his four-week suspension would cost him a place in the Wallabies team, he need not have been concerned. Knuckles seemed to be impressed.

After coming off the bench again in the Waratahs' 17–11 loss to the Crusaders in Christchurch, Rocky was reinstated to the starting line-up for the grudge match with the Brumbies in Sydney. This game was important to Rocky in more ways than one because it pitted him against Brumbies blindside flanker Daniel Heenan, who had emerged as his main rival for the gold number 6 jersey. The Waratahs started slowly, but scored 23 unanswered points in the second half. Rocky scored the Waratahs' fourth try in the 36th minute after collecting a loose ball and running 20 metres to the line. The 37–14 win was exactly the bounce back the Waratahs needed. Rocky's strong performance did not go unnoticed. Former Wallabies captain and blindside flanker Tony Shaw described Rocky as an ideal candidate for a new-look Test back row. 'He's a guy who could really come to the fore,' Shaw said in the press. 'He has aggression, size and impact.'

Secure in his position at blindside flanker, Rocky was emerging as one of the leaders of the Waratahs forward pack. 'One memory about 2006 was Rocky's gradual increase in responsibility,' Al Kanaar said. 'Very assertive, demanding of high performance and really driven to win. I just know at training he was really starting to have a lot of input into the plays, structure and system in the game. He and David Lyons would always be discussing the plays and strategies we would take into the game for forward play. Those barnstorming runs that he does, he was trying to work that into the Waratahs' system. I'm sure there would have been a lot of discussions going on between him and Chris Whitaker and Phil Waugh.

'Throughout 2006 he developed into one of the leaders in the forward pack. He was more comfortable with how things were going and his position in the team and started to take on more responsibility and leadership. He was definitely doing a lot of thinking about how he could better his own game, but also the Waratahs' structure. He has always looked quite deeply into the structures and systems and what's best practice in Super rugby and internationally. In 2006 the confidence and the mateship we had in the team, he was a very strong character within that. He has very strong bonds with his friends and his teammates. He's out for the best for everyone, I guess.'

The Waratahs beat the Highlanders 20-3 in Dunedin, but lost their last two games to the Chiefs in Hamilton (37-33) and the

Hurricanes in Sydney (19–14) to finish third on the table, setting up a semifinal clash with the Hurricanes in Wellington. The Waratahs employed the same conservative tactics — playing for field position, dominating the lineout and using the rolling maul — in the semifinal as they had in the last round and came up with the same result, a frustrating loss. But the Waratahs felt they were robbed when the Hurricanes landed a penalty goal on fulltime after prop Al Baxter was penalised in yet another bemusing call from South African referee Jonathan Kaplan. With the game wrapped up, Kaplan ruled Baxter collapsed the scrum on the Waratahs' feed and gave a full-arm penalty, which was not common practice. It was the end of a tough few weeks for the Waratahs, who had lost Wendell Sailor prior to the last round, and had fought back from their loss to the Hurricanes in Sydney to have their second finals appearance in as many years snatched away from them in such contentious circumstances.

An untested rookie under Eddie Jones, Rocky was one of the first players picked by John Connolly. For Connolly, size mattered. He wanted to build a big, combative forward pack and Rocky was a key part of his plans. 'At that stage we were looking very strongly at where he should play,' Connolly said. 'Cliff Palu hadn't come on the scene then. We were struggling in the back row. We had played a couple of short flankers, Smith and Waugh. I was convinced that wasn't the way to go, although they were both picked in the 22. I thought towards the end of the game you might get away with it, but it definitely wasn't the way we wanted to play the first 60 minutes of a Test match.

'What we were looking for were two back-rowers who could make a difference around the field. That's where we wanted to end up. We weren't sure how we were going to get there. Australia had lost however many Tests in a row in 2005. We started with a blank sheet of paper, knowing where we wanted to get to. Ideally, we wanted one of the small flankers and two back-rowers, who we thought could make a real physical difference.

'There was Hugh McMeniman and Daniel Heenan. McMeniman had just come on the scene. He was a Rocky-type of blindside. We also experimented with Chisholm at blindside. In that combination of players we wanted two big, physical back-rowers. That was the package that we went through the process to find. I always thought Rocky was going to be one of the two. Who the other one was and who was going to be the reserve was the factor.

'Rocky was a player who I thought was clearly important to our side not only in the way he played, but the other stuff he brought to the table. And the confidence other players had in him as well. I can honestly say when the coaches and the selectors discussed teams I don't think he was ever not an option.

'Rocky, to us, was a player with the potential to be a damaging runner. I don't think the rugby instinct comes naturally to him. He's got to work at it. He has had such a narrow base in rugby that maybe that's why things didn't come instinctively. It has got to be natural. Great sportsmen like Tim Horan, he's just got an instinct for it. Rocky did turn into a great player. I thought he was potentially a real running threat once he became comfortable and his game management improved. He is fine with the ball now. He knows where to go. He's got the vision now. In the past when he got caught wide he would stay wide. Now he will work his way back in as a potential ball-runner inside or outside the ten.'

As Connolly got to know Rocky better he warmed to him as a person as well as a player. 'One on one he is incredibly engaging, a very engaging character,' Connolly said. 'He is very similar to Dave Wilson. Dave was a guy who always stood back. There are certain similarities in their personalities. When you engaged them one on one, they would be very engaging. But they would never be at the front of any party or at the front of any photo. Waters run deep with Rocky. There is a lot to him. You can sit down with Rocky and have a discussion about the politics of the day. He has in-depth knowledge of an incredible number of issues. He is an interesting guy. I've got a real soft spot for him.'

As forwards coach, Foley saw Rocky as a key figure in the plan to make the Wallabies forward pack play with more physicality. 'I just thought Rocky had toughness about him, even though he was young, that over the course of the next couple of years the Australian pack would really benefit from,' Foley said. 'Interestingly — where Australia was at that time — we came out of a period where we had looked at smaller back-rowers and Rocky presented us with the first real opportunity to go forward with another dynamic, ball-carrying, hard-hitting back-rower that would complement someone like Cliff Palu. Both of those guys came through at that time and you could see that it was going to take some time, but Australia would have a very different-looking forward pack over the next two or three years, with Rocky being one of the leading figures in it.

'There was a very definite understanding and need to allow Australian forwards to go and be physical in matches. The Australian forward pack had been effective, if you like, in running teams off their feet to some extent from time to time. But it has been well documented that we were losing physical exchanges, whether that was in the more obvious areas like the scrum or in areas like ball-carrying and impactful defence.

'Although at the time Rocky and Cliff hadn't had a lot of experience, there was an understanding that giving them that experience over the next two to three years, Australia could re-establish itself as being a dominant forward pack. It took until 2008 for some of those signs to come through. To just pick teams in the same way they had been picked leading up to that point wasn't going to change one of the real fundamental weaknesses of the Australian team at that time and that was that the forwards didn't have confidence to go out there and play physically against opposition forward packs. Rocky was a very central part of what was being attempted at that time.'

With David Lyons sidelined with a back injury, Rocky was chosen at number 8 for the first Test against England in Sydney as part of an experimental back-row combination with blindside flanker Daniel Heenan and openside flanker George Smith. The new-look back row was designed to help to improve Australia's Achilles heel, the scrum, by adding bulk and support to the front row. It also gave the

Wallabies four genuine jumpers in the lineout, which was something they had not had since the 1984 Grand Slam tour of Britain and Ireland.

Scrummaging was one of the least appreciated aspects of Rocky's play. 'Rocky is one of the best scrummaging back-rowers, particularly behind the tighthead,' Foley said. 'At his best, Rocky has a very good sense to stay with his prop through the engagement phase. It's not that the prop goes and he catches up. He stays with him so they hit with more force. And he has a very good understanding, again at his best, of working off both feet and producing maximum force post contact.

'So you are effectively working with a third lock even though he is on the flank. Ideally, that mentality of having four locks through the middle row of your scrum is critical. Rocky, being as big as he is, you know there is going to be an impact from what he is doing in the scrum. And even if you don't see it in the first scrum, over time, the front-rower that he is packing behind has a real opportunity to wear down the guy he is packing against.'

Rocky won the man-of-the-match award with a superb all-round performance in the Wallabies' 34–3 win against England, playing himself to a standstill. 'Rocky was exhausted,' Connolly told the media after the game. 'Towards the end of the match he was gasping so deeply for air he was sucking the fillings out of [England prop Graham] Rowntree's teeth.' Connolly's humorous comment about Rocky's exhaustion belied a concern in some quarters about his stamina. Foley believed the endurance issue had more to do with Rocky's chronic back and hamstring injuries.

'The discussion about him at the time was he was unable to finish games and his conditioning was an issue,' Foley said. 'The more you watched him the more you were convinced that it may not just be a conditioning issue. It may not even be a conditioning issue. There may be other things that would make it difficult for him to get through games. He is an extremely brave person. He's not likely to complain, particularly at that time as a young player. I really sensed he was earning his stripes. But the more I got to know him through the 2006 season the more I realised there were struggles he was having with his body that NSW had worked hard to help him with, but he hadn't quite overcome yet.

'Some of the volume-based training that was pushed his way may not necessarily have been dealing with the specific issue he had. Maybe when those people way back in Queensland had spoken to Rocky, or had some sort of interaction with him, what might have come out was a sense Rocky was certain about things. I see that as one of his strengths. I see it as strength for him now as a captain. The older he has got the more refined his understanding has become to determine what is required for him to be at his best. That's not just a case of gut feel, although that's an important part of it. Rocky's also done a lot of research that people wouldn't realise. He's not the sort of guy who talks up those sorts of things. He's often mentioned different pieces of strength and conditioning and dietetics literature that he's read.

'In a team sport it's easy to see a guy like Rocky bucking the system and not necessarily conforming. I think, alternatively, if you listen to Rocky as much as you try to tell him what the right thing is to do, there is really good insight there, and instead of asking for his compliance, you tend to get his commitment. That's a really critical difference between Rocky and other players. You can easily get comfortable with the fact that everyone is complying with your wishes, but Rocky will challenge things and if you have a different approach, he is very open to change. But he is really worth listening to. When you listen to him, as I say, those insights are incredibly valuable and there's times where if you give a little scope for him to adapt his program you get the best out of him not just in terms of his performance, but in terms of how thoroughly committed he is to the whole team.'

Foley also took a liking to Rocky the more he got to know him. 'I find his personality appealing,' Foley said. 'I see there are times when he creates division just purely by asking questions that challenge people. I actually find that very, very appealing. It's so important with any group of people that you avoid that group-think where people put their hands up and say I think this would work better, but there is another way, that what we are doing won't allow me to be at my best. For me that's appealing because it gives you other insights. It doesn't mean you always have to agree with them and it might mean that you have to sit down and take time to explain a different perspective.

'I find Rocky's personality as totally engaged in what he is doing when it comes to being part of the team and – the strength for me as an influencer of the team – he has a concern for team dynamic. As much as people might perceive he has a real focus on his individual preparation, which he does, that's very comfortably balanced up with a concern for the team.'

While many people struggle to figure out Rocky, he has his own method for assessing other people's personalities. 'Rocky told me a story about how he measured somebody's personality by saying something that was obviously wrong and seeing whether or not that person went back at him hard, politely corrected him or said nothing,' Foley said. 'He mentioned a couple of results that he got from it and it gave me a fair insight into it being a fairly accurate test. I thought that was a very interesting insight to a bloke – that he would actually say a very obviously incorrect thing and gauge somebody's reaction to determine what sort of bloke they were. I remember him telling me about this test and just thinking how fascinating it was to have a bloke like that in amongst a group of people. That point of difference that people bring to the table and how that makes for a really good energy around the team.

'Highly intelligent, very, very intelligent; it comes back to the time he spends reflecting on things. He doesn't dismiss things lightly. Rocky is the sort of guy who you know, when you've had a chat to him, that he will think about what you have said and he'll either come back with a fairly considered response at the time or at some later date. He is very intuitive. He senses things very well.'

Connolly continued with his new style of back-row combination in the second Test against England in Melbourne, although Mark Chisholm replaced Daniel Heenan, who had injured his shoulder in Sydney, at blindside flanker. The Wallabies recorded another convincing win, 43–18, which was notable for outside centre Stirling Mortlock captaining the side for the first time, while George Gregan came off the bench for his world-record 120th Test appearance. The back row remained intact for the Test against Ireland in Perth, where Australia won comfortably 37–15.

The starting line-up was unchanged for the Wallabies' opening Tri Nations Test against the All Blacks in Christchurch, but this match involved one of the most infamous moments in Rocky's international career. Referee Jonathan Kaplan showed Rocky a yellow card in the 26th minute for a third breakdown infringement. The previous two penalties were awarded as Rocky competed for possession at the tackle contest and at the time players were not given rights to the ball that they have now. On both occasions, All Blacks blindside flanker Jerry Collins took the ball up, Rocky tackled him, got to his feet and fixed himself over the ball. The problem for Rocky was he did not let go and even though the penalties could have been reversed Kaplan was within his rights to penalise him. The third time, however, was different, as Rocky's attempted roll away from the tackle and was halted by a barrage of stomping All Black boots. Noticing Rocky clambering with his upper body to free his legs from the ruck, Kaplan saw red, or in this case yellow. With blood trickling down the side of his face, Rocky watched helplessly from the sin bin as All Blacks hooker Keven Mealamu scored two quick tries to turn a seven-point deficit into a seven-point lead on their way to a 32–12 win.

Rocky had been unlucky, to say the least, to be sin-binned after he was penalised for the third time when making an effort to roll away from the tackle. Significantly, the incident was later held up at a referees' conference as an example of a 'genuine attempt' to roll away. The issue certainly did not count against Rocky at the selection table, with Connolly assuring him his position was safe, but it still had to be dealt with. 'Rocky was really intense around the contest,' Foley said. 'I remember there was a lot of talk about how heavily penalised he was. John's attitude was clearly: the outcome was a negative, but the intent was good. Rocky was playing aggressively and he was contesting. I think John and Rocky had a brief chat about the need for accuracy in that area. There would be no need to be less competitive, but there was certainly a need to be more accurate.

'Rocky received that really well. There was some comment, I believe, at the time that Rocky's position might be in jeopardy and I think John went to a length to let Rocky understand that wasn't the case and once again that gesture from John was a wise one because Rocky respected it. He realised he wasn't playing as he might be able to and to know his position wasn't under threat for the next Test, but he needed to tidy up his game, he answered that well. The next game he went into there was a much higher level of discipline. It's never been an issue since.'

Connolly reverted to a more traditional back row for the Test against the Springboks in Brisbane after the Wallabies scrum was demolished by the All Blacks and the unbalanced back row was beaten at the breakdown. Scott Fava made his run on Test debut at number 8, which allowed Rocky and Smith to play exclusively in their natural positions on the side of the scrum. What the Wallabies lost in height in the lineout they gained in mobility around the field, which was important to playing an expansive game to beat the Springboks' rush defence.

It may not have mattered who Connolly selected for this Test because everything that could have gone right did go right for the Wallabies and conversely, everything that could have gone wrong did go wrong for the Springboks. The Wallabies' extraordinary 49–0 win was a record score against the Springboks. Australia had never scored so many points against South Africa and the margin was 23 points better than their previous best when they won 32–6 in 1999. It was the biggest victory by any team in the 11-year history of the Tri Nations and the first time the Wallabies had held the Springboks scoreless.

While inside centre Matt Giteau was the man of the match after scoring two of Australia's six tries in a sparkling performance, Rocky emerged as the Wallabies' most powerful forward. Jim Tucker wrote in *The Courier-Mail* that 'flanker Rocky Elsom was more aggressive in his running than all the Bok forwards put together' and 'Whispering Jim' was not exaggerating. Connolly's faith in Rocky was vindicated.

There was high drama in the lead-up to the second Test against the All Blacks in Brisbane when the ARU terminated Wendell Sailor's contract after he was found guilty of taking a prohibited substance – cocaine – and suspended for two years. Sailor had been overlooked by Connolly, who was trying to create a new Wallabies culture, so his absence did not have any direct effect on the team's performance.

The Wallabies improved markedly, but they still lost 13-9, which meant they surrendered the Bledisloe Cup to the All Blacks for another year. All Blacks winger Joe Rokocoko scored the only try of the game in the ninth minute when he beat Rocky in a mismatch on the right flank and stepped inside Chris Latham. While Rocky had another strong game, letting Rokocoko get on his outside was a crucial mistake. The Wallabies back row had been outplayed in both losses to the All Blacks, and Connolly conceded he was still searching for his ideal loose trio. Fava was dropped for the Wallabies' Test against the Springboks in Sydney and, in the fourth back-row combination in seven Tests, Wycliff Palu made his run-on Test debut at number 8 in the Wallabies' ugly 20-18 win.

With the Wallabies needing to beat the All Blacks in Auckland to stay in the race for the Tri Nations trophy, Connolly tinkered with the back row again, starting Waugh ahead of Smith at openside flanker. The Wallabies led 20-11 at halftime with Rocky scoring a try just before the break, although it took the Television Match Official (TMO) several looks before deciding he had grounded the ball before losing it, but the All Blacks came back to win 34-27. Waugh maintained his place for the next match against the Springboks in Johannesburg, which the Wallabies lost 24-16. At the end of the domestic Test season the only constant in the Wallabies back row was Rocky.

Connolly had planned to give Hugh McMeniman an opportunity at blindside flanker at the back end of games on the Wallabies' tour of Europe, but the injury-plagued forward lasted only eight minutes before being ruled out for the rest of the campaign. In the absence of any back-up, Rocky further cemented his position with an outstanding performance in the Wallabies' encouraging 29-all draw with Wales in Cardiff. Rocky was a formidable threat, making several rampaging charges and telling tackles. At one point, with the game hanging in the balance, Rocky almost snatched victory when he forced his way through a Welsh maul, ripped the ball away, and set sail for the tryline. Unfortunately, the ball was knocked out of his hands just as he reached the line.

'I remember I talked to a couple of the Welsh players I had coached after we drew 29-all at Cardiff,' Connolly said. 'I talked to them about who had played well. They said, mate, [Rocky] was so tough at the breakdown. It was good to get the feedback from the Welsh guys. He was one they singled out; incredibly damaging.'

While Rocky was performing well individually, the Wallabies were not functioning as a team. A fuming Connolly blasted the players after their insipid 25–18 win against lowly Italy in Rome, although he praised Rocky for his general impact around the field. The Wallabies were then completely outplayed in their 21–6 loss to Ireland in Dublin. The Irish forwards out-muscled the Australians up front and Rocky was one of only three members of the Wallabies' pack — along with tighthead prop Guy Shepherdson and second-rower Nathan Sharpe — to keep their spots for the final Test against Scotland at Murrayfield in Edinburgh. The Wallabies desperately needed a morale-boosting win against Scotland to get their preparation for the 2007 World Cup in France back on track, and they responded with a scintillating 44–15 victory.

For Rocky, the tour was a personal triumph. Arguably the player of the tour, Rocky was one of the first players chosen in the Test team, growing in stature and emerging as the Wallabies' undisputed number one blindside flanker. Rocky looked on track for the World Cup in France, but he would have to survive the wreckage of the Waratahs' worst ever season in Super rugby.

The Waratahs' hopes of building on their achievements in the previous two years were dealt several crushing blows. On top of Wendell Sailor's contract being torn up, Mat Rogers returned to rugby league. The Waratahs also lost second-rowers Dan Vickerman and Al Kanaar to injury, weakening the lineout, a centrepiece of their game.

Kanaar sustained a serious knee injury in a pre-season trial against the Brumbies in Wollongong. He never played again. 'I injured it, spent a year rehabbing and then I had to retire in January 2008,' Kanaar said. 'Every player thinks he is going to make a full recovery. I was very positive throughout that whole year. Rocky was supportive. We would catch up and have lunch and that sort of stuff. I trained really well for a whole year. I was feeling really fit. The fittest I've ever been. We were training at Victoria Barracks, a game of touch or something. It just fell in a heap after that. I was in pain just running. It was quite emotional telling the team at the team meeting. A few tears, yeah.

'In 2007 I was studying for a master's degree in resources with a focus on ecology. I met Al Gore that year. I became a climate change presenter. Al Gore trains thousands of people across the world to present his *Inconvenient Truth* slide show. How climate change is the biggest challenge of our generation and how it has to start with behaviour change and acknowledgement that there is a problem at community level. I was learning a lot about the environment and discussing it with Rocky. In the last two years he has become interested in that area and really exploring it much further. It's something that has kept us in touch. He was the only player from my professional rugby career that I had at our wedding.'

Sitting out the pre-season trials, Rocky won the man-of-the-match award in the Waratahs' 25-16 win in their opening game with the Lions in Johannesburg, pocketing 5000 rand for his effort. A thundering run down the right flank before somehow managing to get the ball over the tryline was the critical moment in the match. After losing to the Sharks 22-9 in Durban, the Waratahs' injury woes were compounded when inspirational captain Phil Waugh sustained a season-ending ankle injury in the opening minute of their 30-26 loss to the Cheetahs in Kimberley. There was strong speculation Rocky would replace Waugh as captain, but McKenzie chose the more experienced Adam Freier, who did an admirable job.

McKenzie claimed Rocky would still be a leader whether he was captain or not. 'He does speak his mind and he has got the ear of the players,' McKenzie told the *Sydney Morning Herald*. 'He's quite worldly. So if he isn't the captain, he will certainly still be having an impact.'

Freier took over the captaincy for the 16-all draw with the Force in Sydney, which was marred by an unfortunate incident involving

Lote Tuqiri and replacement back Sam Norton-Knight. The Waratahs had a chance to break the deadlock in the final seconds when they were awarded a penalty from 45 metres out. Norton-Knight took a quick tap and raced down the sideline, but he was tackled while attempting a chip kick. Force fullback Cameron Shepherd gathered the ball and booted it into touch, ending the game. An angry Tuqiri ran 30 metres to abuse Norton-Knight, first verbally, then bumping him with a shoulder before pushing him in the back. Tuqiri continued to harangue Norton-Knight as the crowd booed the Waratahs off the field.

The Waratahs suffered further losses to the Bulls (23-19), Stormers (16-10) and Blues (34-6), their heaviest ever defeat. The next game was Rocky's 50th Super rugby cap, but this was a season that seemed to have no cause for celebration. The Waratahs faced reigning champions the Crusaders in Sydney. While the Waratahs struggled with the structure in their play, they managed to stay in the game. With less than 10 minutes to go the Waratahs looked directionless, yet they still made inroads in the Crusaders' defence. Rocky was calling the lineout and the last four throws came to him as they maintained possession. Down 34-28 the Waratahs launched one last attacking raid with hooker Tatafu Polota-Nau finishing off a break down the left-hand side of the field to touch down next to the posts and finally give the fans something to cheer about. However, elation turned to disbelief as Peter Hewat missed the conversion attempt from point-blank range and the Waratahs suffered a heartbreaking 34-33 loss.

One major positive from the match was the emergence of rangy 19-year-old NSW winger Lachie Turner, who scored an incredible 60-metre solo try. Turner, whose performance was nothing short of brilliant, revealed he was inspired by Rocky, outstanding in a losing team. 'I really wanted to get up for Rocky,' Turner said. 'He is everything a Waratah is.'

Desperate to bounce back in Canberra, the Waratahs were given a lesson in running rugby. Rocky scored the Waratahs' only try in their insipid 36-10 loss to the Brumbies, which left NSW with the one remaining goal of beating the Reds in Sydney to avoid the wooden spoon. Eddie Jones, now coaching the Reds, nominated Rocky as the danger man for Queensland. 'I think the most outstanding player for the Waratahs this year has been Rocky Elsom,' Jones told the NSW Rugby podcast Tah Talk. 'He looks like he is calling the lineouts. He takes the ball forward. He tackles his heart out. I think if we can quieten him down we will quieten NSW down to a great degree. He and [Adam] Freier are the spirit of the Waratahs team and in these games the blokes who capture the spirit of the team are very important.'

McKenzie acknowledged Rocky's important role in holding the Waratahs together during their horror run. 'The guys who front up every week for you regardless of the situation, they are the ones who are the real plusses and for us, Rocky has been that guy,' McKenzie told *The Daily Telegraph*.

The Waratahs beat the Reds 26-13, but McKenzie still made 10 changes to the team to play the Highlanders, including the dropping of Freier to the bench for Polota-Nau. With Turinui sidelined with a knee injury for the rest of the season, McKenzie turned to Rocky to lead the Waratahs. 'Rocky's been a standout all year and while he hasn't had a C next to his name, he's certainly been one to lead the team around the park,' McKenzie told *The Australian*. Unfortunately, Rocky's Waratahs captaincy debut resulted in a 26-25 loss with Hewat failing to convert his own try in the 78th minute after NSW had clawed its way back from 20 points down. To lose that way again was shattering.

Freier was reinstated as starting hooker and captain for the Waratahs' final match with the Chiefs in Sydney. Despite a gallant effort, the Waratahs lost 28-23 to complete a miserable season. Rocky was one of the few Waratahs to emerge from the devastation with his reputation intact, taking out the Matthew Burke Cup for the NSW Players' Player of the Year award for his outstanding performances in a team that won only three games. 'Rocky is a player that you can rely upon to give his all every time,' McKenzie told the *Sydney Morning Herald*. 'This is due recognition for a truly outstanding season during which he had to modify his game and take a lot more set-piece responsibility for the good of the team. He has a real effect on the people around him, both on and off the field, and he is a real follow-me type of player.' Rocky also won the *Sydney Morning Herald* Super 14 Player of the Year award and the Waratah Medal for his contribution to NSW rugby.

The disappointment of the Waratahs' woeful season behind him, Rocky was the first forward chosen for the Wallabies squad for the two-Test series against Wales. With George Gregan under threat for his starting position from experimental halfback Matt Giteau, Stirling Mortlock and Phil Waugh were named as co-captains for the seven Tests leading up to the World Cup.

Wales' recent dominance over the Wallabies looked set to continue in the first Test in Sydney. Racing to a 17-0 lead early in the match with two tries against the run of play, Wales had the game wrapped up until replacement back-rower Stephen Hoiles crashed over in the right-hand corner after the final siren for Australia to get out of jail 29-23. The Wallabies' poor form continued in the second Test in Brisbane where they led 6-0 at halftime following a disappointing first stanza. The turning point in the game was the injection of Gregan into the match after the break, with Giteau moving back to inside centre. Looking far more cohesive with Gregan at the scrum-base, the Wallabies scored 25 more unanswered points to cruise to an easy 31-0 victory.

Rocky was one of six players rested from the Wallabies' easy 49-0 win against Fiji in Perth to depart to South Africa early to begin preparations for the Tri Nations opener against the Springboks in Cape Town. After leading by nine points early in the second half, the Wallabies suffered a heartbreaking 22-19 loss with replacement back Francois Steyn dropping two late goals. The first was an incredible 40-metre effort from near the sideline in the 74th minute, while the second was coolly struck from 25 metres out three minutes later.

Returning to his birthplace in Melbourne, Rocky celebrated his first win against the All Blacks when the Wallabies came from behind to shock New Zealand 20–15, their first victory against their trans-Tasman rivals since 2004. Stirling Mortlock was a standout in a man-of-the-match performance, which included a huge midfield bust, leading to a try to Scott Staniforth. The Wallabies trailed 15–6 at halftime, but crossed for two tries to Adam Ashley-Cooper and Staniforth, while holding the All Blacks scoreless in the second half.

The euphoria did not last long, however. Perhaps suffering from complacency, the Wallabies had to come back from 17 points down to beat an understrength South Africa 25–17 in Sydney before losing to New Zealand 26–12 in Auckland in the Bledisloe Cup decider. While the Wallabies claimed replacement All Black halfback Brendon Leonard was offside when he took an intercept to score the only try of the match in the 57th minute, the Kiwis did finish the game much stronger. Nevertheless, the Wallabies had shown they could compete with them.

After months of speculation, Stirling Mortlock was appointed captain of the Wallabies for the World Cup with George Gregan and Phil Waugh sharing the vice-captaincy. The Wallabies embarked for France with a certain degree of confidence.

Connolly finally settled on his preferred back row, starting Rocky, Palu and Smith in the Wallabies' opening game of the tournament against Japan in Lyon. In the build-up to the game, Eddie Jones, now working as a consultant to the Springboks, questioned Rocky's work rate, claiming he was a player 'who still drops out of the game a bit too much'.

Rocky guzzled Jones' comments like they were high-octane motivational fuel. In his best performance in the gold jersey up to that point, Rocky produced an astonishing display in the Wallabies' 91–3 win against the wilting Cherry Blossoms, setting a record for the fastest hat trick of tries in World Cup history. Japan is a world rugby minnow, but Rocky showed no mercy in a man-of-the-match effort. Rocky constantly carried the ball through the Japanese defensive line, making numerous busts, covering tackles and lineout steals.

Although Rocky played down suggestions he had a point to prove, the Wallabies coaching staff could not thank Jones enough. 'I remember being asked at a press conference about it,' Foley said. 'My only thought about Eddie saying that was how great – the reality was Rock was never the sort of person, and he still isn't, who is demonstrative. He is not the sort of person who is likely to say that annoys me, but he is proud enough that that would have been a little thorn in his side. It wouldn't have mattered who we played that week, Rocky would have played like that. Probably to this day, Rock would say it made no difference and maybe consciously it didn't, but I was pretty pleased that Eddie came out and criticised Rocky just before the tournament started.'

Jones was good enough to acknowledge Rocky's outstanding performance. 'Rocky is one of the most improved players in Australia,' Jones told the *Sydney Morning Herald*. 'If all the blokes played with his desire, [the Wallabies] wouldn't have any troubles.'

As part of the sub-hosting rights to the World Cup, the Wallabies' crucial pool game against Wales was played in Cardiff. In an unimaginable blow, the Wallabies lost veteran five-eighth Stephen Larkham for the rest of the tournament when he sustained a knee injury at the captain's run. It was a sad way for Larkham to end his wonderful Test career and effectively cruelled the Wallabies' chances of winning the World Cup.

Although he was the last player chosen in the World Cup squad, rookie five-eighth Berrick Barnes wore the gold number 10 jersey when the Wallabies outplayed the Red Dragons to record an impressive 32–20 win. Rocky's powerful running game helped the Wallabies to build momentum early and his interchange passing in the midfield with Wycliff Palu was one of the highlights of the match. Another highlight was Barnes' starting debut. Thrust into the crucial playmaking position at late notice, Barnes shone, parting the Welsh defence in the 15th minute to make a 35-metre dash to the line and land a telling blow. The Wallabies led 25–3 at halftime and were never headed.

After wins against Fiji (55–12) and Canada (37–6) the undefeated Wallabies finished on top of their pool to set up a highly anticipated quarterfinal showdown with England in Marseilles. The veterans of Australia's 2003 World Cup campaign were still haunted by the memory of their narrow loss to England four years earlier and were thirsting for revenge. The Wallabies were confident of beating the ageing English side, but like a recurring nightmare, England eliminated them from the tournament with a dour 12–10 victory. The physical England forward pack dominated the scrum and aggressively counter-rucked the Wallabies at the breakdown. While the Wallabies produced one of their most dominant displays in the lineout to date, they failed to capitalise on their opportunities. Lote Tuqiri scored the only try of the game, but Jonny Wilkinson, reviving bad memories of 2003, kicked four penalty goals to secure victory. Mortlock had a chance to win the game when he attempted a penalty goal from 45 metres with three minutes to go, but the ball drifted to the left of the post, taking the Wallabies' World Cup dream with it. Rocky looked depressed as he spoke to reporters after the game in an almost inaudible whisper.

The Wallabies were shattered not only to be knocked out of the tournament by a team they felt was beneath them, but also because it meant the end of the line for legends of the game such as Larkham, who needed the team to win to play again for Australia before retiring from international rugby. However, Rocky's performance was commendable. 'Rocky was important to us,' Connolly said. 'He was a mainstay of the side. I think he will be a lot better for Australia at the next World Cup because he's got that experience. The problem was we had seven or eight players in their first or second year of Test rugby. History shows — England in 2003, Australia in 1999 and the Springboks in 2007 — you need a lot of experience in your side. Sides haven't won World Cups without hardened professionals. That was an issue for us. We had a number of players who struggled a bit with the intensity of the day in Marseilles.

'We knew what we were going to get from Rocky and he delivered what we thought we were going to get. But rugby is the ultimate team game. A bloke can play well, but the bloke beside him has to play well. You need all the pieces of the puzzle to fit together. There was no lack of effort. It was just a massive occasion. But Rocky delivered.'

Foley rated Rocky as one of the best players of the tournament. 'I thought Rocky played some of his best football in that World Cup,' Foley said. 'There were some commentators talking about – even though we bombed out – Rocky being one of the top players in the tournament. All the other issues of the tournament aside, I thought that was a fair comment for him. Even in adversity Rocky was able to shine.

'Rocky played particularly well in that England match in a pack that was struggling. We've never really spoken about it, but I can only imagine, knowing him as I do, that he would have been deeply hurt by the way we played. Even though his performance was a very good performance you wouldn't be able to escape the [fact that the] team didn't play anywhere near as well as it could have and we had lost a very important game. That's the other thing, being such a quietly spoken guy, people aren't aware how deeply proud Rocky is to wear Australia's colours.

'For any number of reasons, it was a shame Australia bombed out in that tournament, but on a personal note for Rocky I would have loved to have seen him play in those last two games. I think he would have taken on the best back-rowers in the world and done very, very well.'

At least Rocky could say he beat the world champions after playing for the Barbarians in their 22-5 win against the Springboks at Twickenham.

# 6

## THE TALISMAN

*There is no better attribute than when you are out there everyone else plays better. There is no better accolade. You make players around you better because you are on the field.*

Munster coach Tony McGahan

I experienced a Jack Kerouac-style *satori* in Paris while interviewing Michael Cheika, the Australian coach who guided Irish province Leinster to its Heineken Cup victory, at Stade Charlety, the training ground of Stade Francais, the French team he was now coaching. On a cold, autumn afternoon we talked over coffee in a café on the rooftop of the stadium. Wearing a Paris Rugby tracksuit, the swarthy Cheika reminded me of a big cat, perhaps a panther, as he leaned his tall, bearded frame across the table. It was something that Cheika revealed about himself that gave me a 'kick in the eye' and illuminated his relationship with Rocky.

'I had never thought about coaching,' Cheika said. 'I had never coached kids. It really never entered my mind because I wasn't really that way inclined. I was probably more of a selfish player as opposed to a team player. I didn't have that interactivity. Obviously, I had good teammates, but I didn't socialise. I wasn't part of that rugby culture.'

Did he say selfish? When Cheika used that word to describe himself I had the same sudden awakening that I had had when Les Kiss compared Rocky to Howard Roark in that Italian café in Brisbane. There was a little bit of Howard Roark in Michael Cheika too. It was no wonder Cheika related to Rocky so well. He was imbued with the same spirit of individualism. This was the profound connection that forged one of the most successful coach-player relationships in the history of European rugby.

'I think that is a good quality,' Cheika said of individualism. 'He [Rocky] understands that his contribution, how he makes himself, will be how he benefits the team, you know what I mean? That's a different type of player. Some guys have that approach. I don't know what goes on definitely inside his train of thought, but I think he understands if he is playing at his best, the team is going to be better. That is quite a mature way to think because that puts a lot of pressure on a person to do that, to say right, if I play well, I know the team will play well as opposed to thinking of the collective, which is often easier. The team is going to play well tonight. I might not, but the team will play well. He puts the emphasis on himself playing well for the team to play well. In the game at a high level you see the good players are thinking that way.'

Cheika coached Rocky at Sydney club Randwick when Rocky switched back to rugby, and stayed in contact with him partly due to a connection with Sam Elsom in the fashion industry. He started pursuing Rocky for Leinster as soon as the World Cup in France had ended. At first, Cheika did not fancy his chances of securing Rocky, but then the Fates, the three goddesses of Greek and Roman mythology who control human destiny, virtually delivered Rocky to his door.

When John O'Neill returned to the ARU as chief executive in 2007 after running Australian soccer for three years, he signalled his intention to rein in player salaries, which raises the question: how do you place a value on a player? In Europe the players who usually command the biggest euros and pounds are goal-kicking five-eighths, lineout-jumping locks and tighthead props, which accurately reflects the conservative style of rugby played in the northern hemisphere. In Australia it is completely different. More often than not flashy backs are the highest paid players, not just for their ability, but for their entertainment value in a volatile sports market in which rugby is competing with three other football codes. Very rarely, if ever, is an unglamorous tighthead prop on top of the pay scale.

Yet, under the Australian contracting system, it is possible, in theory at least, for a 'fatty' to be the highest paid player in the game. When rugby went open in 1995, Australian rugby officials – who had never had to pay players before, at least not over the table – devised a banding system to grade player salaries. The Wallabies coach, ARU high performance manager and ultimately the CEO and the board would determine a player's status in the game and pay him accordingly out of the golden pot of player-generated revenue, which was largely broadcasting rights money. If you were deemed to be the best player in the world, you would be in the top band. It followed down to best player in your position in the world and best player in your position in Australia and so on.

ARU high performance manager Pat Howard had been put in a difficult – you might say near impossible – position, instructed to re-sign Australia's leading players, but to rein in salaries at the same time. In what band did the ARU place Rocky? Not in one of the higher ones, it seemed. In a meeting with Howard early in 2008, Rocky, now managing himself, was told to explore overseas options if he wanted to secure a contract for the amount he was asking for. Why on earth did Howard put that idea in Rocky's hard head? The ARU probably banked on Rocky not wanting to leave Australia at 25 years of age with his best rugby still ahead of him. It was only veteran Wallabies cashing in at the end of their careers with rich English, French and Japanese clubs and Super rugby players who could not crack the national squad who headed overseas. But an alarming trend was starting to develop where players in the prime of their lives were going to the northern hemisphere in between World Cups, such as All Black five-eighth Dan Carter's sabbatical with French club Perpignan.

The ARU's hardball approach played right into Cheika's hands. 'We got on well, you know what I mean?' Cheika said. 'I didn't know him too well at the time [Rocky started playing for Randwick], but I got to know him and I just sort of kept in contact. I had something to do with his brother, gave him a bit of a hand in his fashion business when he was first starting off. That kept us in contact.

'Then I started speaking to him a while out about coming to play for Leinster. It was probably a low percentage when it first started off actually happening and then time went on and the circumstances I suppose of his situation in Australia and our situation in Europe, the idea of it happening or the possibility of it happening became more and more, a lot higher percentage of it occurring, you know.

'It was really a slow burner over quite a period of time. It was a good negotiation. He was really honest, talked straight with me. He was always straightforward and honest about his position, you know what I mean? That's what I liked about him. He never misrepresented where he stood in the process. He always told me what the other options and possibilities were and what he needed to change his mind or to do this or to do that. He was very honest, which I liked.

'Maybe at first I didn't think it was going to happen. And then the more I got to know him on that level the more I could see that if I presented the right picture, on the field and off the field, it would interest him enough because he is a curious guy, who wants new experiences. He knows what can add to him as a person, you know what I mean? I think I saw that even in the way he left [Leinster]. You could see him prepping the different options in his mind. I think that is the sign of the guy because he wasn't coming just to get the massive pay-out at the end of his career. I think those days are coming to an end anyway. But he saw that it could be an advantage to him, not just financially, but also from a lifestyle point of view. People want to have that experience. Maybe you don't want to be tied into the same routine all the time. I'm sure he could have gone to clubs that would have paid him more money than what we paid him. He based his decision on a composite of factors.'

Vicki tried to persuade Rocky not to go because she thought it would ruin his chances of ever becoming a great Wallaby. 'I was nervous because I always believed he would be Wallabies captain,' Vicki said. 'I wouldn't say it to him, but I thought he would be. Notwithstanding that, he was taking an enormous risk because he was playing really well, the team was playing really well and he was enjoying his teammates' company. I was very worried. I said to him it's a risk and he said, I've got this opportunity and I'm prepared to take those risks. We sat down with friends. People we really did appreciate. They said the same thing to him. Rock, they won't ever make you captain if you do this. He was like, that's okay.

'You have to be careful with Rocky because he doesn't like that kind of talk. If I say to him you are going to be captain one day, I really think you will, he doesn't appreciate it one bit. Just be grateful for where you are and not for where you might go. It was something that we never talked about even though we all thought it and said it to each other, but we didn't say it to Rocky.'

Bob Dwyer also cautioned Rocky against quitting Australia in the middle of his Test career. Dwyer's rationale was basically never to give a mug an even break. 'Given the circumstances that prevailed, I wasn't surprised,' Dwyer said. 'I read or heard that he was considering the move and so I spoke to him and said this is a massive decision. Giving up your position in the Wallabies is a massive step. That's not to say you can't get it back again, but you are giving the opportunity to someone else.

'His reply to me was there was no way I can accept what's being offered to me. We can just put that entirely out of the equation. He is a very serious bloke and he said he understood the significance of the move and potential damage to his international rugby career, but he said there is just no way I can accept it. What happened in terms of negotiation after that I'm not party to. Obviously, things improved and the environment improved and everyone saw it as a positive and acceptable step for him, including the ARU — full marks to the ARU for being able to negotiate their way through that minefield, really.'

And what a minefield it was. At this time there was supposed to be an agreement between the ARU and the Rugby Union Players Association under which players with 35 Tests and five years' service were allowed an early release from their contracts which ran from 1 January to 31 December to allow them to join European clubs at the start of their season or immediately after the Tri Nations. However, this decision was always at the discretion of the ARU. While all professional rugby players in Australia signed one contract, they had two employers, the ARU and their province. This created problems from time to time when players changed provinces and were training with one team, while still getting paid by another until the end of the calendar year. But it was valuable to the ARU because it reduced the attractiveness of Australian players to European clubs if they were not available to them until January,

The Elsom boys – Rory, Dusty, Rocky and Sam – sitting on Santa's knees. I wonder what Rocky wished for.

Rocky and his mother Vicki are very close. The other Elsom kids teased Vicki that Rocky was her favourite.

Still just a pebble, little Rocky floating on the water with his 'rugby bum' sticking out.

The boys with their grandfather Jack Wood, whose motto 'he ain't heavy' had such a profound influence on the family's values.

Brothers in arms – Rocky, Dusty, Robert, Sam and Rory. Although he is the second youngest, Rocky is already the tallest, and growing.

Rocky is highly protective of his sister Kelly, who described him as the 'Don of the family.' Even though he has dirt all over him, Kelly still gives Rocky a hug after a Nudgee rugby match, which became a ritual for the Elsom family.

When Vicki met Rocky's step-father Russell Clarke it changed the course of Rocky's life. It was Russell's idea for Rocky and his brothers to attend Nudgee College in Brisbane. The rest, as they say …

Rocky learnt a lot from Russell, who introduced the Elsom boys to weight-training in the gymnasium he built in the garage. The driving lessons, however, did not go so well.

Former Nudgee boarding master Robbie Martin, flanked by Rocky and friend Jordan Bell, was a mentor to the Elsom brothers.

When I first saw this photograph I thought it was a picture of Rocky and his girlfriend, but it was a youthful-looking Vicki across the kitchen table.

Showing style as well as substance, Rocky became a director of his brother Sam's fashion design company, Elsom Holdings.

Legendary schoolboys coach Peter Gledhill (at right) has a look of quiet satisfaction as Nudgee celebrates yet another win.

Eyes on the ball, fingers spread wide, Rocky still shapes up in the lineout today the way he did at Nudgee all those years ago.

A muddied Rocky chats to a team official after leading Queensland to victory in the under-16 national titles. Notice the number 8 on his back.

Rocky (fourth from left in back row) and his Nudgee First XV teammates in their blue and white blazers. A bolter, Rocky knew the importance of rugby to the school and wanted to be part of it.

Former Wallabies blindside flanker Owen Finegan congratulates Rocky on leading Queensland to victory in the national under-16s titles. Finegan's Test jersey would belong to Rocky in several years' time.

Brother Wal had an affinity with Rocky because he was 80 years old and Rocky wore number 8. The kindly, old brother exhorted the Nudgee First XV players to 'eat 'em alive' before each game.

Former Wallabies number eight Dallas O'Neill presents Rocky with his First XV jersey as another Nudgee old boy, Paul McLean, looks on.

Even as a fresh-faced schoolboy, Rocky had a strong determination and a sense of where he wanted to go.

After less than one full season of rugby at Nudgee, Rocky (third from right in third back row) made the Australian under-16s team.

A dynamic ball-runner, Rocky sizes up a would-be defender while playing for the Brumbies in a Super Rugby game.

Rocky looks pensive as the Bulldogs, including future NRL star Jonathan Thurston, celebrate winning the Jersey Flegg competition in 2001. Maybe he had a foreboding about where his rugby league career was headed.

With a sea of blue in the crowd at Murrayfield, Rocky flies high to secure a lineout ball in Irish province Leinster's historic win against English club Leicester in the final of the 2008/09 Heineken Cup.

Busting through the tackles of two Leicester defenders with sheer will-power, Rocky had his Viking 'bear shirt' on that day.

Rocky loves children and he would spend time with his Irish neighbours' kids while living in Dublin.

Rocky, is that you? According to family legend, the Elsoms are descended from Vikings.

Rocky enjoyed playing for the Barbarians, rugby's free spirits. Here he is taking a lineout catch against England at Twickenham.

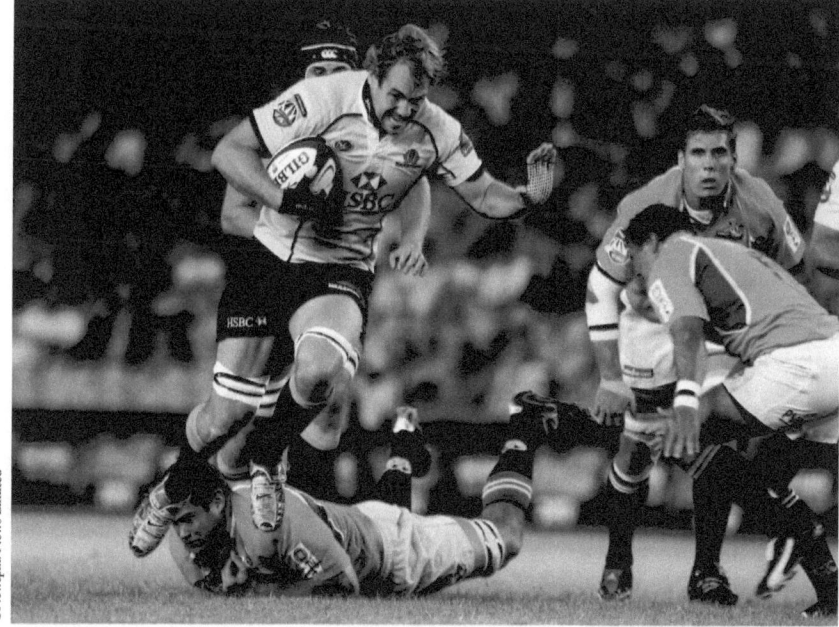

Skipping out of a tackle, Rocky braces himself to palm off another defender with his trademark fend. Rocky's time at the Waratahs coincided with the team's most successful period in Super Rugby.

Eddie Jones' criticism of Rocky motivated him to score a record hat-trick of tries in a power-house performance in the Wallabies' thrashing of Japan in their opening game of the 2007 World Cup in France.

Rocky lifts the Mandela Plate after the Wallabies broke a 47-year hoodoo on the high veld in South Africa, one of his proudest achievements as captain.

Rocky developed into a wonderful lineout jumper, giving the Wallabies a crucial third option in the set-piece.

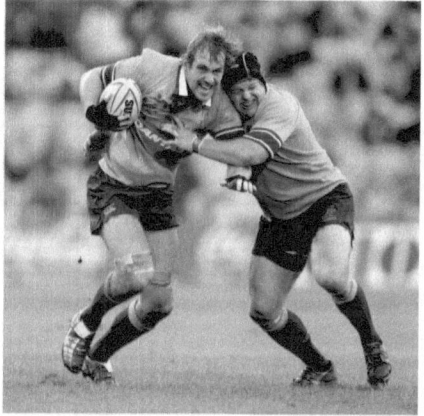

Wallabies prop Matt Dunning appears to be giving Rocky a bear hug as he prepares to launch himself at the opposition defence.

The two Leinster Men, Rocky and Brian O'Driscoll, played key roles in the 20-all draw between the Wallabies and Ireland at Croke Park in Dublin. Here the Irish captain just manages to ankle tap Rocky, who looked certain to score.

All Blacks captain Richie McCaw rates Rocky highly. They are all smiles before a NSW Waratahs–Crusaders game, but the mood will be different at the World Cup in New Zealand.

The Brumbies were described as the 'Real Madrid' of Australian rugby after Rocky and Matt Giteau joined the team, a moniker that would come back to haunt them.

which was halfway through the northern season. To be fair to the ARU, this scenario rarely arose and the list of players granted an early release in good faith is too long to record here. But in Rocky's case it seemed the ARU was prepared to follow the letter of the law, or rule.

What the ARU was probably not aware of was that even before Rocky received its initial offer and was subsequently encouraged to look abroad for employment, he had already been vigorously courted by some wealthy French clubs, which were desperate to secure his services. Rocky had had a fantastic World Cup in France and had just returned from playing in the Barbarians' win against South Africa at Twickenham in which he scored one of the best tries you would ever see from a back-rower. Performing a quick wraparound play on the halfway line with Munster prop Federico Pucciarello, Rocky sliced through the first line of defence and set off for the tryline, somehow managing to hold off defenders with a mixture of speed and deception as he ran nearly half the length of the field to score. As far as an advertising sign for European clubs goes, Rocky's try was blazed in neon light.

With big euros on the table it was not a good time for the ARU to be throwing a low ball, but how was it to know? Details of contract negotiations are usually leaked to the media by player agents who are trying to heat up the market or by over-zealous clubs attempting to woo other players on the back of a marquee signing. It is common practice for players, or their agents, to play the negotiation game through the media if they are unhappy with the process because in short it seems to work. The public pressure increases on the ARU, which cannot afford to be seen to lose a battle over a player it wants to keep.

As always, Rocky was different. The interesting thing about Rocky's negotiations was that nothing was leaked about what was being put on the table or that there was even an interested party. Even as talks broke down, Rocky preferred to keep things so close to his chest that almost no one knew what was happening. Exactly why he did it that way I am not too sure, but it just seems to be the way he prefers to do things.

I suppose Rocky would have been unnerved by taunts that he could not secure a better deal anywhere else. Given that he was being offered substantially more overseas, he had the perfect opportunity to embarrass those who doubted his capacity to command big bucks by revealing details of his negotiations with foreign clubs. But he didn't. For reasons known only to Rocky, he chose to closely guard his dealings. As twisted as it may seem to others, Rocky has his code and lives by it.

While still the underdog in the race for Rocky's signature, Leinster did have some strong attractions for him as Bob Dwyer explained to me. 'I obviously knew the coaching staff that he was going to and I was very happy that he was going to them because I thought that will only add to his ability and his capacity as a rugby player. He will come back a better player than he went away. And the experience of a new culture, et cetera, et cetera, will be good for him also. And so it was. He loved it. He played better and he got significant praise, which brought him back as one of the top half-a-dozen players in the world.'

Regardless of who was coaching Leinster, Rocky was still a 25-year-old giving up an Australian jersey, which he had a mortgage on, to play on the other side of the world, and most would have seen it as a risky move if he intended to come back. John Connolly, however, did not see it as a risk at all. 'I think Rocky is the type of guy who would back himself,' Connolly said. 'He wouldn't see it as opening the door for anyone else. He would have the confidence to back himself. "When I come back I'll play well enough." I've got no doubt that's his attitude.

'I knew he was keen to go overseas. I think he wanted to experience something else. All players go through that stage. Ireland loved him. They would love him still to be over there. I think it was part of his development. What is he now, 27? I think he was at the stage where he wanted to experience something else.'

As Wallabies forwards coach at the time, Michael Foley was disappointed to lose Rocky, even though he understood his reasons for going. 'I was disappointed, not in him, but disappointed to see him go,' Foley said. 'People have to take those decisions based on their own circumstances and the full gamut of those circumstances would probably be only known to Rock, but I would say Australia missed him. It was a hit to a team that was progressing. In 2008 you saw the progress. There was work done leading up to 2008. There was work done by Robbie [Deans] arriving in 2008. Rocky was a big part of the team gaining confidence to go and win in South Africa, to beat New Zealand and beat England in England. To suddenly have him and Dan Vickerman disappear overseas was a massive blow to Australia.

'In terms of where Australia had been, where they had come from and where they were going, to me there were other players Australia could have done without in favour of losing Rocky to overseas. That's not to devalue any other players. We were blessed with a lot of players who had been through some hardship and were really starting to galvanise as a team in 2008 and it was highly disruptive. Very few sporting teams who are on that upward curve after being in a difficult time can have two such influential players as Dan Vickerman and Rocky Elsom torn out of it and for that upward curve to continue. There was another dip. It was the last thing Australia needed.

'Was he valued enough, I'm not sure. From a coaching perspective I know he is highly valued by Rob. He is extremely highly valued by me and the team and we would have liked to have seen him stay. While any negotiations come down to dollars and cents, if the negotiations are handled with respect to the player, then I think there's opportunities sometimes to not necessarily have to match the offers that are on the table from other areas.'

Les Kiss did not believe Rocky was valued highly enough in Australia. 'I don't think he was recognised in negotiations as someone who should be looked after in terms of contracts,' Kiss said. 'He was frustrated, very much so. I won't speak for him. I remember reading in the paper if he thinks he is going to get big dollars overseas, he's kidding. He got big dollars overseas and he performed overseas.

'I wasn't surprised because I knew there was frustration with what he was worth here compared to what he was offered. I remember having a conversation with Michael Cheika when I was considering going to Ireland and he mentioned Rocky over a coffee. I knew that he was going to be one of his best signings. If people were saying no, you are worth this much and you won't get that money over there, he said let's find out and he did. And he got it. Cheika, to his credit, smelt it. He knew something was there and he got onto it.'

After a stand-off that lasted for months, Rocky agreed to terms with Leinster, and while whispers from Dublin even came across my desk there was no announcement. It was as if everyone was being purposefully kept in the dark about the value, length, and even the validity of the contract itself.

Despite the fact Rocky had agreed to join Leinster there was still plenty of work to be done. The ARU could scuttle any European deal by enforcing the full length of Rocky's contract because missing the pool stages of the Heineken Cup would be unacceptable to most teams. A marquee import usually cannot attract top dollar if he only signs for half a season. The ARU was also aware Rocky only wanted a year-long European sojourn. Just how Rocky was going to convince the ARU to release him to play for Leinster in the 2008/09 Magners League and Heineken Cup competitions was quite literally the million-dollar question.

Rocky's future was up in the air as the Waratahs opened their 2008 Super 14 campaign with a 20-3 win against the Hurricanes in Sydney, but he was playing with great assuredness. In the loss to the Chiefs in Hamilton and in the victories against the Highlanders (15-12) in Dunedin and the Brumbies (24-17) in Sydney, Rocky was outstanding. Even in the Waratahs' 34-7 loss to the Crusaders in Christchurch, he was finding ways to consistently break the line. However, there was trouble in the Waratahs' ranks.

Senior Waratahs, including Rocky, believed they could never beat the Crusaders playing conservative, percentage-style rugby. After Christchurch the Waratahs changed the way they played. In their next outing the Waratahs faced the Cheetahs and started like they had been shot out of a cannon. Again, man of the match Rocky was in the thick of it, scoring an impressive try off a switch play and beating the last line of defence. Making numerous line-breaks, stealing balls at the front of the lineout and ironing out would-be Cheetahs attackers was doing Rocky's bargaining position at the ARU's negotiating table a world of good. It seemed also that the Waratahs had found their rhythm against the Cheetahs, but no sooner had the wagon got rolling than the wheels started to fall off. In an unimpressive second half by the Waratahs, the Cheetahs almost did enough to come back, but time was against them.

The result had wide-ranging ramifications for the Waratahs. On April Fool's Day the Waratahs announced that Ewen McKenzie's five-year reign as coach would end after the 2008 season. The news that McKenzie's contract would not be renewed did not seem to have any adverse effect on the Waratahs' performance.

Rocky sustained a thigh injury and was ruled out of the Waratahs' match with the Blues. The *Sydney Morning Herald* reported that Blues coach, David Nucifora, could 'hardly contain his glee' when told of Rocky's unavailability. In any event, the Waratahs kept on winning, beating the Blues 37-16, the Force (17-12), Lions (26-3) and Sharks (25-10). Rocky returned for the Waratahs' tour of South Africa where they lost 16-13 to the Bulls in Pretoria and drew 13-all with the Stormers in Cape Town. The Waratahs secured a home semifinal with an 18-11 win against the Reds in Brisbane.

Rocky shone again in another man-of-the-match performance in the Waratahs' 28-13 win over the Sharks in the home semifinal in Sydney. He was in everything: breaking the defensive line, laying on try assists and looking to be thoroughly enjoying himself.

It was around this time that John O'Neill seemed to become personally involved in the negotiations with Rocky. O'Neill, who was known at the time as one of the best – if not *the* best – sports administrators in the country, would have appreciated the importance of a player like Rocky to the Wallabies, and the game, but with the resignation of Pat Howard, the ARU was behind the eight-ball in the negotiations.

I doubt whether Rocky is a gambler, but it appears he did take a calculated risk with his Leinster deal. Even though his preference was to return after only one season abroad and miss just a handful of Tests, Rocky agreed to a two-year deal with Leinster with an option stating that should he be given an early release in time to register for the first round of the Heineken Cup on 18 September, he would have the option not to take up the second year of his contract. In effect, if his early release was denied, Rocky would be lost to Australian rugby for two years instead of a possible nine months. I am sure Rocky was hoping the ARU would play ball, but with his hands now tied, he had little room to move if they did not.

Les Kiss saw Rocky's move as a show of strength. 'He was never going to be pushed around by people. He stood his ground. He is very determined about certain things. He said, I'll go. It just fit perfectly. He went away. He did a job. The Brian O'Driscolls have huge respect for him as a person and as a player. In the end Australia said please come back. He had them on a plate.'

Stephen Moore believed Rocky would be a huge loss for the Wallabies, but he knew his mate would not have taken the decision to leave lightly. 'Obviously, there were whispers around. He wasn't giving much away. It all sort of happened. I don't think he got the chance to tell anyone. One day he was here, the next day he wasn't there. It's not something he speaks to many people about. His decisions about his rugby, he keeps very private, very personal, until it actually happens. I didn't hassle him about it. I respected his decision and it turned out to be a great period for him.

'We didn't know whether he was coming back. It was a big loss for the team and Australian rugby. He was leaving a big hole in that position. It was certainly a big loss, but I suppose it comes back to what I was saying about him having a different training regime. I could see his reasons for it. He had a great opportunity both rugby wise and culture wise, and financially as well. He would have weighed all that up and you can guarantee it would have been a well-calculated decision. He wouldn't have decided in a blink of an eye. Away he went. I've got plenty of family in Ireland and they were certainly happy to see him turn up.'

Simon Poidevin was disappointed to see Rocky go, but he was confident he would come back. 'I could understand why Leinster at the time was an option,' Poidevin said. 'He is a pragmatic guy. He said, okay, this is what I'm going to do and he did it. But I always knew he would be back because he's got great nationalistic blood in his veins. That always brings you back to the real thing.'

In Limerick Tony McGahan's ears pricked up when he heard the news Rocky had signed with Leinster, Munster's arch-rivals. 'He was a huge signing for Leinster,' McGahan said. 'Even getting the name of a quality player like that on the world stage, who was willing to go for twelve months, whether he stayed longer or not was still up in the air; he certainly left it that way with his dealings with the ARU. He'll do what he is going to do. If he is good enough, he'll force his way back in. If he isn't, so be it. He backed himself to go over there and he was a huge coup.'

With O'Neill seeming to take over the negotiations from the ARU's end — which was a rare occurrence — the question was raised about whose fault it was that Australia had lost one of its top players in the prime of his career, possibly forever, to the lucrative world of European rugby. Rocky's outstanding form was not helping to calm down the situation. But O'Neill is as shrewd an operator as you could come across, and immediately sized up the situation. If Rocky was forced to join Leinster in January and spend two years away, the chances of him returning to Australia would diminish significantly. O'Neill would also have sensed that Rocky would prefer a good, working relationship with the ARU rather than confrontation, which did not serve anyone's interests. With a better understanding of Rocky's deal with Leinster, O'Neill no doubt would have seen solutions, perhaps even opportunities, instead of problems.

In the interim, the Waratahs played the Crusaders in the Super 14 final in Christchurch. Despite outscoring the Crusaders two tries to one, the Waratahs lost 20-12 with Dan Carter kicking the Kiwis home with four penalty goals from five attempts and a field goal. Rocky's time at NSW coincided with the Waratahs' most successful period, reaching the Super rugby semifinals in 2006 and the final in 2005 and 2008. However, losing two finals in the space of four years would have been difficult to accept for someone as competitive as Rocky. It was sad to say, but the Waratahs were the nearly men of Super rugby, and I could only imagination the frustration and disappointment Rocky would have felt.

Two days after the Super rugby final the victorious coach of the Crusaders, Robbie Deans, was in Sydney announcing his first Wallabies squad as Australia's new head coach. A former All Black fullback and descendant of a pioneering Scottish family, which settled the Canterbury plain, Deans was the most successful coach in the history of Super rugby, guiding the Crusaders to a record five titles. Deans accepted an offer from the ARU to coach the Wallabies after the New Zealand Rugby Union rejected him in favour of retaining the coaching triumvirate of Graham Henry, Steve Hansen and Wayne Smith following the All Blacks' quarterfinal exit from the 2007 World Cup. The ARU turned to Deans, the first foreigner to coach Australia, to restore the Wallabies to the glory days of the Rod Macqueen era, which seemed more and more like a distant memory.

I caught up with Deans in a café adjacent to the ARU's headquarters in St Leonards on Sydney's lower North Shore, two weeks after the Wallabies returned from their highly successful tour of Europe at the end of 2010. Deans was wearing a dark blue, collared T-shirt and black slacks. A serious squash player, Deans looked fit enough to play for the Wallabies, not just coach them.

For five years, Deans had seen Rocky on the opposite side whenever the Crusaders played the Waratahs. I was curious to know what Deans thought of Rocky as an opponent. While Deans can be a man of few words, he poured out volumes of praise for Rocky. 'Rocky was a player that you noticed,' said Deans, who has a habit of pausing and nodding his head after he has made a point. 'That's probably as much about his physical presence as anything. He's a bloke who had the ability to stand up against the tide and when he did things they tended to stay done. I noticed his physical prowess from a distance before I got to know him. That was his most obvious quality from a playing perspective.

'Clearly, he was a trigger for the group. You are aware of not wanting to provide excitement for the rest of the group by allowing him to do what he wants to do. He is one of those blokes who others gain confidence from. He is very single-minded in everything he does. You need blokes in your group, in your mix, [who] others draw from. The game is about momentum. The game is about the tide coming in and going out. You've got to have people who not only have the capability to do it, but the willingness, first and foremost, to actually stand up against the flow or the momentum and make a dent or an impression from which others draw confidence and belief.'

Deans revealed to me that he met with Rocky in his home in Christchurch in the week of the Super rugby final to discuss his role in the Wallabies and his future plans. 'I had the opportunity to speak with him before I actually started in the role,' Deans said. 'It was in the week of the Super rugby final. He came around to my place. We had dialogue and it was really evident to me, his ability to compartmentalise. The fact we were opponents at the end of the week didn't matter. It was a connection that was man to man. It was about the game and obviously what was coming beyond the weekend.

'What I experienced of him there was clearly a bloke who thinks a lot more than he discloses, always a good trait. It was evident to me how much it meant to him in terms of the Wallabies. Even though he took an option — which others would suggest [indicated] he was leaving the jersey for a period of time — the motivation was more around ultimately being able to play for the Wallabies and achieve some things that hadn't been done. It was evident he had a flame inside him that was strong.

'Over time I've come to know him more, obviously. You've got to earn that right with Rocky. That's an element I like, enjoy, to be honest. He is not verbose. He doesn't fill the airwaves. But he won't mislead you. He is a good communicator, albeit minimalistic at times. But so be it. He is very consistent as a bloke, and a quality bloke. He doesn't have any habits that you need to concern yourself about. He is very disciplined. You only have to look at some of the physical challenges he has had and he has had a few. He has played professional sport for a long period of time and it hasn't been without challenge in terms of his body. The work that he does away from the eye of the public to get himself in the right shape to get out there is more than significant. It's actually quite enormous. Most blokes wouldn't and don't — aren't prepared to go to that length and hence they are no longer here, some of them. You don't get longevity lightly.'

With his future somewhat more certain, Rocky joined the Wallabies the week after the Super 14 final playing under the coach he had played against 48 hours earlier. An integral part of Deans' plans, Rocky was one of the first players picked, starting for the Wallabies at blindside flanker in their thrilling 18–12 win against Ireland in Melbourne and their two-Test series win against France. Two days before the Wallabies' 34–13 win against France in Sydney, O'Neill announced that the ARU had granted Rocky an early release on 'compassionate grounds' from his contract so he could leave Australia after the Tri Nations to play for Leinster. The ARU usually gave an early release to players as a reward for long service to the Wallabies or if they were not required by the national team. Rocky did not fit either category.

'It would be inappropriate for us to comment further on the conversations we have had with Rocky,' O'Neill said in a media release. 'He took us into his confidence and this remains a confidential matter between Rocky and the ARU. What we can say is that we have offered Rocky valuable advice moving forward.

'We also factored into the equation that not giving him this assistance, in the form of an early release, meant we could have lost him to Australian rugby permanently. As it stands now we hope to have Rocky back in Australia by the middle of next year.'

O'Neill stressed the ARU had not given Rocky a Dan Carter-style sabbatical because he did not want to set a precedent where Australia's best players would have short stints overseas, devaluing rugby in Australia. In many ways Rocky had an even better deal. If Rocky had taken a sabbatical, he would have been obligated to return to Australia the following year just as Dan Carter was committed to come back to New Zealand from France. I doubt Rocky would have asked for a sabbatical. As it was, there was nothing to stop Rocky staying overseas, which left his options open, just the way he liked it.

While O'Neill did not have the ironclad guarantee that New Zealand had with Dan Carter's sabbatical, he was probably more confident about Rocky returning sooner rather than later than he let on. O'Neill left himself open to criticism, but he seemed happy to wear it. Maybe he was comfortable in the knowledge of Rocky's extraordinary circumstances or perhaps just knowing Rocky the man a bit better than he had before.

After three impressive in-bound Test wins against Ireland and France (34–14 and 40–10) the Wallabies opened their Tri Nations campaign with a gritty 16–9 win against South Africa in Perth, which had been a favourable ground for the Springboks. Rocky, who had received a handful of man-of-the match awards in his last 10 outings, picked up another for a strong, all-round performance, but it would come at a cost. Early in the match Rocky's boot got caught in the ground. With his toes literally dug in, the rest of his foot collapsed back on itself, tearing the medial ligament among other things.

With the highly anticipated first-up clash between the Deans-coached Wallabies and the All Blacks, coached by his rival Graham Henry — who had blocked him from the All Blacks job — seven days later, the timing of Rocky's injury was terrible. Rocky was in real doubt. Deans' policy was a player had to train to play, but Rocky got through the session on Thursday, although he looked uncomfortable, and was included in the match-day 22.

In the absence of the injured Stirling Mortlock, George Smith led Australia to a stunning 34–19 win. While Rocky was struggling with his injured foot, he still managed to score a crucial try 15 minutes into the second half. With the Wallabies looking directionless, the ball landed in Rocky's hands, standing flat-footed at first receiver just outside the All Black 22. Showing great acceleration off the mark, he went straight through a cluster of defenders and beat fullback Mils Muliaina on his way to the line to put the Wallabies back in front. Matt Giteau kicked a field goal to cap one of Australia's best performances in years and it seemed like the beginning of a new dawn under Robbie Deans.

There was a euphoric feeling in Australian rugby circles that the Deans magic was already working, but the coach was nothing if not a realist, stating that he feared the Wallabies had made a 'rod for their own back'. Few understood what Deans meant and his comment was pretty much dismissed at the time, but he knew better than anyone what the All Black response would be like, as the Wallabies would soon find out.

The return match in Auckland was scheduled for the following Saturday and it could not come fast enough for an All Black side smarting from losing to Deans for the first time. Rocky, however, was ruled out. He may have paid a painful price for his involvement in the Sydney Test victory, but I doubt he regretted it.

Deans reverted to the small, mobile Eddie Jones-style back row of George Smith and Phil Waugh. It was the first and last time he did. The Wallabies came back to earth with a thud, humbled 39-10. The All Blacks out-muscled the Wallabies forwards in the contact zone and completely dominated the lineout, although the return of towering second-rower Dan Vickerman from elbow surgery midway through the second half helped them in the set piece. At one point, the All Blacks attacked straight through the lineout to score a crucial try. For one of the world's best lineouts to be so thoroughly outplayed by one of the lesser lineouts in the game was not well received.

The chastened Wallabies set their sights on South Africa and their first victory in the republic for almost a decade. Rocky's rehabilitation was ahead of schedule and he was included in the touring party, then surprisingly named in the team to play the Springboks in the first Test in Durban. It was expected that Rocky would have to wait until the second Test in Johannesburg, but Deans threw him in and it proved a masterstroke. Rocky produced a man-of-the-match performance in Australia's 27–15 win, their first on South African soil since 2000, yet another milestone for Deans, but it was not without drama and, in retrospect, humour.

Rocky almost missed the game after arriving so late for a team meeting that the departure of the bus to take them to ABSA Stadium had to be delayed. 'There were some challenges with the lifts, but to be fair if they were running perfectly, I don't know if he would have got there on time,' Deans said, smiling. 'I never put the question to him whether he was aware he was late. He wandered in like everything was the way it should be.

'He was significantly late. He wandered in, took his seat, we got on with things and things unfolded well. He was a big part of that. That's just the nature of the beast. Sometimes he can give you the impression he is a mile away, but he is generally thinking about something that is important to him and us. Others would suggest he beats to a different drum – he does enjoy the drums – he is a very calm man. Within that he is very focused as well and very clear in what he wants to do and what he wants to achieve. When you transfer that to the group context, it's powerful.'

Deans touched on an important part of Rocky's make-up, his absent-mindedness, which is a characteristic of intelligent, creative people, hence the expression, 'the absent-minded professor'. While Rocky's absent-mindedness could cause stress as when he was late for a team meeting, it could also be a source of humour.

'I know a lot of coaches used to hate the fact he would be the last to run out onto the field from the dressing shed because it would be, where is my mouth guard?' Les Kiss said even though Rocky doesn't wear a mouth guard. 'There is an absent-mindedness about him. I remember once he borrowed a mate's car, his BMW – Chris Whitaker tells the story – [Leinster] flew back from Wales or wherever and Rocky said the car's been stolen! He had just forgotten where he parked it. The next day there it is. Another one was his keys. [Leinster] trained and went back in and he said he had left his keys out [on the field]. Felipe Contepomi and Whits are with their mobile phones on their hands and knees on the training paddock until they found them.'

Rocky is conscious of the fact he is forgetful from time to time, which is why developing habits is very important to him. The way Rocky explained it to me once was it was easier, and more reliable, for a forgetful person to rely on a fully developed non-conscious habit than to try to remember everything they have to do. For example, some people only put their wallet in their left pocket, while others get ready to leave a place several minutes before they have to, to give themselves time to think about what they have to do. When I asked Rocky about running out last, he told me he did not need to run out dead last, but somewhere at the back of the line to give him time to re-check everything before running out onto the field. This practice seems to work for Rocky most of the time, although he may need to develop a more effective habit for car keys!

Covering the Wallabies' tour of South Africa for *The Australian* I wrote that Rocky, although not yet captain, was starting to exert the same talismanic influence on the Australian team that Richie McCaw had on the All Blacks. Michael Foley, then the Wallabies forwards coach, agreed. 'I think that's fair,' Foley said. 'Richie obviously had the formal role of captain and therefore there were formal mechanisms through which he could have influence, and that's not to suggest he didn't have that talismanic effect anyway.

'But certainly while Rocky didn't have a formal role he was a presence. That started to happen in the World Cup in 2007. Some of those dominant performances stood him out as a guy who had progressed beyond being a young rookie who was finding his feet to somebody who was now a fully-fledged Test player, who was capable of having match-turning impact.

'By 2008, if you like, the expectation of players around him was that he could do that so therefore when he played he was influential and beneficial for other players. There are players who are talismanic that you can't possibly measure the benefit of them to other players. Other players play 10 per cent, 20 per cent better by virtue of them being in the team and certainly by 2008, and even more so now, he is one of those players.'

Tony McGahan, watching Rocky's progress from Limerick, believed being described as a talisman was the highest compliment a player could ever be paid. 'By the time he left [for Dublin] he was such a leading figure,' McGahan said. 'He galvanised the players and they followed him. There is no better attribute than when you are out there, everyone else plays better. There is no better accolade. You make players around you better because you are on the field and playing.'

Stephen Moore believed that first season playing under Deans was a highly positive period in Rocky's career. 'That was a really good period for him and the team,' Moore said. 'That was probably the closest we've come in recent times to winning the Tri Nations and the Bledisloe. Rocky was a big part of that. We knocked over the Boks in Durban. It was as good a win as I can remember having in my career. You need figures like that against the big teams, the South Africans, New Zealand, particularly in the back row. It's such a confrontational part of your team. You need guys to step up to that challenge and he certainly did the job.'

Rocky had already emerged as a leader even if he did not have a letter C next to his name. 'He had been around for a long time, more so than most,' Deans said. 'He has now seen the transformation of the group, but he has grown with that. He is smart enough to do that. Even from a leadership perspective he is smart enough to have embraced the different emphasis. Our emphasis around leadership is not about title. It's about what you do and what you can do and what you are prepared to do at any given moment. And everyone being prepared to take initiative and take ownership and be responsible and accountable as opposed to waiting for instruction or biting your tongue because you don't think you're old enough or have been around long enough. It doesn't cut it anymore.

'Rocky has come through an era where leadership was probably owned more by the back seat than by those further up the bus, but he has embraced where we are going and he's no slug. He can see the value in it.'

After Rocky's suspension for tackling Springbok captain and second-rower, Victor Matfield, in the air in a lineout was successfully appealed, a much-changed Australian team was handed an embarrassing 53–8 defeat in Johannesburg. A pattern, which Deans described as 'undulation', was starting to emerge where the Wallabies would achieve a wonderful win one week only to suffer a woeful loss the next week. This trend had to be broken if the Wallabies were to become a power in world rugby again.

The Wallabies returned to Australia to challenge for the Tri Nations in the final round of the tournament, but they were dealt a heartbreaking 28–24 loss to the All Blacks in Brisbane. It was Rocky's last game before he departed for Dublin. I remember seeing Rocky in the lobby of the team hotel the morning after the game, signing autographs for fans. I wanted to go over and say goodbye and wish him good luck, but I was stuck in a media scrum, interviewing Robbie Deans or another player. I tried to make eye contact with him, but I had to concentrate on the interview that was taking place. When I looked around again he was gone. Just like that.

Deans was confident Australian rugby had not seen the last of Rocky. 'Essentially, he had some things he needed to do and wanted to do, but what was evident to me was the underlying motivation and the underlying intention from his perspective was always to come back and see Wallabies rugby re-establish itself and to play a big part in that,' Deans said.

'From a contractual perspective that wasn't always obvious or necessarily guaranteed, but from the discussions I had with him I was confident he would come back and he would continue to give a lot back to the game in Australia. There were no guarantees, but I was reasonably confident – off the back of having got to know him – that he wasn't finished yet. He had things to do. Things he wanted to do. History has shown that is the case.'

Under ARU protocols foreign-based players are not eligible for Wallabies selection, even though the IRB states clubs must release players for Test duty during the international windows in June and November. Convinced in his own mind Rocky was coming back the following year, Deans explored the possibility of him playing for the Wallabies on their end-of-season tour of Hong Kong and Europe.

'Oh yeah! Rocky wanted to play every game,' Deans said. 'We had to deal with protocols, obviously, that were in existence and still are in existence. We asked the question in terms of his ability to play on the end-of-year tour and so forth because sure, he was leaving, but the likelihood was he was coming back. But protocols are protocols and he understood that you have to draw a line in the sand somewhere. The [ARU] board did that and they were resolute in that and they have been consistent in that.

'Players are obliged to be available according to IRB protocols. Players have to be released to play international rugby, but according to the [ARU] protocols he couldn't. That's the way it is. He knew that going into it. As is often the case, others get an opportunity and you build the base. He had a great experience off shore and did something he had been close to, but hadn't been able to achieve: he won a premier comp and he was obviously a big contributor to that.

'Of course [we missed him]. You have to cut your cloth to suit the time and you adapt. You are so busy you don't think about who's not there. You just get on with it. When you see him in the stadium in Hong Kong for our very first Test and he's there and keen and he can't play … as it would have crossed his mind because his emotions would have been running high. It was the first time he had been in attendance and not had the gear on.'

# 7

## A BIT OF CRAIC

*We wouldn't have won the Heineken Cup without Rocky Elsom. He is a remarkable player, probably the best I have ever played with and I have played with some very good players.*

**Leinster and Ireland centre Brian O'Driscoll**

Rocky could have played for any number of European clubs, perhaps for more money, but I have no doubt he gravitated towards Leinster because of one reason and that was Michael Cheika, although the presence in Dublin of Australians Chris Whitaker and Alan Gaffney would have made him feel more at home. Rocky's brother Sam was pleased to learn Rocky would be playing for Cheika. 'I think Michael is a great guy,' Sam said. 'I think that their personalities gel very well. They are both a similar kind of person. Michael is a little bit more passionate. He makes business very personal whereas I think Rocky is a little detached. But in every other way ... they are dry and to the point and honest.

'I thought it was good in a sense for Rocky [to go to Leinster] because he had people that he knew. A lot of people are probably closer to Rocky than they think they are because I don't reckon that he lets you think you are very close. Not that he doesn't let you think, but I think his personality is such that when people are friendly or they're close they act that way and there are certain things in Rocky's dry kind of personality that he doesn't let on.'

The son of a Lebanese immigrant, Cheika was a talented and uncompromising number 8 for Randwick, captaining the Galloping Greens from 1997 to 1999. He represented NSW and Australia under-21s. Although Cheika did not play for the Wallabies, he played in Randwick teams that included a host of internationals such as Simon Poidevin, Gary Ella, Tony Daly, David Knox, Ewen McKenzie, Lloyd Walker, Warwick Waugh and David Campese and played for the club against the touring All Blacks.

Cheika spent the Australian off-season playing in Europe with French clubs Castres Olympique and CASG Paris and Italian side Livorno. At the same time Cheika was building a successful fashion distribution business, consciously avoiding becoming financially dependent on rugby. 'I've always liked to have my business as my way of earning money because I don't want to earn money from rugby,' Cheika said. 'I get paid. It's good. But I don't want to be dependent on the salary because then my decisions become compromised.'

David Campese asked Cheika if he was interested in coaching his old Italian team, Padua. Cheika applied for the job and was successful, taking former Randwick and Wallabies five-eighth David Knox to Padua with him as his backs coach. Cheika and Knox guided Padua through a Heineken Cup campaign and while it did not yield any wins, it gave the young coaches valuable experience. Cheika returned to Sydney in 2001 when his father fell ill and he secured the Randwick coaching job, winning the premiership in 2003 and 2004.

On the recommendation of Alan Gaffney, Leinster's Australian backs coach, Cheika was appointed head coach the following year to replace Declan Kidney, who had left Dublin to coach arch-rivals Munster. 'The opportunity came to interview for the position at Leinster, which, to be honest, I'm not quite sure how I got because I wasn't really qualified,' Cheika said. 'I'm sure they had people with CVs that were much more detailed than mine. I did two or three interviews there and it went well. I allayed their fears that I wasn't going to have the reputation maybe to control some of their bigger players. It worked out really well. I was at Leinster for five years. It was a great project, really enjoyed it.'

Mick Dawson, the Leinster CEO, described Cheika's appointment as a 'calculated punt'. A former hooker with Dublin club Lansdowne, Dawson had worked as a stockbroker for 20 years before taking on the Leinster job. Cheika was a speculative investment. I took a taxi to Leinster's headquarters on Main Street in Donnybrook, situated above a branch of the Bank of Ireland, the team's sponsor, opposite Lansdowne Road stadium. From street level I had to scale a narrow stairwell, whose walls were adorned with photographs of Leinster heroes. When I reached the top of the stairs I saw a photograph of Rocky roaring with delight with his victorious

Leinster teammates after the Heineken Cup final. Dawson greeted me and ushered me into his office. With his spiky hair, Dawson looked like he could have been a guitarist with Rod Stewart's old group, the Faces, although he was dressed more like a respectable businessman. I did not want to come all this way and have a tape recorder malfunction like I did with my interview with Rocky's mother so I placed two recorders on Dawson's desk, prompting him to exclaim: 'To be sure! To be sure!'

'I had never heard of Michael Cheika,' Dawson told me. 'But Alan Gaffney, who was with us at the time, rang me and said there is a young fella called Michael Cheika, who has done a great job at Randwick, and I should meet him. I remember I flew to London and I met him at the Hilton at Heathrow. We had a long chat and Michael is a good talker. He was very, you know, bullish about the job he could do. He thought he could make a big contribution. I must say I was very impressed with him that first meeting.

'I came back here and I spoke to our chairman, Brian McLoughlin, and the team manager, Paul McNaughton – the current Irish team manager – and said I thought we should interview this guy. Michael put back his trip to Australia, flew over here, and he was interviewed on a formal basis by the three of us. As they say, the rest is kind of history.

'He was a risk, but it was his drive, energy and enthusiasm that we needed. We had a lot of high-profile players and we were probably looked upon as slightly under-achieving. He spent five years here. In the early years the team were kind of a mirror image of him. Michael drove himself and I suppose in later years he gave more control to the players. History will treat him well here. He did very well and won the ultimate goal, which is the Heineken Cup.'

Leinster was said to be in disarray when Cheika and Knox arrived in Dublin, but in his very first season Cheika was a runaway success, guiding the under-achieving team to the Heineken Cup finals where they met European heavyweight Toulouse in Toulouse, a graveyard for opposition sides, in the quarterfinal. But Leinster produced some of the greatest rugby ever seen in the club's dark blue colours. Leinster's game plan was filled with well-thought-out and perfectly executed plays, glittering with moments of brilliance. Leinster's unlikely win entered folklore and pitted them against arch-rival Munster in the semifinal. While Munster toppled Leinster in Dublin on their way to lifting the trophy, Cheika had made his mark. Cheika's second season was a difficult one, with Leinster being knocked out of the Heineken Cup quarterfinals by London Wasps. The following year ended in triumph for Cheika as Leinster won its first Celtic League trophy since 2001. Disillusioned with Irish rugby, Knox returned to Sydney in 2008 and missed Leinster's greatest triumph.

Known as the 'Ladyboys', Leinster was considered soft, particularly in the forwards. Something was missing and Cheika knew just where to find it. The recruitment of Rocky strengthened Leinster's forward play and defence to complement the traditional attacking brilliance in the backline, but he offered something much more, something intangible: an indomitable spirit. 'What I do in a lot of my recruitment is profiling, not just talent, but also character,' Cheika said. 'And we really needed what Rocky's profile was to add something that was missing in our squad. It was very much about an anchor. A player who could drive the team like an engine, you know what I mean? He was that very solid player who could carry the team, who could change the game with an action, but maybe didn't brag about it.

'He did his thing. He prepped very well and he was a very good example to a lot of the players as far as his preparation was concerned. He was very professional and meticulous in getting himself ready. He knows his own body and how he wants to get it. I like a player who will take charge of his own game. If he's got his own way of getting himself right and he performs on the field, who am I to change it, you know what I mean? The thing about that, too, is he is open to suggestion. He is interested to know what he can add to his arsenal and he is also interested in sharing information to make the team better.

'What you are investing in is the player's character and his potential as well as what he has done already and then I as a coach and my staff and the rest of the team have to try to get the most out of that player. You are not just going to get Rocky and say, here you go mate, here's the ball, go and score. We had to help him find his feet as much as he helped us and that's what made us a good team, you know.

'It's a big change. I've played overseas as a foreign player. It's a massive change. You've got no support structure that you are used to. Your girlfriend is in another country or your family is a long way away. You are playing rugby that is completely different. I remember when he came I think we lost the first two or three games. His first game was against Munster in Dublin and we lost at home. It wasn't a great start. We may have lost another game after that back to back. He likes his way, but he was mature enough to have a look at the landscape, see what the rugby was about, right, because it's different rugby compared to the southern hemisphere, and adapt his game accordingly. Once he got on top of that part he really started to excel. He started to invest in the team. He probably took less time than most foreign players to acclimatise. It's not easy.

'First of all his on-field performance was outstanding, not just because they were outstanding games, but because of their constancy. He repeated pretty much week after week, after he got settled in, a really high level of play. Technically and emotionally he really contributed to the team. He got right involved in the identity of the team and people respect that. As soon as he asserted himself as someone to be respected, that was it, you know. Once that happened it went two ways. The team loved him and the players really liked the way he went about his business. They knew that was a bit of profile we needed. And I think he got turned around by the team as well. There was a really good fit.

'His investment in the strategic side of our game as well was good through his initiative whether it was the set piece or general play. He was good counsel for me because I liked bouncing ideas off him. I had a good group of senior players. In the end they just ran it themselves. I just got in the background a little bit and brought the cones out onto the field. They had good interactivity with him and Brian O'Driscoll, Leo Cullen, Felipe Contepomi. They worked it out themselves. He gave good example and he knew when the team needed him.

'I find him a charming guy. He's intelligent. He is articulate. He can be hard when he has to be and a bit down in the gutter. I enjoy his company as a person and even though he's got those qualities he is more than prepared to take instruction given by the coach or the captain or whatever. He understands his place in the order. He knows what he can give and he knows when to give back. That's the sort of intuition that has made him a successful player. He assesses what he has been given and what he gives back, you know what I mean? I just found him to be a really good character fit for what we needed in the team.'

Cheika's astute management of Rocky was a much underestimated part of Leinster's success. Thrown straight into the team's training a week after the Tri Nations, Rocky had a number of uncomfortable standoffs with strength and conditioning staff and earned the ire of some of his teammates for his special treatment.

One incident in Rocky's first week involved a strength coach scowling at him to lift a weight more appropriate to his strength. When Rocky refused, the whole gymnasium went quiet as players awaited the outcome of the confrontation. Even though it was an awkward situation, and probably not a good first impression to make on your new teammates, Rocky stood his ground.

When I heard this story I asked Rocky why he wouldn't just go along with the strength coach's instructions, at least in the beginning. He explained to me that after two shoulder reconstructions, lifting anything heavier than a 30-kilogram dumbbell above his head caused crunching and irritation in his shoulder capsule. Even though the weight the strength coach wanted him to lift was relatively light, it was important not to push it in that position because it was the only position which caused problems.

Bob Dwyer's philosophy that 'you only train to play better' also seemed to be Rocky's mantra and he was prepared to stand up for what he believed. Eventually, the Leinster strength and conditioning staff would play an important role in developing Rocky's incredible durability over the next nine months in Ireland, but at the start, the relationship was well, rocky, to say the least.

Similarly, some of Rocky's teammates were not overly impressed at first with his removal from most of the contact drills and his total removal from fitness drills. For Rocky, halfway through what was effectively an 18-month season, crashing into bodies and running laps was likely to do more harm than good. It was not worth the risk of possible burn-out or injury. As uncomfortable as those early confrontations surely were, ultimately Rocky's strong-mindedness benefitted the whole group because of his performance on the playing field. Rocky's self-management was always going to be critical to his success. 'He has learnt the hard way he has to take control,' Dr Angus Bathgate said. 'He manages himself. He picks the eyes out of different options and self-directs. He has done this well.'

However, to say that giving this kind of special treatment to a foreign player, who was new to the club, was a high risk would be a gross understatement. But Cheika knew what he was getting with Rocky and he knew how to get the best out of him.

Mick Dawson knew Rocky was a good player, but he had no idea just how good he would be when Cheika recommended they sign him. 'Michael came to us and said listen, I tell ya, if we are going to be really competitive, we need to add to what we are going to do. And we signed CJ van der Linde, Isa Nacewa and Rocky. CJ had been a World Cup winner with the Springboks. I thought the South Africans wouldn't look for CJ while he was up here, which meant he would be available to us all the time. Isa seemed like a real good buy to me because he would never be required for international duty again because he said he wasn't going to play for Fiji.

'Rocky Elsom? Obviously, with a name like Rocky Elsom we had all heard of him, right, and I knew a bit about him. My impression of Rocky Elsom was that he was a very good player. I think he had been capped 46 times by Australia at that stage. But what I was really impressed with was he was young. He was only 25 when he arrived here. Also, what I liked with the Australians is that they wouldn't pick him while he was here. That meant he was going to be available to us all the time.

'I knew he was a good rugby player. He turned out to be an absolutely fantastic rugby player for us. I really didn't know how good he was, but Michael Cheika wanted him and we went with it and we paid a lot of money for these three guys, but we made a decision that's what we were going to do.

'I didn't know Rocky Elsom personally. I rang up and said tell Rocky to drop in and see me and he came up here. He was a very soft spoken, quiet, unassuming guy. In terms of how he performed on the pitch he was understated off the pitch. We had a reasonable relationship. Obviously, the relationship was with the coach and the players. Rocky seemed to get on well with the players, but he kept himself to himself. He doesn't seem to court controversy or want to be overly friendly. I'm the CEO so I didn't see him every day of the week, but I would see him on match days and he would always say, how are you doin', Mick? He would always be friendly.'

Dawson agreed with Cheika that once Rocky got going there was no stopping him. 'His first match I think was a Leinster–Munster match and we were beaten up here. The intensity was quite ferocious and you were kind of saying to yourselves, I'm sure he didn't expect that. I don't know whether it was Rocky's impression. I don't know. Some of the people who came from the southern hemisphere don't think the Magners League will be as intense as Super rugby and can be just as at times.

'Post-Christmas Rocky just ... he was just outstanding. I think he got man of the match nearly every match. He had kind of a five-month window where he was just awesome. Played every match, never injured, always available for selection, and was scoring tries and was at number 6 being a dominant force in every match he played. I think it's safe to say that we wouldn't have won the Heineken Cup if Rocky Elsom hadn't been around.

'And the other phenomenal thing and, I say it touch wood, he doesn't seem to get injured. He is unbelievable. That's where his real value is – obviously, his real value is that he is such a good player – but the fact that he actually gets out and does it every week is amazing. I think Cheika looked after him fairly well here in terms of he monitored him. He let him off once or twice to go on holidays. Rocky saw a bit of Europe and that sort of thing. But nobody minded because every time he played he pitched up and played, you know.'

Leinster went into the opening round of the Heineken Cup against bogey team Edinburgh at Murrayfield on the back of two defeats in the Magners League. Leinster had experienced difficulties playing against Edinburgh in the past, but Rocky did not carry any of that emotional baggage. Rocky scored Leinster's first points of the campaign after breaking away for a long-range, solo try in the 27–16 win. The sight of Rocky in full flight in the open spaces would be spread across the Irish newspapers and soon become a familiar one to Leinster supporters. Cheika knew right from the start what type of player he was getting with Rocky and incorporated his powerful running as a key component in Leinster's game plan.

'Every coach has a game plan, you know what I mean?' Cheika said. 'How you want to use the guy. What we tried to do was just find his strong points and put him into those positions as much as possible, you know what I mean? As the leaguies say, the good players make their own luck. He puts himself in the right position so many times because he understands the game and he makes the effort to be in it.'

But Rocky even exceeded Cheika's expectations. 'He played better than I thought,' Cheika said. 'I knew he was a good player, but he had some games there where he was just — I think not as much as some games — it was his consistently high level of preparation and if he did dip even in his own mind you rarely saw it. It never had an influence on the rest of the team. Often when players dip — and everyone does you know — they can let their body language or their mindset influence the rest. He was like ice. The guys felt good about that. They knew they had a cool guy in the middle they could rally around. There was a really good camaraderie between him and the players because they had a massive amount of respect for him in that short space of time he spent with them.

'Rocky was so consistently a stand-out player in a team that had a lot of good players. He was very respected, not just because he was a good player, but he represented the identity ... he helped Leinster find the identity it had been looking for for a while, you know. To not just be the show boys, but to be able to have both, a bit of steel, not that we didn't have it, but he just made a little extra, filled the little hole there was that pushed the team in the right direction.'

Les Kiss, whose defensive expertise helped Ireland to win the Six Nations grand slam the same year Leinster lifted the Heineken Cup, said Rocky provided Leinster with a critical edge. 'The edge that he brought was all his trademark stuff,' Kiss said. 'He did critical things at critical times. That's the measure of great players. He could meet moments and they are critical. They become turning points. That's what he gave to the team. He would find a magic moment when it was most needed and most unexpected. That could be a busting run or a huge, turnover tackle. He wasn't a guy who would tackle legs. He would tackle a man and monster him on the ground and rip the ball out and get a turnover, which was critical and would lift the team. The guys were in awe that it wasn't just a one-off. It was a regular thing. He is nonplussed about it.'

Stephen Moore's cousin, Felim O'Rourke, was a dairy farmer in County Meade, which is part of Leinster province. I asked Moore for his cousin's contact number because I was intrigued to know what an average Irishman thought of Rocky and his impact on Leinster. I met O'Rourke in the lobby of the Jurys Inn Christchurch in Dublin. It was a Friday evening and he'd brought his pretty wife, Fiona, for a night out afterwards. Given that he was not a player, coach or even an administrator, O'Rourke, who played Gaelic football, seemed surprised that I wanted to interview him about Rocky. But like any good Irishman, O'Rourke enjoyed a chat.

It turned out that O'Rourke supported Munster, and although Rocky had not quite swayed him to change his allegiance, he cheered for Leinster too. 'Munster were more successful and they had a better team attitude or team morale,' O'Rourke said. 'They had a never-say-die attitude. They got stuck in and everyone liked them for that, you know. The country kind of got behind them because they were the most successful team.

'Gradually, it started building as people got to know his style of play and his sort of attitude. He was the main reason Leinster done so well. But he changed people's attitudes towards Leinster because of the way he played and approached the game. Leinster were a very Dublin-based team and people in Leinster really didn't follow them because of that. When Rocky came and brought his style of play and they became more successful, that was the start of it with Leinster. You definitely go to watch anything that Rocky played in. No problem watching them. He was a stand-out in every game. He was man of the match nearly every game. Huge, huge, huge — everyone loved him. He was in every paper, just huge.

'Leinster definitely wouldn't have won the Heineken Cup without him because they changed their style of play and they became even better in the pack while he was here. They were a better team to watch. And more people turned out to watch Leinster. And they improved. They have overtaken Munster in many aspects. Now people watch Leinster more than Munster or equally as much. I'm easy. I don't really get time to go to games that much, but I would go to a Leinster game or a Munster game. Rocky changed my attitude towards Leinster.'

At the end of the Wallabies' tour of Europe in 2008, Moore visited his relatives in Ireland and took Rocky to the family homestead in County Meade for a traditional Irish spread after a day's pheasant shooting. 'Stephen brought him out to our house to go pheasant shooting,' O'Rourke said. 'It's a family tradition. Down the years we've always been involved in shooting. From November to the end of January you can go shooting pheasants. We have a couple of guns at home so we decided to go for a walk for a couple of hours. He didn't shoot any pheasants. There were a few missed efforts, misfires, but the pheasants all got away. The pheasants were safe enough when he was there. Far more chat went on than shooting that day. His shooting wasn't up to his rugby standards.'

While O'Rourke was amused that Rocky could not hit the side of a barn, I doubt he would have enjoyed shooting a defenceless pheasant. But he would have enjoyed the Irish hospitality as much as the O'Rourke family would have enjoyed having him as a guest. 'Spent an afternoon at the house, got to know him, got to talk to him,' O'Rourke said. 'It was an enjoyable day. We had a good few of our family there. We came back and Mam had dinner ready for us all and we all sat down and had a big feed. It was great. It's something that everyone remembers. We have photos there at home. To have a superstar doing something that we do, our sort of stuff, you know, was great. As for the pheasants they were happy enough to see Rocky come. They knew they were safe.'

The craic is an Irish expression for fun, entertainment and enjoyment. Whatever the craic is exactly, Rocky certainly experienced it during his time in Dublin. Rocky became a cult hero at Leinster. The fans chanted: 'Rocky, Rocky, Rocky' and dressed up like Rocky Balboa. 'To get your name chanted you have to do something special on a regular basis,' Dawson said. 'It doesn't happen that often. Rocky just became … I can't explain it really, but it was definitely his contribution on the pitch. And then he was very good with his time, signing autographs for the kids afterwards.

'The crowd chanted his name and he became a firm favourite of the crowd. I think it works two ways. Obviously, our fans love Irish players to do well, but they also value the contribution of real quality overseas players and Rocky was a real quality overseas player.'

Rocky was lauded in Dublin. 'No matter where he went he was well looked after,' O'Rourke said. 'He could do what he wanted. Everybody would have loved to have Rocky at their pub or in their company.' And Rocky responded positively to the hero worship. 'I think it had an effect on him,' Cheika said. 'When you hear forty to fifty thousand people yelling out your name, that has an effect on you. You can't go past that you know.'

There is no doubt Rocky was afforded hero status in Ireland because of his outstanding play, but maybe, just maybe, there was even more to it than that. The Vikings ruled Ireland for three centuries. Perhaps Dubliners saw something of their own Viking past in this ferociously competitive Australian who had that Scandinavian warrior look. I visited Dublinia, a heritage centre in the heart of medieval Dublin. At the entrance to the Viking museum was a frighteningly realistic wax dummy of a Viking warrior, standing in a long boat, holding a sword and a shield. Dark blond hair fell below the Viking's helmut. As I stared into the Viking's dark blue eyes I thought for a moment I could see Rocky staring back at me.

As I wandered through the museum I came upon an exhibit of Viking words. 'You may know more Viking words than you think,' was written on a panel. 'English, and to a lesser extent Irish, contain many everyday words derived from the language of the Vikings,

Old Norse.' A list of English words of Old Norse origin included window, egg, ice, fish, boat, skip, rope and rock. Rock! It suddenly occurred to me that both Rocky's Christian name and his surname were of Viking origin. Hey, this guy is a real Viking!

Some Viking warriors worshipped the god Tyr and copied his clothes, which were made from bear skin. They were famous for working themselves into a frenzy, both before and during a battle, and it's from the Norse word for 'bear shirt' that we get the word beserk (funnily enough, Bob Dwyer, when describing Rocky's play back in 2003, would often describe him as a 'beserker'). Their opponents were often unnerved because the Vikings appeared to be completely fearless. It made me wonder whether Dubliners had made some sort of psychic connection to their Viking heritage through watching Rocky play.

While the Irish were treating Rocky like a rock star, family and friends back home were keenly following his progress. 'I was so excited for him,' Vicki said. 'We all were. We all sat up, all of our friends. Everyone was watching every minute of every game.' Kelly did not have the pay TV channel which showed the Heineken Cup in Australia so she would have to go to a pub in the early hours of the morning to see Rocky play. 'We'd have to get up at two o'clock in the morning and go to some pub in Kings Cross because we didn't have the channel,' Kelly said. 'Toia wasn't allowed in so I had to stand out in the street and watch through the window. When they won it was like the greatest moment of our lives. It was happening to him, but it was happening to all of us as well.'

Stephen Moore, who had considered playing in Ireland earlier in his career, kept in contact with Rocky and followed his progress closely. 'Irish rugby was going through a huge renaissance,' Moore said. 'They were doing well internationally. The Irish team had had a real resurgence. Also, Munster had been very successful. Munster were always seen as the dominant provincial side in Ireland and the only successful one. Leinster had always had a good team or seemed to have a star team, but had never won the Heineken Cup, which is what they are all after. One way or another when Rocky arrived and they started to do well he gave them that real catalyst to make that next step.

'I watched as many games as I could. I was getting told what he was doing by my relatives over there. They are in and around Dublin. I used to speak to him quite a bit while he was over there. Obviously, I caught up with him when we went on the spring tour. We didn't play Ireland that year, but he came over and caught up with us. I think that period in his career has been the most enjoyable for him. I think he really, really enjoyed being in Ireland, not just the rugby, but the whole lifestyle. He found the people really friendly. He just got on well with the people there. They looked after him. He did the right thing by them.

'Things just panned out for him really well. He was dominating games. He immediately developed a cult following for Leinster fans. They probably hadn't seen anyone like him before playing in that jersey.

'They win their group. The next thing they are in the semis. All of a sudden there is a semi at Croke Park against Munster in front of

85 000 people and it's just an absolute zoo. It's like a circus and he is the star of the show. They win that pretty well. They go and win the Heineken Cup. Bang, bang, very quickly. It was like Spain winning the World Cup. It was that sort of feeling I think just from talking to people and talking to him.

'He was massive. They did have a good team and you need it to win that tournament. He was the key figure there's no doubt, particularly in the finals. Once again, physically, he had to really manage himself through that period. I think he hardly trained. He just had to really look after himself to make sure he could play well. That all comes back to him knowing his body.'

Some southern hemisphere players approach a stint in Europe as a working holiday, but Michael Foley knew Rocky would be determined to prove himself on that stage. 'If you imagine the situation, there's a foreign player arriving at a club,' Foley said. 'The assumption from the players at that club will be that the foreign player is well paid. And there are a lot of internationals in that team.

'Rocky would have been extremely determined to ensure that people saw him as somebody who wasn't letting the team down based on the perspective of his performance matching up to some of the other internationals in the team and also whatever people assumed he was earning. I'm sure he would have wanted them to understand he was worth it. I don't know if those thoughts were particularly a conscious thing, but when you are overseas as a coach and you are looking to bring players in, Rocky is just the sort of guy you want in your team because that's the way he will respond, his great pride in his own performance.'

Foley was right. Questions were raised about Rocky's motivation for playing for Leinster, albeit comical ones. In his second game against Connaught, Rocky was seemingly buried beneath a pile of players when suddenly he popped up and made a clean break around halfway. With the game in the balance, Rocky streaked towards the tryline only to be pulled down just short, prompting one cynical journalist to write: 'I wonder if he would have run faster in a gold jersey.' Tough crowd!

'Leinster had this Irish backline that had wonderful skill and flair and had been playing great rugby, but probably what Leinster lacked was some real class in the forwards,' Foley continued. 'They had a good, hard-working forward pack, but Rocky presented them with a big, physical forward, who could suddenly adapt and play with the backs and be a real running option in midfield. It added another dimension to their game, culminating in one of the world's best players, Brian O'Driscoll, nominating him as the world's best player.

'There was no doubt he learnt that year some more about the game. Rocky is the sort of guy who reflects a lot on what he does. If I was to sum Rocky up as a different type of person to a lot of players, he is very reflective. That's what makes him so unique in terms of improvement. From my own point of view people would say gee, he has improved as if it was a good job done by the coach, but in actual fact he improves anyway. He improves irrespective of the circumstances because he reflects on his performance. He considers how he might do things differently and he'll often talk to you about it. But he is very intrinsically motivated. You saw in that year in Leinster – a guy who was playing very good rugby in 2007 and 2008 in Australia suddenly goes overseas and in a totally different type of game, different environment, takes another step forward.'

Simon Poidevin admitted he was surprised Rocky was so dominant in Europe, but he expected him to work well with Cheika, who is one of Poido's closest friends. 'I played with Michael at Randwick and Michael was a fantastic back-rower, probably should have gone further than what he did in the rep scene,' Poidevin said. 'Michael's ability to harness the qualities Rocky brought to that Leinster team was just like the natural mix.'

Robbie Deans took a personal interest in watching Rocky perform so well for Leinster. 'We all watched the final, but by that point he was coming home,' Deans said. 'We had good reason to take an interest. From my and our perspective it was fantastic to see him be such an integral part of a team winning what is such a tough competition because that comes with him. That's the habit we are trying to acquire.'

After entering the campaign as outsiders, Leinster went into the November international break at the top of the pool after beating Wasps 41-11 and Castres Olympique 33-3, both in Dublin. The first three matches could not have gone better for Leinster. In the Wasps game it was Leinster who had the sting both in attack and defence. Leinster and Ireland centre Brian O'Driscoll scored a truly remarkable try and followed it up with another before halftime as

Leinster's backs had a field day. Rocky contributed to the scoresheet, but his game will be remembered more for the big hit, and subsequent turnover, on French flanker Serge Betsen. It was one-way traffic for the full 80 minutes and the Castres game was much the same. However, Leinster lost the return leg to the French side 18-15 in Castres. A lot of the media started writing off Leinster's chances of getting out of their group. The old perception of Leinster as being 'soft' and 'having no heart' was reinforced and morale was low as the team broke up for Christmas.

Leinster began the New Year with another loss, with Wasps reversing their earlier defeat, winning 19-12 at Twickenham. Rocky was again a very positive influence on the side, not only with powerful charges into the fray, but also his calmness under pressure. Leinster lost three second-rowers in the first half as captain Leo Cullen was replaced and Malcolm O'Kelly was given 10 minutes in the sin bin. Self-appointed, Rocky called a very makeshift lineout with great success even though it was obvious some of the movements had never been rehearsed. While the result was disappointing, and the bookies had Leinster as outsiders to make the finals, and around 18-1 to win the final, they pushed on.

Now faced with the first of four season-defining games against Edinburgh in Dublin, Leinster needed a bonus point to be assured of advancement ahead of Wasps. Leinster ground out a 12-3 win in a muddied arm wrestle, without the bonus point, but it did not matter as Wasps lost to Castres. Leinster scraped into the final eight of the Heineken Cup, but they gained momentum with three successive Magners League wins starting with Scarlets where Rocky, dominating the match at number 8, came up against his former Wallabies and Waratahs teammate, David Lyons, who had been somewhat of a mentor to him in his early years. Playing number 8 again, Rocky performed well against the star-studded Ospreys in a tight match. Next was Ulster, coached by Australian Matt Williams, and Rocky was unstoppable. 'Rocky was far and away the best player on the field today,' Williams told the Irish media.

With a string of close wins, Leinster was also back in the running to retain the Magners League title when they faced a showdown with front-runners Munster. Although there were still several weeks to go in the Magners League the points on offer were critical to both teams' title aspirations. Leinster travelled to Limerick with high hopes, spurred on by the bitter memory of their 19-0 thrashing at the hands of Munster earlier in the season. However, their hopes were dashed as Munster inflicted a demoralising 17-point defeat on them, ending their chances of regaining the Magners League title.

With no team ever winning the Heineken Cup from below fifth place in the top eight, Leinster were rank outsiders. The first challenge was English premiership front-runners Harlequins at the Twickenham Stoop on Easter Sunday. Quins had knocked out French powerhouse Stade Francais in the pool stage and were expected to do the same to Leinster.

Leinster scored the first six points off the boot of Argentinian Test centre Felipe Contepomi, which grew in value as the rain poured down in a classic northern-hemisphere-style struggle in which every inch of ground was fought over. Rocky was again dominant in an outstanding display. Quins halfback Danny Care was running riot in the domestic English league, but Rocky was like a heat seeker to his thermal energy, constantly crashing through the ruck and knocking him to the ground, forcing his team backwards.

As the Leinster supporters, corralled together in one section of the ground, chanted his name, Rocky embraced the battle the game had become. At one point, Rocky stole a Quins lineout throw and took off with his opposite number, Chris Robshaw, in hot pursuit, but only the sheer pace of British and Irish Lion wing Ugo Monye could save a try. With tries hard to come by, Rocky had a chance to land a telling blow early in the first half, but as he buried has palm in Monye's face, the winger slid around behind him and clipped his legs, stopping him just inside the quarter and 50 metres away from where the play had started. Leinster had another chance just before halftime when Brian O'Driscoll went close to pulling off one of his trademark chip-and-chase tries, evading two sweeping defenders before being dragged down centimetres before the line. It was the kind of magic only O'Driscoll could conjure up, but Leinster was still without a five-pointer.

While Leinster had more opportunities, the tries were not forthcoming. When Mike Brown scored the only try of the match in the 65th minute to take it to 6–5 the momentum seemed to be with the home team. But Leinster dug in. Although Rocky, bloodied from a nasty head clash with Cook Islander prop Stan Wright, would receive the man-of-the-match award, every member of the Leinster team, none of whom were substituted, produced outstanding efforts. The Leinster back row of Rocky, Shane Jennings and Jamie Heaslip outplayed the Quins loose trio of Will Skinner, Nick Easter and Robshaw, who would go on to win the Guinness Player of the Year. Brian O'Driscoll conjured up his own special magic. Halfback Chris Whitaker was forcing turnovers the best number 7s in the world would be proud of. And Isa Nacewa proved his worth with a flawless display.

New Zealander Nick Evans, who had come on as a blood replacement in suspicious circumstances, missed a last-minute attempt at field goal and Leinster hung on in the most stressful of circumstances. It was a truly remarkable game in so many ways. For a team to score six points early and then defend the narrow lead for the rest of the game is almost unheard of in modern rugby. For a coach not to make any tactical substitutions in a match that was so physical and intense was almost unbelievable. And of course the incident that became known as the 'Bloodgate' scandal will never be forgotten.

An investigation revealed that Harlequins winger Tom Williams had come off the field with a faked blood injury in order for the team to make a tactical substitution. It came out that Harlequins had faked blood injuries on four previous occasions. As a result, Williams was banned for four months, Harlequins director of rugby, Dean Richards, for three years and physiotherapist Steph Brennan for two years, as well as a £260 000 fine for the club. Harlequins chairman, Charles Jillings, resigned and club doctor, Wendy

Chapman, was suspended for cutting Williams' lip to hide the use of the blood capsule. Harlequins chief executive, Mark Evans, said it would be naïve to think the Bloodgate stigma would ever disappear.

'We got out of our group and we were all delighted and we got an away fixture with Harlequins,' Dawson said. 'I think Harlequins made a mistake. Harlequins put all of our fans into one section of the crowd, which really galvanised them. There were about four or five thousand of them there and they really got stuck in on the day and the team really had to perform.

'When Michael Cheika and David Knox arrived here their attitude had kind of been: if the opposition score three, we'll score four. Now in the northern hemisphere at times when the weather is shite, that philosophy just won't work. You need to be able to dig out a 9-8 victory or a 6-5 victory, which is anathema, I think, to Australian teams, who just don't play in those sorts of matches. And actually, our supporters love the intensity.

'Michael agreed eventually he needed more fire power up front and that you do actually have to learn how to eke out those sorts of victories. No matter how well you play you are not going to score two tries. It just doesn't happen. You just can't do it. That 6-5 victory, as the match went on, you could actually see that both teams became more and more into themselves. A drop goal or a penalty was really all they were hoping for.'

Leinster teams of the past would have succumbed to the pressure in that quarterfinal against Harlequins. 'They were camped on the Leinster line, Harlequins, for the last few minutes,' Felim O'Rourke said. 'In other years they would have folded, but it was just the way it was, they got out of it, you know.'

The scene was set for an all-Irish semifinal between Leinster and Munster, 'the mother of all local derbies'. Earlier in the year on Valentine's Day, Rocky's birthday, the Gaelic Athletic Association Central Council had provisionally made Croke Park in Dublin, the cathedral of Gaelic football, available in the event of both Irish teams reaching the top four. What a birthday present!

The Leinster–Munster rivalry transcended rugby and even sport itself. It was like Athens and Sparta, an epic struggle between two very different ways of life. It is rare that fierce rivals from the same country would meet in a Heineken Cup semifinal. Leinster fans may have thought they would have to wait a decade to challenge Munster again after their devastating loss in 2006, but in a fortuitous twist of fate they were given another shot much sooner than expected. 'The Leinster–Munster thing was in a lot of people's psyche,' Dawson said. 'We had been beaten by them badly in a semifinal here at Lansdowne Road a couple of years beforehand and at the time I suppose a lot of people felt Munster had the psychological edge on us.'

Rocky gave Felim O'Rourke two tickets to the semifinal, but there was a condition attached. 'He knew my liking for Munster so he sent me a message about two hours before the game: Just one thing, wear blue. He knew I would have been wearing a Munster jersey and the tickets were in the Leinster family section. It wouldn't have gone down well. I swapped jerseys with my brother for the day.

Unbelievable — the country was divided. The crowd was blue and red. The atmosphere when the teams came out was electric.'

On a beautiful spring day, Munster entered the semifinal as hot favourite after winning its two Magners League matches with Leinster, scoring 40 points and conceding only five. A world-record 82 208 spectators crowded into Croke Park to watch the two rivals battle it out for what seemed like much more than passage to the Heineken Cup final.

Munster had demolished an almost all-international Ospreys side 45–6 in Limerick and were overwhelming favourites to win back-to-back titles. The Munster men were justifiably confident, but also wary of their traditional rivals, particularly a bloke named Rocky. When Munster and Lions captain, Paul O'Connell, was asked about Rocky's impact on Leinster, he replied dryly, 'He's certainly not here for a holiday.'

The tone of the match was set from the kick-off. As a high drop-kick by five-eighth Felipe Contepomi reached the Munster 22-metre line, Rocky and Leinster openside flanker Shane Jennings flew through like scud missiles, skittling the Munster receivers and blockers.

Contepomi was the Leinster player the Munster fans loved to hate and he received more attention in the build-up to the game than any other player. Contepomi's clash with Munster five-eighth Ronan O'Gara, which reached epic proportions when Argentina ended Ireland's World Cup dream in 2007, could have filled the stadium on its own. Over the years Contepomi was targeted by the Munster players, who tried to unsettle him, a potentially damaging outcome given he was the Dubliners' first-choice goal-kicker. Acutely aware of Munster's intentions, Contepomi sent a clear message to the men in red with his first carry of the ball, charging straight into O'Gara like a rugby league prop. Although Contepomi's run did not amount to much statistically, the Leinster fans understood its symbolic importance and let out a deafening roar.

Leinster had made their intentions abundantly clear in that opening minute of the match, but then disaster appeared to strike. Powering through a couple of would-be defenders Rocky got his right leg tangled up. He tried to push off his leg, but he was trapped. Enveloped by the Munster defence, Rocky fell awkwardly with his leg outstretched and twisted. As referee Nigel Owen blew his whistle to award Leinster a penalty, the team's medical staff rushed towards Rocky, who was slowly getting to his feet. Rocky seemed to ignore the medical officer as he struggled to put weight on his leg. The camera caught a close-up of his face, which had a look of quiet concentration, focusing on something in the distance, while Contepomi took the kick at goal. Later scans would show a crack in Rocky's tibia, which would fill with fluid and sideline him for three months, but wild horses could not drag him off the field now.

Rocky's fitness was tested a few minutes later. In a well-rehearsed backline move, Munster's Irish centre Keith Earls sliced through a hole between Brian O'Driscoll and Gordon D'Arcy. As the ball was cleared quickly from the ensuing breakdown three Munster attackers lined up against a Leinster defence which was still getting back into position. A cut-out pass found Munster winger Ian Dowling five metres from the tryline, but Rocky crunched him with a ball and all tackle that would not only save a try, but lead to a vital turnover. As the Leinster fans chanted 'Rocky', the Munster supporters may have noticed the replay on the big screen showed Rocky, instead of retreating to the ruck, had headed straight to Dowling's wing and may not have made it back onside.

For all their enthusiasm, Leinster were being outclassed by the Big Red Machine. Then Leinster hit back, inspired by one of those match-turning moments that Rocky has become renowned for. On the halfway line, Contepomi sent Rocky surging through a gap and he raced upfield only to be brought down by his former Nudgee College schoolmate, Paul Warwick, metres from the line. The ball was cleared to Contepomi, whose leg buckled as he stepped off his right foot, rupturing the cruciate ligament in his knee. Contepomi was carried off, leaving Leinster to continue the battle without one of the world's best midfielders and goal-kickers.

Enter back-up five-eighth Jonathan Sexton, who walked straight into a difficult shot at goal. Somewhat patchy early in the season, Sexton's skills were now under the most enormous pressure imaginable. With a face of serene calm, Sexton stepped forward in the deathly silence and sent the ball sailing between the posts as if it were no bother at all.

Leinster began to lift, while Munster started to fade, but the men in blue could still not find a way through. With the match locked at 3-all Sexton, Nacewa and O'Driscoll combined in a sublime backline play to put D'Arcy over in the corner. Leinster's stars were shining just when they needed them the most. At halftime the scoreline and the psychological advantage favoured Leinster, but the game was far from over.

Leinster opened their account in the second half when slick hands and excellent finishing resulted in a try to Luke Fitzgerald. The two ancient combatants continued to slug it out with Leinster seeming to gain the ascendancy as the game wore on. Then, on the hour, O'Driscoll landed a killer blow, intercepting a wide, cut-out pass and racing 70 metres to score while the passer strained every muscle in his body trying to catch him. While 20 minutes is a long time in a game of rugby, Leinster were not giving an inch and the margin seemed unsurpassable. The final minutes were a kind of pre-celebration for Leinster supporters, who had waited so long for redemption.

Rocky produced yet another incredible performance in Leinster's upset 25–6 win. Matt Williams described Rocky's try-saving tackle on Ian Dowling early in the first half as the 'watershed' moment in the match. Again, Rocky was not alone, with Nacewa, Whitaker, O'Driscoll and Sexton outstanding. No longer the 'Ladyboys', Leinster's game plan was to do the unthinkable: out-muscle Munster in the collisions and force turnovers at the tackle area. Rocky revelled in the hand-to-hand combat as Leinster put the Munster men on their backs. Just like the week before there were no weak links in the Leinster line-up and they performed as a perfect unit.

It would be arguably Leinster's finest hour, coming back against a fast-starting Munster to totally dominate the match. Blue flags waved in celebration every time a Leinster forward put a Munster man on his back or one of Alan Gaffney's backline plays peeled open the Munster defence, while the Red Army looked on in utter disbelief.

You had to commiserate with losing Munster coach, Tony McGahan, who had helped Rocky to develop his game in his formative years at Nudgee — something that had now come back to haunt him. 'It was such a big moment for both clubs,' McGahan said. 'We had beaten Leinster in 2006 in the semifinal at Landsowne Road and to come back two seasons later in the semifinal again at Croke Park in Dublin with 84 000 people, it was a special occasion for both organisations.

'Rocky that day had an absolute screamer of a game. He was everywhere. Attack, defence, breakdown, he lifted the side with one-out moments, but the consistency and quality of his involvements put Leinster in a very good position. He had a huge impact in that game with his running and uncompromising attitude in every impact and tackle contest area. He gave the rest of the side the ability to row in behind him and it got a great result for Leinster.

'It's an unfortunate thing that someone comes over for 12 months and plays in the Heineken Cup final and wins it. To come in when Leinster had been just a little bit away from it in the past, to maybe be that final part of the jigsaw that really pushed them across the line and play such an integral part in not only the final series in which he was so dominant, but all the way through to get to that point. He won't have to buy a Guinness in Dublin for a long, long time.

'We had a brief conversation [after the game]. Well done, congratulations and all the best for the final. We were too disappointed to be sharing too many accolades. It's a bit like NSW and Queensland. They are our biggest rivals. It probably suited Rocky because he lived in Sydney after leaving Queensland. He was in the latte set in Dublin. Europe gave him a different perspective on not only the rugby side of things, but life too. Any time you move away from a comfortable environment and start again, it gives you those sorts of values.'

McGahan claimed no foreign player has ever made such an impact in a single season as Rocky did at Leinster. 'I think he picked up nine or 10 man of the matches,' McGahan said. 'It was form you would hope to reproduce every season. Obviously, you can't. I don't think Leinster would have won it without him.

'It wasn't just the game that he played so well in. It was the things that he brought to training, what he brought to the other players. That "follow me" attitude that was a huge impact on the European scene. It was a different environment. I'm over here and I'm really going to prove myself. These blokes over here know who I am, but I want to make sure I leave a stamp here and make sure my credibility stands over here. It's not just come over here, take a bit of money and go again. It was a different environment in which he had to prove himself again. I don't want to come back down the track in 10 or 20 years' time and Rocky Elsom was a dud. I'm sure that would have been a motivating factor for him.

'They were an ambitious club and they were trying to make their mark in Europe. He was there at that time and it was well put together. They seemed to suit each other.'

As Leinster marched towards its first European Cup final, the city of Dublin was awash in celebration of what the team had already achieved and hope for what it might yet still accomplish. The three weeks Leinster had to prepare for its date with destiny must have been a wonderful time for Rocky to be alive, albeit he spent much of it on crutches. Here he was, the hired gun, brought over specifically to help take Leinster to the next level of European glory. He was just one step away.

While preparations drew to a close in the week of the final an unexpected drama hit the club. Just days before Leinster played English club Leicester at Murrayfield, Rocky was involved in a frightening car accident. As he drove through the junction at Donnybrook Church on his way to training, his car was hit by a van that had run a red light. Rocky's car was a write-off and with the airbags deployed on the driver's side where he had been hit; onlookers feared serious injury. After slowly wrenching himself out of the wreckage, Rocky made his way over to the driver of the van, who had veered off the highway and barely touched the brakes before colliding with Rocky's car. The driver looked shaken as Rocky approached the side window. A newspaper reported that Rocky told the driver not to worry about the accident, that he had been looking for a new wing mirror for two months and now he need not bother.

One of the first to hear the news was Mick Dawson. 'It was funny because my mother in actual fact was driving behind him,' Dawson said. 'She rang me and said one of your players has just been milled in a car crash. The car has been milled, but he got out of it okay. Yeah, it was very worrying. He was very lucky.'

Someone rang Michael Cheika at Leinster's training ground and told him one of his players had been in a car crash.

'Who?' Cheika cried. 'No, not Rocky!'

Cheika jumped on the nearest bicycle and pedalled madly to the scene of the accident. 'They told me Rocky's car had been written off,' Cheika said. 'It was just down the hill from the training base. I just grabbed a pushbike and I rode down the hill. First of all I was worried about the guy. I saw the car and it was just poleaxed, you know. He's just got out, walked up the street and come to training, you know what I mean? It didn't bother him. That sort of calm, complemented by a real aggression and a hard-nosed attitude, was a great combination in a rugby player.'

With the drama behind them, Leinster headed off to Edinburgh where they would meet one of the most successful teams in European Cup history and the newly crowned Guinness Premiership champions, Leicester.

As the Leinster team bus approached Murrayfield on the day of the final, Rocky would have noticed a 40-foot banner of himself on the back of every stand. It was an appropriate image because his performances for Leinster had indeed been gigantic. But on this day he would be truly superhuman. Leading Leinster from the front, he received his most important man-of-the-match award. Rocky had his Viking 'bear shirt' on that day, terrorising the Leicester defence every time he touched the ball. It was an extraordinary display of powerful, aggressive running.

The two teams faced off in front of a crowd of 66 523. The game did not start well for Rocky, who dropped the first ball thrown to him by Chris Whitaker. It seemed like an uncharacteristic mistake, but in fact it was not that uncommon. Rocky often bounced back from an early fumble to produce a match-winning performance and Leinster would need that from him today. The Leinster fans erupted into the 'Rocky, Rocky, Rocky' chant as the two teams packed down for the ensuing scrum. I doubt whether the fans could have made it more obvious that they expected the world of him, which left me wondering just what that must feel like. I also wondered what the reaction would have been from the Leinster players and fans if Rocky had gone into his shell after making that mistake like so many players do. But Rocky delivered.

The set-piece was a major focal point for Leinster. While not a noted lineout stealer, Rocky pinched three of Leicester's first four throws to destroy the English side's confidence on their own throw. In the scrum much rested on the broad shoulders of tighthead prop Stan Wright, who was grappling with one of Leicester's favourite sons, an Argentine Bull named Martin Castrogiovanni, who was so damaging in the semifinal against Bath that the Bath front-rowers' shoulders noticeably drooped whenever a scrum was called regardless of who had the put in. It was assumed that Wright and the Leinster front row would be given the same treatment. But in a great example of rising to the occasion Wright, Bernard Jackman and Cian Healy held the Leicester scrum at bay and while they did little better than gain parity with their opponents, their effort sent a powerful message that they would not be intimidated.

But as far as sending powerful messages was concerned, the best was yet to come. Seizing the opportunity on a turnover, Shane Jennings quickly shifted the ball to Rocky, who set off down the left-hand side of the field. Holding the ball in two hands, textbook style, Rocky threatened to use Jamie Heaslip on his outside, keeping the defenders at bay. As Heaslip switched back inside Rocky, powerful Leicester winger Alesana Tuilagi balanced himself for a trademark rib crusher. But Rocky crashed straight into Tuilagi, who fell over as if a chair had been pulled from beneath him. At the same time Leicester and England centre Ayoola Erinle leaped on Rocky's back. Rocky virtually carried Erinle until he was brought down metres from the line. The ball was shifted from the breakdown only to be knocked on. It was unfortunate that Leinster did not capitalise on that opportunity, but in a strange way it was better for the play to break down. Rocky crashing into Tuilagi and then carrying Erinle on his back was shown again and again on the big screen, prompting the Leinster supporters to chant 'Rocky, Rocky, Rocky'. The message that Rocky and Leinster had come to play could not have been made any clearer.

They say a team has to lose a final to win a final, but Leinster won the Heineken Cup in their first appearance in the decider against a Leicester side that had been there five times before, having won twice. In front of a crowd of 66 523, Brian O'Driscoll gave Leinster an early lead with a field goal, but Leicester halfback Julien Dupuy levelled the score with a penalty goal a few minutes later. Leinster moved ahead again 9-3 with a field goal from halfway and a penalty goal by Jonathan Sexton. Stan Wright was sin-binned in the 30th minute for an off-the-ball challenge on Leicester flyhalf Sam Vesty and while he was off the field, Leicester reduced the deficit to three with another Dupuy penalty before taking a 13-9 lead at halftime following a converted try to flanker Ben Woods. Dupuy increased Leicester's lead to seven points with a third penalty after the break, but a converted try to Leinster's Jamie Heaslip had the teams level again with 30 minutes to go. Then, with 10 minutes left, Sexton raised the flags with a penalty to win the game, 19-16. On the final whistle, in a rare display of emotion, the usually undemonstrative Rocky hugged Leinster winger Shane Horgan like a long lost friend. Or maybe Horgan hugged Rocky?

It was in the ecstatic glow of Leinster's historic victory that Brian O'Driscoll uttered his immortal words about Rocky being the best player he had ever played with. As Mick Dawson said to me, 'that was a hell of a statement for Brian to make'. Indeed it was. You simply could not receive a greater compliment. As they say in Ireland – in BOD we trust. O'Driscoll was the greatest Irish rugby player in history, perhaps the Emerald Isle's best-ever sportsman. He had played on star-studded Leinster teams, Irish Grand Slam-winning Six Nations sides and the British and Irish Lions, a who's who of international rugby. And yet, he offered the ultimate praise to

Rocky, and why not? The meteoric impact Rocky made for Leinster in one shining season was beyond compare.

One of the features of Rocky's play in the Heineken Cup finals was the bigger the occasion, the better he performed, which is the pattern of his career anyway. 'What you could noticeably see was him lift his intensity the higher the stakes became, you know what I mean?' Cheika said. 'He took a more active role when he felt he was needed. He spoke a little bit more. He took a bit more control of the situation the higher the stakes got. He came out of his shell a little bit more. He wanted to take more responsibility when there was more at stake, which is obviously a real good quality.'

To Mick Dawson, Rocky just seemed to grow and grow and grow in the finals. 'Rocky was just outstanding that day [against Harlequins],' Dawson said. 'As always he seemed to have two streams of blood coming out of his nose, which is nearly a trademark of his. He was phenomenal on that day and then again against Munster. We go to Croke Park. There's 85 000 people there and he just seemed to warm to his task. He made a fantastic break in the middle of the pitch at one stage. You looked at him and if you remember back, the bigger the occasion the better he seemed to be able to play.

'Then you go to Murrayfield and we were under the pump a bit there. But Rocky caught a ball well into our own half and he sold a dummy and made a surging run and the fans and the team just seemed to rise with him. In those three games he was just a bit special you know.

'If you get christened with a name like Rocky, to be five foot three isn't great. It's a big plus to be six foot five. It's a great name, a catchy name, but then you've got to deliver on that because it can be used against you if you don't perform. Rocky delivered from pillar to post in terms of his professionalism and his contribution on the pitch and really you can't say an awful lot more than that, and contributed to Leinster's biggest day in history.

'I've often been quoted as saying that to win a Heineken Cup you need a good team, which we had, you need a bit of luck and you need your star-quality players really performing when they have to perform. During that campaign Brian O'Driscoll and Rocky, and a number of others, were just playing on top of their game and really wanted to win it.'

For all the plaudits and praise for Rocky's performance, the best thing about his stint in Ireland for Vicki was that he was so happy. The sheer joy on Rocky's face after the final was an image Vicki had never seen before. 'The biggest thing was how happy he was,' Vicki said. 'He was very, very happy over there. I've never seen him quite so happy. He was always so serious here. He was so happy over there.

'To see him laughing with the guys I could see how happy he was. The photographs of him, I've never seen him like that at a game here. You see his face, singing at the top of his voice. He really enjoyed the company of the people there. He loved his teammates and I would say that's what he will remember most about Ireland. He's very lucky to have had that.

'I just knew they were going to do it because they had momentum. I said to him you know what's going to happen? You are going to win this game against such and such and then you're going to win the thing. And sweet Rocky goes, are we? Yes, you are Rocky. It was like I looked into a magic ball.'

Naturally, Leinster attempted to re-sign Rocky, but he was ready to go home. 'It's easier to accept anything like that when people are honest with you,' Cheika said. 'He always told me it was going to be an option. If not, he would have signed a two-year contract, you know what I mean? I sort of knew it might happen, it might not. He made his decision. I hope it works out for him going forward now and especially to the World Cup.

'There wasn't a bad word said about the guy when he left — even though he had stayed just a year — because they knew that he gave everything to the cause. And that's all people can ask. That's all a rugby supporter, coach, teammate ... all you can ask is that a bloke gives his best and that guy gave his best.

'We didn't try to replace him. I said we are not going to replace this guy because we are not going to find anyone like him. And anyone who comes in his position is only going to be compared to him. We brought up one of our young blokes [Kevin McLaughlin] to play that role and he ended up playing for Ireland that year, which was great. And we tried to bring in a player who maybe had some character traits. We ended up using [Australian-born Scotland lock] Nathan Hines, who became the replacement. Even though he played in the second row, he sort of brought some of those same qualities in the middle of the pack. Obviously, a different player altogether, but from a character point of view ... we knew if we brought in another foreign player they would always be compared to him. There wasn't much point because the guy would have been living in his shadow the whole time.

'It worked out really well you know. We had a pretty good season the next year. We lost the semi of Europe and we lost the final of the Magners so we were close to going for a double. We had lost Rocky, we lost Chris Whitaker, and we lost Felipe Contepomi. We had good players coming through, but we lost a lot of experience. I think the year before left a lot for that team of the next year. Rocky and those guys who left the team left something for the next team to build on. We had a really good season. It was a real pleasure for me to see the continuity in the performance of the team from the year before.'

Most Leinster fans had resigned themselves to Rocky leaving. 'When it came out he was thinking of leaving, everyone understood because of the player he was, and Australia needed him,' Felim O'Rourke said. 'We knew the situation. He couldn't play for Australia when he was off contract with the ARU. Everyone knew he was seriously thinking of leaving, needing to go back for that reason. Everyone was hoping he wouldn't go or he wouldn't be able to organise a contract. But people were fairly resigned to the fact that he was going back because he wanted to play for Australia.'

Asked whether he thought Leinster missed Rocky, Felim said: 'Oh hugely, yeah. Even though the players for Leinster have improved, he would still walk in the team. He would walk in any team. Even for publicity, they have missed him that way. He was a huge draw to go to the games even.'

Mick Dawson believed the lure of Test rugby was too strong for Rocky to resist. 'We were trying to get him to stay for the second year, but I think he missed international rugby from what he said to me, because we were having a chat here one day and he had gone over to see Australia play England at Twickenham or something like that and he said he would never do that again,' Dawson said. 'I suppose he felt he should have been there. The lure of international rugby finally got him home I suppose, now, I don't know.

'He just rang me up and said, listen, I'm going to go home. I just wished him all the best. It wasn't as if he had let me down or anything like that. I knew exactly where Rocky was and we had pushed as hard as we could for him. I think his heart was in international rugby in Australia.

'You wouldn't ever say about a person like Rocky Elsom that you wouldn't miss him because he just made an immense contribution. Yeah, sure, you miss someone of Rocky Elsom's quality. You can't say any more than that you know. Last year we did really well without Rocky. We got to the semifinal of the Heineken and we got to the final of the Magners League. We had a good season. Didn't win a cup and if Rocky had been here maybe he would have made a difference because he is an immense man and a great player. Yeah, he was missed.

'And he'd had a wonderful experience here, I would say. I hope he went home saying he enjoyed it here. I'd say anybody would try to keep him, but I just think he wanted to be somewhere else. I think and I hope he did enjoy his time here. We enjoyed having him here anyway.'

# 8

## COME TOGETHER

*If you are going to rely on someone, you need to choose wisely who you rely on.*

Wallabies coach Robbie Deans

Arguably the bravest decision in Robbie Deans' coaching career was his appointment of Rocky as Wallabies captain. It would be the first time Rocky had led a team on a regular basis since the Nudgee First XV nine years earlier and he had almost no experience as a captain in professional rugby. Just about everyone else thought Rocky shouldn't be captain. Rocky was too laidback, individualistic, rough around the edges. When Rocky spoke in public he sounded like he had studied method acting at the Actors Studio in New York with James Dean. Maybe Rocky was too real for some. There was talk at the time that sections of the ARU hierarchy preferred playmaker Berrick Barnes as captain, but Deans would not be pressured, if indeed any pressure was applied. Deans knew who he wanted.

'Rocky is a bloke who has a presence,' Deans said. 'He likes to win. He was a guaranteed selection and to be honest, if you go back to that time, there weren't too many. He obviously didn't have a lot of background in the role, but he had a burning desire and that's a start. You can work with that. And he is smart enough to work his way through it and get better at it. No one enters the role good to go, so to speak. It's a fast learning curve. You look at the profile of the group and you look at the reality of our circumstance at the time ... we had a young group and clearly it was not going to be plain sailing so we needed someone who was going to be resolute enough and strong enough in their own convictions and beliefs to not only survive, but ultimately thrive in that circumstance and come out the other end.'

I asked Deans whether he thought there was an element of risk in appointing Rocky captain, given he had so little experience in the role. 'Oh yeah, totally, people were voicing it left, right and centre,' Deans said. 'But every choice is a risk. Every decision you make is a risk. But the decisions you make have to be founded on something. And you need to be sure that people you back, you can rely on to keep turning up, first and foremost. There's no short cut to success. You can't talk your way there. The first requirement was for someone: A, prepared to stand up against the tide; and B, inspire others to do the same.'

How did an individualist such as Rocky not only fit into the Deans team culture, but lead it, nurture it? It would appear to be a contradiction, but even though Deans had only known Rocky for a relatively short period of time, he intuitively understood his capacity to bring people together. In many ways, Rocky was a more dynamic version of Reuben Thorne, Deans' former Crusaders captain and blindside flanker, who was the glue who kept the perennial champion team together.

'You look at many of the teams over time,' Deans said. 'If you want to go back and look at some of the Crusader sides and look at some of the blokes who have been integral triggers, go right back to '99 for example. Norm Berryman was probably the critical spark in the group and yet people from the top of the country to the bottom would have said he is not a Crusader, he doesn't fit — and he was the ultimate Crusader. The team offered him a lot. He offered the team a lot. It's a two-way street. It's a me–we. Sure people arrive in different states. They arrive with different backgrounds and histories and habits. It's how you come together and how you get all your needs catered for.

'Rocky's deep. He is smart and he is capable. Most people wouldn't be aware of his capabilities away from the playing field. He's got his pilot's licence. He is gifted with the drums. He can play the piano. But he'll never tell you. That's a good point. It's an unappreciated point with Rocky. They don't see him as verbose and going out of his way a lot, but it doesn't mean it doesn't happen. It happens in his time and in his way and he does connect. And he connects across the generations. When you look at the profile of our group it was a critical element.'

Deans' observation that Rocky was a trans-generational communicator was an astute assessment of his character and how that personal quality would benefit the Wallabies. Rocky was the one leader in the group who could bridge the generation gap. If you watch Rocky in social situations, it is evident that he is just as at ease talking to a rookie such as James O'Connor as he is a veteran like Nathan Sharpe. Maybe it's because Rocky really is some kind of transcendental soul, as his sister Kelly claims, and a person's age is irrelevant in the timelessness of the cosmos. Whatever the reason, Deans had perceived this quality in Rocky and understood its intrinsic value to a team that was going through generational change.

Of the playing group Deans inherited in 2008 only a few had experienced any real success and none had played on a winning team over a long period. After introducing seven uncapped players in his first Wallabies squad, Deans continued to shape and re-shape the team like a sculptor trying to carve an ideal form out of a block of marble. In the space of three years, Deans blooded 27 Test players, almost an entire World Cup squad. While the benefits of Deans' youth policy would start to emerge towards the end of 2010, it would take a captain with Rocky's strong yet compassionate character to help the team cope with its growing pains.

If the Wallabies had had an older captain who could not communicate with young players, it would not work. Similarly, it would have been unfair to saddle one of the young players with the burden of captaincy, even a born leader like David Pocock, who will no doubt succeed Rocky as captain one day. The Wallabies have split along generational lines in the past, most notably the 1981/82 tourists to Britain and Ireland, but Rocky had the ability to bring all the disparate elements of the team together, not just age, but personality and cultural differences as well. It reminded me of the Beatles song 'Come Together'. Rather than a gamble, making Rocky captain could have been a stroke of genius.

Rocky returned to Australia from Ireland in June, but his comeback with the Wallabies was delayed until August because of a leg injury, which he had carried towards the end of his stint with Leinster. All players carry niggling injuries, but very few can play through severe pain. Deans was impressed by Rocky's ability to perform to a high standard while carrying or recovering from injury. 'He came back with a lot of physical challenges,' Deans said. 'He came back with the accumulative effect of the rugby and the nature of the injury, which was a little bit elusive initially, the gravity of it. While he came off a high he didn't really re-enter in ideal shape. The accumulative effect of all the rugby he had played was starting to kick in. It's a reflection of him and his toughness – if you like, his belligerence – he kept going where lesser mortals wouldn't have, almost to his detriment.'

Rocky's return to the Wallabies for the Test against the All Blacks in Sydney coincided with Stirling Mortlock being sidelined for the rest of the Tri Nations with a knee injury. It may not have seemed terribly significant at the time, but it would prove to be the beginning of the change-over of captaincy from Mortlock to Rocky. There was a growing concern that Mortlock, who would be 34 in 2011, would not make it to the World Cup and a new captain needed to be groomed in time for the tournament. Even if Mortlock was in his prime, Deans still might have made the change. While Mortlock was an inspiring captain on the field, his off-field leadership was not as effective. In Mortlock's absence, George Smith led the Wallabies, but he was a reluctant captain, struggling with the spotlight and off-field responsibilities. Smith was also being strongly challenged by David Pocock for the number 7 jersey and could no longer be assured of a starting position. Deans had to find someone else.

While Rocky's presence made a big difference to the Wallabies, it was not enough to prevent them losing to the All Blacks in Sydney (19-18) and Wellington (33-6) and the Springboks in Perth (32-25). Their only win in the tournament was a 21-6 victory against the Springboks in Brisbane.

Three weeks later when Deans announced the Wallabies squad for the Grand Slam tour of Britain and Ireland, Rocky was named captain. I wondered what Peter Gledhill, one of the few coaches to recognise Rocky's leadership qualities, thought about his appointment as Wallabies skipper. 'I always thought there was a chance of him being captain, but it would depend on the type of coach,' Gledhill said. 'Rocky is his own man and slightly left of centre. If you are going to appoint him captain, there is a bit of a risk.

'Deans has shown he is more than willing to take risks with selections and bringing people up from nowhere and giving them a break. When Deans was appointed coach I think Rocky's chances of being captain increased massively, once Deans saw what type of man he was and the aura he had around the place. And he is an attacking player. Still to this day his attack is slightly higher than his defence.

Rocky loves having a crack at the opposition. Loves having the ball in his hands and he won't die wondering. That's Robbie Deans, isn't it? Won't die wondering.

'There are perceptions of him and they are probably perceptions of people who haven't taken the time to get to know him. When he was here — Rocky hasn't changed much, leopards don't change their spots — there were teachers here who would have said Rocky had a touch of arrogance. Champions have a touch of arrogance. I can kind of understand how people could have that perception.

'Rocky is a good one at shutting himself off, too. I'm going to train until I drop, but when training is over, it's over. I'll put on some relaxing music. I'll do what I think I need to do. He won't be one of the boys if he doesn't want to be one of the boys. He is his own man. I could see how some people could perceive that as not being a good captain and how other people could see that it would be good to have him as captain.'

Robbie Martin remembered telling Rocky he would captain the Wallabies one day. 'I thought it was fantastic,' Robbie said. 'But it didn't surprise me at all. I said to him years ago, you can captain the side one day. Just in conversation. He didn't aspire to be the captain, but it sits with him well. It suits him. When he was at Nudgee he was a destined leader. It was part and parcel of his make-up. He has a certain aura about him. He is calming, but he has a bit of mongrel. He is the full package. He's got it all.

'I don't know what light switch went on, but I think the chemistry between Robbie Deans and Rocky is good. They have a good working relationship. Robbie is no fool and neither is Rocky and I don't think Robbie tolerates fools, listening to him talk. He is used to success. Rocky wants to be just as successful as Robbie does. If Robbie thinks Rocky's got the goods to lead the side, Robbie has a track record second to none. He wouldn't have picked someone he thought wasn't up to the job.'

Bob Dwyer was curious to know what it was that Deans saw in Rocky as a captain. 'Has Deans ever said anything about why he made him captain?' Dwyer asked me. 'It would be interesting to know what he saw in him.

'A captain obviously needs to be a leader, but all leaders are not necessarily captains. Leaders are people who other people want to follow. They want to listen to what they have to say and watch what they do and follow them. It doesn't have to be stated, but they obviously emerge. If some of those leaders are quiet and don't want the responsibility of having to lead, they do lead, but they don't want to have to lead.

'It was clear right from the start Rocky was a leader. He was a leader by example. He doesn't say much, but when he talks, people listen. That was clear. What hadn't yet become clear was whether he would become a captain. All people you identify as leaders you identify as potential captains. And you see how things develop.

'Some people develop from the leadership role along one path towards captaincy, like Nick Farr-Jones, who had an enormous capacity to understand the needs of the individual and direct himself quietly and unassumingly in that way. And so his leadership role became stronger and stronger so that he became the obvious captain. Some people, like Ealesy [John Eales], did it in a slightly different direction. Not as personable, but very good with people anyway. But his deeds became so superhuman that it was clear that everyone wanted to follow him.

'Whether Rocky was going to develop along those lines was just a matter of time and no need to force it because ... I always say to people if you are looking for good players, don't look for them, they will find you. If you are looking for a captain, don't look for him, he'll find you. Otherwise, you tend to force things and excuse things and find certain things more important because you are looking for that guy to be a captain so you find what he does more important than perhaps it really is in order to strengthen your own direction.

'Obviously, Rocky developed that way for Robbie Deans. There is no doubt he has the strength of character, the morality, to be a captain. I'd like to see him [be] more vocal, but my idea of captain is not someone else's idea of captain.'

John Connolly revealed he would have considered Rocky as Wallabies captain if he had continued as coach after the 2007 World Cup. 'He was a senior player,' Connolly said. 'He had the respect of all the players. He had an opinion, but you did have to pry it out of him sometimes. At times you had to ask him. He was quite happy to stand back a bit and let other people talk instead of pushing himself to the fore.'

Stephen Moore was not surprised at all by Rocky's elevation to the captaincy. 'He was exactly the type of guy Robbie wanted to lead the team,' Moore said. 'He was a good choice. He has grown into the role. It's never an easy role for anyone. There's plenty of added pressure when you are named captain, but I think he has handled it well. It's very much a follow me-style of leadership, but not by what he says, by what he does. He tries to inspire the guys around him by his actions on the field and hopes the way he plays will bring people along with him.'

Michael Cheika said Rocky showed leadership qualities at Leinster. 'Yeah, all day,' Cheika said. 'Through the way he prepped himself. He spoke when he needed to. He didn't waste words when he didn't think he needed to. He took ownership of parts of our game that he thought needed improvement. Defensive lineout and bits and pieces that he thought we needed to improve. He asked me about it and I said, you go and own it, mate. There it is. Take charge of it. He took charge of it and it improved. It's in him, there's no doubt about that. The core qualities of a captain are there.'

But Cheika admitted he was surprised Rocky would have wanted the responsibility of Wallabies captaincy. 'I wasn't sure he would want to be the captain, you know what I mean?' Cheika said. 'I like the fact he is prepared to evolve. Maybe two or three years ago he wouldn't have done that, but he is prepared to evolve and become a better man, a better person, instead of hiding away from it. Now I think it was a really good thing for him to do.

'I spoke to him earlier in the day for five minutes. You can see he has changed a little bit as far as now he talks about the team. I just thought he thought more about the collective as a whole. I thought good on him. And he'll be learning about how to do that job. It's not just going to come and you are going to be a great captain in your first year. It takes time to build that knowledge of how to be a good captain and how to get the best out of everyone while at the same time not diminishing your own performance.'

One person who was concerned about Rocky leading the Wallabies was Les Kiss, but for entirely selfish reasons. Kiss feared the adverse effect Rocky's captaincy could have on the Irish team at the World Cup. Australia and Ireland are in the same pool and the outcome of their pivotal game will determine which team gets the more favourable passage through the finals. Rocky is still regarded with awe in Ireland and the last thing the Irish needed to see was him leading the Wallabies out onto the field. 'I said, oh, strewth! Because I knew how many people revered him over there [Ireland] and knew his influence,' Kiss said. 'They know he is a great player. I hope we don't paint this thing bigger than *Quo Vadis* and now we can't beat the Wallabies. I said we've got to manage this and not make him bigger than he is. It's been managed well because the players understand it's not just one man. It's a team. I think we've got through that now and I'm glad it was done last year and not this year.'

Simon Poidevin believed Rocky played a key role in helping Deans change the culture of the Wallabies. 'I thought Rocky was someone who they should consider for that role and that wasn't a mainstream view out there because people again didn't understand who Rocky was,' Poidevin said. 'All credit to Robbie Deans, who is a quite introverted guy himself, but when you sit down and dissect things with him he is fantastic. He would have been all over the candidates and he clearly identified Rocky as someone who brought standards to the team, which Deans demanded and needed.

'And again, this is where people don't understand Rocky. Rocky brings standards to the Wallabies that had drifted off a bit. He was the right personality for the job. Deans had to undo a lot of player-power, bad habits that had come into the Wallabies, and that was a major job. Deans came in and people underestimated what he had to deal with in changing the attitudes. Clearly, there were some very good guys in there at the same time, but the overall attitude was not good. That's why we were not being that successful. It took time to turn that around. Deans recognised a guy like Rocky Elsom — who set very high standards and took no shit and was a warrior leader — was the right person to work with him to change that culture.'

Rocky could not have asked for a tougher initiation to captaincy than a Test against the All Blacks followed by the first Grand Slam tour to Britain and Ireland in 25 years. There was pressure on the Wallabies not just to break their run of losses against New Zealand, but also to emulate the feat of the 1984 Grand Slam-winning Wallabies. In the end they achieved neither goal. After leading the All Blacks at halftime for the fifth time in six Tests, the Wallabies let another opportunity slip in Tokyo, losing 32–19. In his first touch of the ball as captain, Rocky dropped a pass, albeit directed at his head, from Adam Ashley-Cooper on halfway. Things had to get better, right?

The Wallabies began their quest for the Grand Slam with a lively 18-9 win against England at Twickenham before flying across the Irish Sea to Dublin. Rocky's return to the fair city was big news, with memories of his heroic deeds for Leinster still vivid in the minds of the Irish. He tried to keep a low profile, but the Irish media was all over him like he was Bono.

Vicki and Russell gained first-hand experience of 'Rockymania' in Dublin when they flew over for the Irish Test. 'We were at the airport and we were waiting for the bus,' Vicki said. 'It was like a tourist bus and people were all lining up for a lift into Dublin. This old guy was coming along with brochures and maps. He said you'll be needing, you'll be needing. I said thank you. I opened it up and it had a picture of Croke Park. I'm sort of looking at it. He said, you won't be needing that, give it to me. I said I am interested in it because I'm going to the rugby. He said, are you now? You've come all this way to go to the rugby, have you? I said yes. He said you know we had one of your fellas over here last year. Oh, he was a champion. His name was Rocky, can you believe it? Do you know him? I said, he's my son.

'He goes, Holy Jesus, Joseph and Mary! I retreat from you into insignificance as I bow in reverence in your presence. And then he goes do you know who we've got here, everyone? Rocky's parents! Jesus, me wife's not going to believe it. Can you take me photo? People were going is your son Rocky? And we were getting our photos taken with perfect strangers. It was very funny.'

The build up to the Irish Test could not have been scripted any better. On one side was an Irish team unbeaten for the first time in five decades, Six Nations Grand Slam champions, and the man who had done more than any other to deliver that success, Brian O'Driscoll, captain in his 100th Test for his country. On the other side were the Wallabies on their quest for the Grand Slam with Rocky, not only returning to Dublin so soon after his Heineken Cup heroics, but as the captain of Australia. The Irish team was brimming with Rocky's former Leinster teammates; the last time they saw him was when they lifted the Heineken Cup together.

Even though there were standout performances by Wycliff Palu and David Pocock, almost all of the decisive moments of the Test revolved around the two Leinster men leading their respective teams. Right from the start Ireland was under pressure. A wayward pass thrown way out in front of O'Driscoll was slapped down by the Irish centre and fortuitously landed in the hands of a swooping Drew Mitchell, who sprinted to the line untouched.

Ireland kicked off and Rocky scooped up a loose ball, straightened up and burst through a gap. Rocky kicked into top gear with who else but O'Driscoll in hot pursuit. It seemed Rocky was pulling away, but as he was just about in the clear, O'Driscoll stretched out his hand and managed to clip the back of one of Rocky's boots causing his legs to tangle up and bringing his charge to a halt.

The Irish responded with a well-worked sequence of phases which saw them march all the way to the Australian line, with David Wallace eventually carrying the ball into the tackle of Wallabies outside centre Digby Ioane. As the Irish set themselves for an attack on the thinly defended Wallabies line, Rocky crashed into the tackle contest, retrieved the ball with a critical turnover and ended the emergency.

The two sides continued to attack each other, but the only points came from penalty goals, Rocky and O'Driscoll conceding one each. Then in a break-out set of phases started by Irish prop Cian Healy, halfback Thomas O'Leary found a gap in the defensive line and put winger Tommy Bowe through it. Bowe slid over the line and the score was locked up at 13-all. The Wallabies had seemed to have the upper hand throughout the match, but now there was nothing in it. As the afternoon sun disappeared, leaving the night sky in darkness, 80 000 spectators all leaned forward in their seats at once. The only thing that was certain was that neither side was prepared to give an inch.

With loosehead prop Benn Robinson having a damaging impact on the Irish scrum, the Wallabies gained a decisive edge in the set-piece. As penalties began to flow the Wallabies' way it became obvious this weakness would threaten to become Ireland's Achilles heel. Gaining field position, the Wallabies launched an attack in the Irish 22. At a breakdown on the right-hand touchline, halfback Will Genia cleared the ball to five-eighth Matt Giteau, who threw a floating ball behind the Wallabies forward-runners to inside centre Quade Cooper. Cooper then threw a flat ball to tighthead prop Ben Alexander, who, under pressure from Tommy Bowe, flung the ball backwards to a sweeping Rocky, who had to reach back to grasp the pass. As Rocky got the ball under control just inside the quarterline it became a race for the corner with the Irish defence flying across in cover. With Irish fullback Rob Kearney crashing into Rocky just before he reached the line and halfback O'Leary clutching his back, Rocky slammed the ball down before careening into touch. With the Wallabies leading 20-13 with 20 minutes to go, it seemed Rocky had delivered the killer blow.

As the match entered its final stages Ireland was intent on making the most of what little opportunity it had left. Almost camping on the Wallabies line, the Irish sent runner after runner into the Australian defence with no success. Then, as play stalled at an Irish breakdown a five-metre scrum was called with just seconds to play. With the Wallabies' Grand Slam dream and Irish hopes of an undefeated season on the line, the pressure in the stadium reached breaking point as the two sides lined up for the last play of the game, which would decide it all.

On the referee's call of 'engage' both packs launched into each other with tremendous force. At first it looked as if Benn Robinson, as he had done all game, had put the Irish scrum in an awfully uncomfortable position. The delivery of a bad ball would have been disastrous for Ireland's planned attacking move, but before it came out the scrum collapsed. As the Wallabies forwards rose to their feet they looked at each other the way a bowler looks at his fielders after a plum LBW, not even waiting for confirmation from the umpire. But referee Jonathan Kaplan did not see it the same way. Instead of awarding a match-saving penalty to the Wallabies, Kaplan re-set the Irish scrum.

Taking no chances, O'Leary fed the ball into the scrum quickly. This time Irish tighthead prop John Hayes, the only other man to play 100 Tests for Ireland, lived up to his nickname 'The Bull' and the Irish managed to clear the ball lightning fast before the scrum collapsed again. As the Irish scrum began to retreat, number 8 Jamie Heaslip passed the ball off the ground to O'Leary and the attack was on. As the Wallabies defence closed in on four Irish runners, O'Leary found the one Irish runner who was inexplicably left unaccounted for. Of course, it was Brian O'Driscoll, who timed his run perfectly to slice through and touch down under the posts. What a way to end your 100th Test! The Irish expression 'in BOD we trust' came immediately to mind.

If the 20-all draw with Ireland was not shattering enough, worse was to come. The Wallabies' spirits sunk even more heavily when they were upset 9–8 by Scotland at Murrayfield the following Saturday. It was one of the most bizarre Tests ever played. The Wallabies completely dominated the game in terms of possession and territory, but could not translate it into points. Rocky looked to have put the Wallabies in front in the 49th minute when he crashed over, but French referee Romain Poite ruled no try after consulting the video referee. Rocky appeared to ground the ball, but nothing was going the Wallabies' way. Still, when outside centre Ryan Cross scored the only try of the game in injury time to put Australia one point behind with a kick to come, it seemed like they had got out of jail. However, Matt Giteau's attempted conversion sailed away on an ill wind and the Wallabies lost their first game to Scotland in 27 years.

The Wallabies entered the final Test of the tour against Wales in Cardiff under immense pressure, but the team's attitude was still positive. Writing a column in *The Australian*, Rocky provided a rare glimpse into the Wallabies mindset. 'The notion losses don't "hurt enough" is something I struggle to cop. The truth is, in any given situation you don't know what someone is feeling high or low, no one really does. Just like when someone experiences physical pain, some guys roll around Ronaldo-style, screwing up their faces like they're having their appendix removed with a spoon and others just get up showing no emotion; either way it's not possible to always tell exactly what they are feeling. As a player in an extremely high-contact sport you intend not to show pain or weakness. It's a very big part of your job.

'The first question asked after our loss last weekend was "What happened?" and I think that after watching the match several times I can assume that anyone watching the match has a fair idea of what happened. A better question would be "What is going to happen?" We have a clear focus of what we want to do this Saturday and how we want to go about doing it. Some of the emotions resulting from last Saturday might be very useful this week, but some are not so we'll do what we can to harness what we can use and discard the unwanted baggage. We have an opportunity to show some of the character we displayed earlier in the month and exorcise some of the demons from the past and we intend to make full use of it.'

The Wallabies needed to produce something special and they did just that. In one of the best performances by any Wallabies team of the professional era, Australia defeated Wales 33–12 in a brilliant display of attacking rugby, outscoring the Red Dragons four tries to nil. The Wallabies created a template for how they wanted to play in the build-up to the World Cup in New Zealand. For Deans, it was a Crusaders-like display and despite the pressure on the team following the previous disastrous loss, the Wallabies appeared fearless the way they approached the game.

'That Welsh Test was as good as we have played for a while,' Stephen Moore said. 'We came back with a lot of confidence.'

When Rocky returned to Australia he did not re-sign with the Waratahs. He has never really explained why he did not come back to Sydney. I doubt whether he had any problem playing under the Waratahs' new head coach, Chris Hickey, who had replaced Ewen McKenzie. There was a rumour that Rocky was disgruntled over the Waratahs insisting he was obligated to return to them because they had been party to his early release to play in Ireland. Maybe he had had a falling out with the NSW Rugby Union administration? Or perhaps he had become frustrated at the Waratahs, who had gone so close to winning the Super rugby title but had come up short, and needed a change of scenery? Only Rocky knows.

But Simon Poidevin has a theory. 'I think Rocky has a very strong view on organisations he is employed by and the cultural standards they set,' Poidevin said. 'I don't think he was happy with the NSW management and board's direction and the Brumbies provided an environment where he could be Rocky, but NSW didn't. I think playing at Leinster where Michael Cheika has been very formative in his career ... Michael went to Leinster and Leinster was this typical top-heavy, blazer-heavy organisation and [he] really turned that around culturally in a big way and created a great success — took the club from playing a style that was mediocre to very exciting and memberships went through the roof. I think Rocky, clearly, took a view that the Brumbies could provide that kind of environment.'

Rocky's preference, however, was to join the Reds because he had family and friends in Queensland and saw the re-building of the team as a great challenge. But negotiations broke down. Why? Did it have anything to do with Poidevin's theory? It was the third time the Reds had missed the opportunity to sign Rocky, but there was nothing too surprising about that. For years, the Reds' biggest problem was the retention and recruitment of players, which was one of the main reasons why they were so unsuccessful for so long.

So Rocky sought out the Brumbies. Brumbies chief executive, Andrew Fagan, was described as a 'super recruiter' for signing Rocky in three days, but he really fell into Fagan's lap.

'Rocky just contacted Andrew Fagan and said, is there a spot there?' Stephen Moore said. 'If there is, I'd be interested to talk. From what I understand he pretty much instigated it. I don't know the workings of it, but things panned out and next thing he has signed. I had spoken to him. I knew near enough to when it was announced. He keeps everything pretty guarded. I was obviously saying mate, you should consider us, we've got a good bunch of fellas, and the next thing he is on the books. It happened really quickly. Andy Friend [Brumbies coach] was a bit surprised by how quickly it all panned out because they hadn't really chased him that hard. We were fortunate that's the way it went.'

When I thought about Rocky playing for the Brumbies it occurred to me there was a shade of blue in the colours of every team he had played for — with the exception of the Wallabies. From the blue and white butcher stripes of Nudgee, to the blue and white hoops of the Bulldogs, to the sky blue of the Waratahs, to the dark blue of Leinster, to the navy blue of the Brumbies. I wondered if this meant anything to a colour symbolist. I googled the colour blue and found that people who wear light blue are analytical and practical, while those who wear dark blue are intelligent, self-reliant and take on a lot of responsibility. Blue evokes wide open spaces, calm and serenity. It symbolises peace, escape and dream. Blue also has a more dynamic side, promoting creativity and inspiration. Blue is associated with freedom, strength and new beginnings. Blue is the colour of loyalty, faith, power and protection. Sound familiar?

With the recruitment of Rocky and Matt Giteau's return home to Canberra from Perth, the Brumbies were dubbed the 'Real Madrid' of Australian rugby. It created unrealistic expectations for both Rocky and the Brumbies. The Brumbies had not reached the Super rugby playoffs since they won the second of their two titles in 2004, yet they were now regarded as one of the favourites, especially among the Australian teams.

Even though he was Wallabies captain, Rocky was more than happy to play under Stephen Hoiles' leadership at the Brumbies, although there were murmurings that the team had too many chiefs and not enough Indians. Rocky missed the Brumbies' season-opening 24–15 win against the Force in Perth because of a hamstring strain and made his debut for his new team against the defending champions, the Bulls, in Pretoria, a place with highly dramatic memories for Rocky. Three months after last playing for the Wallabies against Wales in Cardiff, Rocky looked very determined. Rocky was as powerful as he had ever been on the rugby field, crashing into the Bulls with tremendous force. His damaging runs were unmistakably Rockyesque. I wrote at the time that the Brumbies missed Rocky's power in their forward pack against the Force, but even I did not expect this in his first outing.

Rocky scored the Brumbies' first try on the left flank after brushing off two defenders and carrying another two across the line with him, demonstrating impressive strength and dynamism in his 20-metre burst. The Bulls then kicked off to Rocky, who immediately charged right back at them as if *he* was a bull. It was a message the Bulls took heed of. Soon after he peeled off the back of a lineout and cleverly read a switch play between Bulls halfback Fourie du Preez and number 8 Pierre Spies. Ripping the ball off du Preez, he took off towards the line. As defenders closed in on him he found Hoiles, who sent George Smith strolling over. While the Brumbies lost 50–32 it was an outstanding 80-minute performance by Rocky and a welcome return to Super rugby.

While Rocky battled with a hamstring injury through the Super rugby season, he noticeably lifted for the Brumbies' local derbies against the Waratahs and the Reds. However, with George Smith missing much of the season with a shoulder injury and Stirling Mortlock ruled out for many games with a back injury, the All Star

Brumbies produced mixed results, which was not what was expected. The intense pressure on the Brumbies boiled over the week of the Waratahs game when Rocky and Andy Friend exchanged angry words in a team meeting. 'What happened was Friendy brought something up at the meeting and Rocky questioned it,' Moore said. 'Something to do with the lineout or something ... lifting ... something like that. Rock just questioned it and it was a little bit heated, but that was it. There was nothing personal in it. Guys weren't being thrown around the room or anything. It was merely, "I disagree with that."

'Sometimes guys get a bit spooked by that kind of thing. Some of the young guys in the room might not have seen something like that before, but that's [Rocky]. He's going to challenge something if he doesn't believe it's right and that's the way it should be. That's a healthy work environment if guys are challenging each other because it means they want it to be right. If he doesn't think something is right, he'll tell you. He won't be huffing and puffing and yelling. It will just be, mate, I don't think that's right. This is why. Take it or leave it. He thinks pretty deeply about the game and about everything. Usually, he's got a pretty valid point.'

It would have irked Rocky to lose to the Waratahs 19–12 in Sydney, not just because they were his old team, but because the Brumbies now had to win their last three games with bonus points to reach the playoffs. With media speculation about rising Queensland back-rower Scott Higginbotham challenging him for the Wallabies' number 6 jersey, Rocky launched an almost brutal attack against the resurgent Reds in the Brumbies' 32–12 win in Canberra. Following Rocky's example, Stephen Moore was also a stand-out against his former team, physically imposing himself on the celebrated Reds forwards. After recording another bonus-point win against the Highlanders in Canberra, the Brumbies fell at the last hurdle, losing 40–22 to the Crusaders in their 'quarterfinal' in Christchurch to just miss the playoffs yet again.

'Rocky played some really good games,' Moore said. 'From playing with him he has a very high work rate in defence and probably didn't get to carry the ball as much as he would have liked. He's on the back of a fairly long stretch of playing rugby without a break. It's hard to maintain that level day in, day out for that long. He has settled in well in the team environment and the boys accepted him pretty well.'

Rocky and Moore shared a house in Canberra and also a mutual interest in music. 'He plays the piano and drums. I play the bass and drums,' Moore said. 'Hopefully, we didn't disturb the neighbours too much. We were in a pretty quiet area: Forrest. It's where a lot of the embassies and consulates are. We had the Swiss embassy behind us and the UK deputy high commissioner next door. There are Federal police everywhere. We kept it within school hours, regular hours.

'We are looking to get the band together again in Sydney, hopefully. It's hard to get everyone together. We had a couple of people coming and going. Rocky's brothers are into music. I think he's got his drums set up in Sydney. I'll head over there and have a bit of a bash.'

Despite Rocky's good job of leading the Wallabies on the Grand Slam tour, critics continued to question whether he was the right man to captain the Test team. Writing in his column in *The Courier-Mail*, Eddie Jones claimed that halfback Will Genia, not Rocky, should be Wallabies captain. 'The more I watch the rise of Queensland Reds halfback Will Genia, the more I am convinced that he should be named Wallabies captain ahead of Rocky Elsom for the June Tests,' Jones wrote. 'He looks a natural leader to me, and Rocky, as great as he is as a player, is not. This is not aimed at tearing Rocky down. He's an individual, a player who performs best when worrying about himself. There's nothing wrong with that mindset. The Wallabies need their powerful flanker to play at his best, and I'd suggest he'd be happy unencumbered and performing at his optimum.'

Jones' comments may or may not have been applicable when he was coaching Rocky in 2005, but they were way out of touch in 2010. Once again, the core criticism of Rocky as a captain was that he was an 'individual', a Howard Roark.

'I can understand the logic of why people would say that,' Les Kiss said. 'Some of his actions might be perceived as selfish or mistaken. There is part of him that is misread, I truly think that. When you read about Howard Roark you will know what I mean. Could he be a little more diplomatic? Perhaps, but again he is not going to be determined by other people.

'I can understand why people think that, but tell me where it is written that a captain has to be this or that. I don't think personality type is an issue. The guy who delivers, the guy who leads by example, holds his composure and doesn't respond to outside influences and distractions. They are the people you need, strong characters. And I think he represents that. Again, it's people looking at what he doesn't have rather than what he actually gives. That's the key to it. I understand why people say what they say, but it doesn't mean it's right. He's different. He is who he is and he does a good job with it.'

The push for Genia to take over the captaincy gained momentum when the media jumped on comments by ARU high performance manager and Wallabies selector, David Nucifora, that Rocky was not guaranteed the role. It was just one of those clichéd answers to a question that people sometimes gave when they did not really want to say anything, up there with 'we are taking it one game at a time'. But it gave rise to wild speculation that Rocky's position as captain was not secure and that Genia was poised to replace him. Rocky seemed unfazed by the controversy, even when sitting next to Deans at an ARU lunch for a new sponsor two weeks before the Test season and the coach refused to publicly endorse him as captain. Speculation about the captaincy was rife virtually the whole Super rugby season, but only once did Rocky make any comment about it. Asked whether he would like to continue captaining the Wallabies, he simply replied, 'Yes, I would.' And he did.

Rocky celebrated his 50th Test and his first as Wallabies captain on Australian soil with a 49-3 win against Fiji in Canberra, but there were bigger Tests and greater demands on his leadership lying ahead. The Wallabies would experience the worst injury crisis in the front row for as long as anyone could remember. Tighthead prop Ben Alexander sustained a knee injury in the Fiji Test, joining Benn Robinson, Stephen Moore, Tatafu Polota-Nau and Sekope Kepu on the sideline. Added to this, experienced back-five forwards Wycliff Palu and James Horwill were also injured. As a result, Rocky led the greenest Wallabies pack ever into the first Test against England in Perth. If Rocky thought the Grand Slam tour was a tough start to his captaincy, it was about to get a whole lot harder.

Deans resisted calls to bring back veteran props Al Baxter and Matt Dunning, preferring to blood young talent. Such was the level of turnover in the Australian team only four players remained in the run-on 15 from the starting line-up when the Wallabies beat England at Twickenham in November. Rocky was the only survivor from the starting pack. Tighthead prop Salesi Ma'afu and hookers Huia Edmonds and Saia Faingaa had made their Test debuts against Fiji, while props Ben Daley and James Slipper were selected to make their maiden Tests against England. It would take all of Rocky's leadership skills to hold this young and inexperienced forward pack together.

Rocky scored one of the Wallabies' three tries in their 27–17 win against England, but the powerful English forwards demolished Australia's scrum. It was the fieriest of baptisms imaginable for the rookie front row of Daley, Faingaa and Ma'afu, who was sin-binned for repeatedly collapsing. At the end of the game as the Wallabies celebrated their victory, Rocky walked off the field in quiet conversation with Ma'afu. I would imagine reading the riot act to the front row in that situation would be the first thing to enter a captain's head, but Rocky seemed calm and supportive, possibly offering a brief insight into his unique style of leadership.

'Leadership isn't about the obvious,' Deans said. 'A lot of the public look for the obvious. They look for the speeches and the remonstrating. Ultimately, it's about the ability to connect with people around you and care and help them to grow and develop from the ground up. He takes the responsibility seriously. You look at any good leader over time they grow into it. It's not easy, but he's up for it. And the people around him know that.'

Stephen Moore said Rocky's attempt to comfort Ma'afu was a typical example of his leadership. 'That's the way he does it,' Moore said. 'He's not going to come in and yell and carry on. He is going to give you his words and as with everything with him it will be carefully thought out what he says.'

Nathan Sharpe, who led the Wallabies in two Tests, including Rocky's debut against Samoa in 2005, described him as a 'fantastic' captain. 'I wasn't on that trip [to Britain and Ireland],' Sharpe said. 'I came into camp this year [2010] after the spring tour and I hadn't experienced playing under Rocky and because over the years Rocky has just managed himself and turned up and played really well, I had no idea as to how he was going to be, but I have been nothing but impressed with the way he has gone about things. He is a guy who thinks deeply about what is good for the team and he works at it all the time. You couldn't ask for any more from him.'

Richard Brown, Rocky's old Nudgee teammate, described his captaincy of the Wallabies as refreshing. 'He is very honest with his opinions and genuinely wants to get the best out of the team,' Brown said. 'He is willing to communicate that with the boys and the coaches.'

The Wallabies scrum showed signs of improvement in the second Test in Sydney, but England reversed the result, winning 21–20. Both teams scored two tries in slippery conditions, which negated the brilliance of the Australian backs, but Jonny Wilkinson booted England to victory, again. Conversely, a missed attempt at goal from in front of the posts would have won the game, but that did not change the fact that it was the Wallabies' first loss to a European team on Australian soil since the World Cup final against England in Sydney in 2003. An unconvincing 22–15 win against Ireland in Brisbane the following Saturday did little to ease the pressure on the Wallabies heading into the Tri Nations.

In one of the best ever games by a blindside flanker for Australia, Rocky was outstanding in the Wallabies' 30–13 win against the Springboks in the tournament opener in Brisbane. With Rocky leading the charge, the rampant Wallabies overwhelmed the Springboks with their brilliant running game.

But with Quade Cooper, who had emerged as Australia's chief playmaker, suspended for two weeks for a dangerous tackle, the Wallabies lost the first two Bledisloe Cup Tests against the All Blacks in Melbourne (49–28) and Christchurch (20–10). While the Wallabies were stunned by the All Blacks' counterattack in

Melbourne, they showed great character when they fought back in Christchurch with only 14 men after Drew Mitchell had been red-carded.

After an improved, but unfruitful, night in Christchurch, the Wallabies took that fortitude with them when they flew to South Africa to play two Tests against the Springboks on the high veld. Given that they had not won at altitude since 1963, the trip was regarded as mission impossible. But it also presented a wonderful opportunity. I remember talking to Rocky at Sydney Airport before the team flew out. I said if the Wallabies could achieve a historic victory on the high veld, the team would etch itself into Australian rugby folklore. Rocky nodded in agreement. I think the thought had already crossed his mind. Against all expectations, the Wallabies broke their 47-year-old drought and went close to winning both Tests in Pretoria and Bloemfontein.

It looked as if the Wallabies would break their hoodoo in Pretoria after racing to a 21-7 lead with their 'run and stun' style of game, but the Springboks came back to win 44-31. After Drew Mitchell had a try disallowed in the second minute, Will Genia and James O'Connor scored three quick tries between them. Rocky was heavily involved in O'Connor's first try. In the Wallabies' 22 Rocky slipped the ball to fullback Kurtley Beale, who stepped past five defenders before racing 50 metres up field and popping a pass back to Rocky in support. For a moment it looked like Rocky would score himself, but he was brought down five metres out by Springbok halfback Francois Hougaard, a former winger. It is amazing how many tries are bombed in exactly this position, but Rocky recycled the ball quickly and Beale was at the base of the ruck to fire a pass to O'Connor, who crashed over next to the posts.

The Springboks responded to trail 28-24 at halftime and then outscored the Wallabies 20-3 in the second half. The Wallabies had let slip one of their best chances to win on the high veld in many years. While they played with enthusiasm, Rocky was furious with their lapses at critical times, particularly in the set piece. In the last 10 minutes the Wallabies lost four lineouts on their own throw in attacking positions. After the game, in a rare display of frustration, Rocky vented his anger in a dressing-room dressing-down. In a blunt address, Rocky told the players their performance was not good enough.

Robbie Deans regarded Rocky's preparedness to question and challenge as a positive trait for a captain. 'He is smart enough and cares enough not to just meekly accept,' Deans said. 'He wants ultimately to do well. He is prepared to challenge. That is another thing that he brings. He is experienced. He is intelligent. He has seen a lot. To that end you want him challenging as opposed to just accepting everything and the group needs him to challenge.

'We had an instance on tour this year through a review process where he challenged a statement essentially and what it allowed us to do was to elaborate. We actually ended up with a better understanding off the back of it and the motivation behind the challenge was to get that elaboration for the group to fully understand the meaning as opposed to just accept it or walk away — worse than that, walk away with a sense of dissatisfaction and unfulfilment in terms of understanding of why and have gripes behind the scenes. He is prepared to table issues and that is the only way ahead in a team context.'

Asked whether Rocky had input into the Wallabies' strategies and tactics, Deans said: 'Yes, he does. The lineout is the most obvious. He understands it intimately and he understands what is required to have a functional lineout. He is able to help drive that process. He's not calling it, but everyone involved knows that he knows. You don't have intuition without understanding the big picture. Every week we talk before we talk to the group. We have an opportunity for proactive dialogue. He offers a lot.'

The Wallabies rebounded from their disappointment in Pretoria with another chance to create history. The second game followed a similar pattern to the first, with the Wallabies speeding to a 31-6 lead after 24 minutes only for the Springboks to respond with 24 points in 13 minutes and take the lead in the 61st minute. Rocky scored one of the Wallabies' five tries next to the posts after he supported a charge downfield by James O'Connor, who had left Bryan Habana in his wake.

If support play is not the most underrated aspect of play in rugby, I do not know what is. When I was a kid I played rugby league for the Asquith Bears. We had two coaches, Phil and Ron, knockabout blokes, who stood on the field at training, beer in hand, teaching us how to play. We used to do a drill where we would run in a line passing the ball. After we made the pass we would run around to the end of the line and receive the ball again. It was my first lesson in support play and it has remained with me ever since. You do not have to be the best player on the field to be a good support player. You just have to make the effort. It's almost childishly simple, but it's not something Rocky takes for granted.

The lead changed two more times, with a superb goal-kicking performance from Matt Giteau keeping Australia in touch. However, when the Wallabies were reduced to 14 players after Saia Faingaa was sin-binned in the 68th minute for a dangerous tackle, the momentum seemed to swing towards the Springboks. It got worse for the Wallabies when fullback Kurtley Beale experienced one of the most embarrassing five minutes of his life. With the Springboks hammering the Wallabies' line Rocky made a crucial turnover at the breakdown. Beale was acting as halfback and I am sure he intended to fire off a pass to a kicker in the goal area. Instead, he threw a wild pass over the dead ball line, giving the Springboks a scrum five metres out. The Wallabies held out the Springboks yet again and a couple of minutes later they were on the attack inside their own half. A simple pass was thrown to Beale, who slipped over as he attempted to accelerate, and the ball hit him square in the face. The Wallabies would nickname Beale 'Gilbert' because of the mark that the ball left on his face. The loose ball was regathered by the Springboks and carried to just outside the Wallabies' 22. Beale chased the play hard and contested at the breakdown, but was penalised. With golden boots Morne Steyn kicking it was a guaranteed three points and it looked as if another game would slip through the Wallabies' fingers. In the final minutes, with the Wallabies trailing 39–38, the Springboks played safe, protecting the ball at the breakdown, but they went too far and were penalised for sealing off.

There were 34 seconds on the clock. The Wallabies were on the halfway near the right touchline. Rocky had the ball in his hands and Kurtley Beale, despite his run of bad luck, stepped forward to take it. Beale had been practising long-distance kicking with South African goal-kicking guru Braam van Stratten and had been knocking them over regularly from halfway, but kicking at training and in a pressure-cooker situation like this are two entirely different things, especially as Beale would not have been high on confidence right at that moment.

Beale hit the ball sweetly and it sailed through the thin air straight between the posts, giving the Wallabies a 41–39 win. When the flags went up the Wallabies erupted in ecstasy. There is a photograph of Beale in which he is raising his right hand, his legs pumping with excitement and a look of utter jubilation, possibly disbelief, on his face. Rocky and Stephen Moore, who had celebrated his 50th Test, hugged each other in the centre of the field. Rocky had not looked this happy since Leinster won the Heineken Cup. In fact, he looked happier, if that were at all possible. It must have been a tremendous feeling for Rocky to lead the Wallabies to victory on the high veld for the first time in 47 years. The Wallabies had not only made history, but they had retained the Mandela Plate and regained the number two world ranking behind the All Blacks, all achievements of which Rocky could be justifiably proud.

'I suppose in my career, and [for] most guys involved in that game, that's right up there,' Stephen Moore said. 'To win it like that was very, very special. I know Rock was hugely satisfied. I guess there was a sense of relief as well to finally win a big game like that, which was something we hadn't done as a group. And for him to be leading the ship was a really big moment in his captaincy.

'I had the ball in my hands actually when the ref blew the whistle. I looked around at the boys and I thought it certainly won't be me kicking it. Which one of you blokes is going to take this? We had a fair few goal-kickers. I remember there was a bit of talking among the boys and then KB [Beale] just stepped up and grabbed it.

'I guess [Rocky] was the nearest bloke to me. I just grabbed him. It was a pretty special sort of moment I guess. You don't get those things often in your career. It was my 50th Test as well, which made it pretty special to share it with some of my best mates in the shed afterwards.'

From afar Michael Foley sensed Rocky was starting to have a greater influence on the way the Wallabies played. 'When you think about that role of captain you think about influence and what influence a person can have on a team,' Foley said. 'I don't think anybody is as good as they'll end up being first up. I think about John Eales in that light.

'When you are given something as important as the Australian captaincy you probably wrestle with a couple of things. Firstly, what am I supposed to do? How am I supposed to be? That's often a flaw because you've been given the captaincy because you are who you already are. And secondly, how can you influence the environment most appropriately?

'Sometimes a captain is going to influence a team from a strategic perspective and that will be a real strength for the team. At other times it will be in how the team prepares. Other times it's just down to their philosophy of how they are trying to play generally.

'It's only this year [2010] and probably a little way through the Tri Nations that I've seen Rocky's influence come about with how Australia are trying to play. The last three Tests of the Tri Nations — and it's important to note here Genia's and Cooper's influence can't be underestimated — but as a team, Australia are now playing the type of rugby that is threatening and I think people will underestimate Rocky's influence in that.'

Stephen Moore noticed Rocky had grown into the captaincy role and was comfortable with it on and off the field. 'Throughout that Tri Nations series, Rocky stamped his mark on the team and played well himself, which always helps the whole thing go well,' Moore said. 'He certainly relished that role.

'The sort of bloke he is, he's a reasonably quiet sort of bloke. He only speaks when it's necessary. It probably took him a little bit of time to adjust to the captaincy in the sense that there were a whole lot of things that he had to do. Just little things like meeting with the ref the day before the game and things like that, that would definitely take a bit of time to get used to. And also the increased media interest in him, not just because he was the captain, but because of what he had achieved at Leinster. He has certainly grown into that side of things. Initially, he wasn't as comfortable with it as he would have liked. Once he realised what he had to do he just got on and did it.

'He has also developed a good relationship with Robbie Deans, which is crucial. I think they work really well together. They would sort things out and present it to the team and we would just get on with it. Any issues we had were dealt with pretty quickly as far as how we wanted to play, and stuff like that. Rocky and Robbie had a good combination in sorting that stuff out.

'Robbie is similar to Rocky in that he doesn't speak for the sake of it. When he talks he is pretty forthright and he's always got something pretty important to say. That works well in the sense that when you hear something from either of them you know it is worth listening to. They are both reasonably reserved. I think right from the start their relationship has been pretty good and I know they definitely challenge each other and that's great. That's how it's got to be. That's a good thing for the side. You have a captain who bounces things off the coach and you'd like to think at the end of the day you'd come out with a better outcome.'

The Wallabies travelled home from South Africa to play the All Blacks in Sydney in the final Test of the tournament. The All Blacks had the advantage of two weeks' rest, while the Wallabies were suffering from jet lag after flying across the Indian Ocean. Once again, the Wallabies got off to a great start, leading 22–9 at the hour. In an all-too-familiar pattern, the All Blacks made an inevitable comeback to steal a 23–22 win. The All Blacks were accused of being cynical for bending the rules like Uri Geller, but they kept finding ways to beat the Wallabies, or perhaps more to the point, Australia kept finding ways to lose. It was the Wallabies' 10th straight loss to the All Blacks and the biggest heartbreaker of them all. There was no doubt the Wallabies were bridging the gap with the All Blacks, but close losses in some ways are even more agonising than big defeats because you know that you could have, or should have, won.

Successful sportsmen and women and sporting teams are always looking for a competitive edge whether it is a winged keel or some tactical innovation. Since 2008 the Wallabies have been working with neuroscientist Evian Gordon, who, through his biotech company Brain Resource, is at the forefront of brain fuction and has the largest brain database on the planet. It was Simon Poidevin who introduced Evian Gordon to Robbie Deans, and the Wallabies coach immediately understood the value of harnessing the intricate details of the non-conscious brain. 'Evian is one of the world's leading brain researchers,' Poidevin said. 'The basic premise is that 99 per cent of sports training is physical and only one per cent is mental. There's a big gap.

'Evian and Robbie Deans sat down in the same room with me and straight away Robbie Deans was on the same page. Robbie knew the All Blacks were doing similar sort of stuff. It's not about sports psychology. It's all about basically players learning to communicate with each other and respecting that communication and understanding how actions on and off the field can affect the team. Rocky probably surprised a few people with his grasp of how important that was and worked pretty closely with Robbie and Evian on that particular project. We did a fair bit before the team went off on the last spring tour. Rocky's leadership in that has been really spectacularly strong.'

Poidevin suggested I interview Gordon for this book and provided me with his contact details. I emailed Gordon and he responded almost immediately, saying he would be happy to do an interview with me about Rocky, who he described as a 'genuine, phenomenon peak performer, unique in ways that will surprise people'.

Gordon invited me to join him on his 6 a.m. Bondi to Tamarama beach walk. What! Does this guy know I am a journalist? The only time I see six o'clock in the morning is when I am coming home from the night before. With my publisher's deadline fast approaching, I reluctantly agreed and set my alarm, which was used lightly. Wiping the sleep from my eyes, I met Gordon under the Seiko clock at the surf club at the northern end of Bondi Beach. Of average height and build, Gordon's short salt-and-pepper hair kind of matched his black sweatshirt and shorts. Pressed for time, we only walked to the southern end of Bondi and back again, which did not upset me. On an overcast morning there were more people at Bondi Beach, walking, jogging, exercising and swimming, than in the centre of Sydney at lunchtime and almost every one of them seemed to know Gordon.

We had breakfast at Speedo's Café, which is Gordon's regular haunt. When we sat down at our table I noticed he was wearing an exceptionally large, black watch with a white dot on the band.

'This is a titanium watch,' Gordon said in a South African accent. 'Titanium is a big metaphor, the strongest, lightest metal on the planet. You'll notice on my watch is a dot. That dot is my trigger for my circuit breaker. When I'm in a difficult situation, that's my trigger, just look at the dot. Break the negative cycle.'

On his way to the USA 30 years ago, Gordon stopped in Sydney to visit an uncle. He swam at Bondi in the morning, had a barbecue lunch, watched the cricket in the afternoon and by evening had decided to migrate to Australia. Gordon's cutting-edge work in neuroscience brought him into contact with Poidevin, Deans and, ultimately, Rocky.

'When I met Rocky I really had a sense of his physical presence, his power, his courage and his relentless determination,' Gordon said. 'That's pretty much what I saw initially, someone who didn't say much. His stand-out characteristics were his physical attributes. I didn't expect to find much more than that, but I did. And what I found really surprised me. What I found is his smarts are as much of a unique attribute as his obvious physical strengths. And his smarts are his intuition and it's an intuition to get the patterns right.

'I only discovered this for a very simple reason. In creating this culture for the Wallabies, Robbie needed a translator. A translator first and foremost is the captain. Robbie, Rocky and I began to meet to see if Rocky would be an effective translator. And I suppose that's when I got to see how smart he was. Information is not that valuable. It's the training of that information into a habit that is everything and that is going to determine who is going to win the World Cup.

Who came with the better habits to withstand the cauldron of those seven games? What surprised me was how he saw what he was going to do on and off the field was going to be really important in training what was required.

'I began to see a very thoughtful person emerge who could see the patterns and, even more intelligently, he knew what was critical. He knew what was critical and he knew what was noise. And the reason his intelligence became more and more evident was that he was able to match the Australian culture of the players he was working with — that deep sense of pragmatism, that dislike of authority, that sense of fairness. Mateship is an easy word to say, but Rocky called it the quality of their connectedness and he began to see that he was the key catalyst to make sure the quality of their connectedness was going to happen.

'Rocky knows just how to nudge, and I use that word very specifically. He knows if you push, you'll get pushed back. You nudge to get the desired outcome. He is focused on outcomes. He is very solution focused, very, and that's the highest level of intelligence. Basically, he is a neuro-leader. And he doesn't try to be. It's just intuitive intelligence. He switches it on and it's like a rocket firing.

'Rocky has grown into what I think is a really unique leader. The difference between unique and great is the capacity to win. I think he has the potential to touch genuine greatness if he pulls this [World Cup] off.'

While paying for our breakfast at the counter of the café, Gordon gave me his business card. Then, as we were saying our goodbyes on the footpath, he offered me his business card again. Surely one of the world's leading brain researchers would remember giving me his business card just a few minutes earlier. Then, I realised maybe he was just like Rocky: an absent-minded professor.

Rocky had played every minute of every Test so far in 2010, which was why you could have knocked me over with a feather when I learnt that he was turning out for Randwick against Eastwood in the Sydney club rugby preliminary final at Woollahra Oval. No one could remember the last time Rocky had played for Randwick. Why was the Wallabies captain running around on a field the Brumbies would not even train on? Robbie Deans encouraged the Wallabies to play club rugby at every opportunity to keep the players grounded and Rocky may have felt a sense of loyalty to the Galloping Greens. But I was plagued by a portent.

I watched the game on television. When Wallabies and Randwick second-rower Mark Chisholm looked like he'd dislocated his knee, I yelled out to Rocky to 'get off the field!' Even if Rocky could hear me, I doubt he would have listened. Rocky remained on the field for the whole game, assuming the captaincy in the final moments of the match, and when he bumped off Lachie Turner and threw a cut-out pass to an unmarked player who strolled over for a five-pointer to give Randwick a 23–21 win, it all seemed worthwhile. However, at some point in the match he had torn his hamstring, which put him in doubt for the fourth Bledisloe Cup match with the All Blacks in Hong Kong in four weeks on the way to Europe. The Wallabies were closing in on the All Blacks and a breakthrough victory could not be too far away. After all the work Rocky had done to help rebuild the Wallabies, I thought it would be grossly unfair if he did not play in that strikingly important win that was surely coming. Rocky did lead the Wallabies to their famous 26–24 victory against the All Blacks in Hong Kong in a game that will be remembered as one of the great trans-Tasman battles.

While there was no Tri Nations trophy or Bledisloe Cup at stake, the Test against the All Blacks in Hong Kong was not a dead rubber. There was still a valuable prize on offer: psychological ascendancy. The All Blacks were determined to maintain their edge on the Wallabies, who were equally intent on ending the Kiwis' dominance. The Wallabies led 12–0 after 23 minutes after tries to Quade Cooper and Adam Ashley-Cooper and they seemed to be playing all over the All Blacks.

Rocky played an important link role in Cooper's try in the ninth minute. The Wallabies were attacking in the All Blacks' 22 when Rocky received a pass from David Pocock. He looked to pass to number 8 Ben McCalman, but flicked the ball instead to Cooper, who turned on some fancy footwork before racing over for five points.

You could never accuse Rocky of having a beautiful pair of hands like Quade Cooper and he does not have a natural fluency in his passing movement. But Rocky knows the importance of being able to shift the ball and he can now appear in the try-assist column as often as Quade Cooper, Matt Giteau or Berrick Barnes.

I covered basketball for 15 years and I once asked Andrew Gaze, Australia's greatest scorer, what was the best technique for shooting the ball. The best technique, Gaze said, was the one that put the ball in the hoop. You did not have to adopt any particular pose or stance other than the one you were comfortable with. It was whatever worked for you. Passing a rugby ball is similar. You can have the most beautiful-looking pass in the world, but if there is no intent behind it or if it does not hit the right man in the right place, it is as useless as a triple somersault on a rugby field. If you watch Rocky pass the ball, there is always a calculated thought behind it and he invariably finds a player in a better attacking position than himself. Whether his execution is crude or not is irrelevant.

But getting back to Hong Kong, when the Kiwis scored 24 unanswered points in 21 minutes it looked like we were seeing a re-run of the same old horror movie. This time, however, the Wallabies came back from 24-12 down to win. In the final, desperate minutes, the Wallabies, trailing by five points, maintained their composure as they attacked the All Blacks line, patiently waiting for an opportunity to strike. Then in the last play of the game, in the 82nd minute, winger James O'Connor scored a try out wide on the right-hand side of the field to level the scores at 24-all. Significantly, Rocky was running alongside O'Connor in support. If he had not been there, on O'Connor's outside, the winger would not have scored because there were enough defenders to stop him. It was Rocky's presence which kept the defence guessing and allowed O'Connor to slip through. After spending 80 exhausting minutes slogging it out in the forwards against the best pack in the world, Rocky was able to squeeze out one last drop of energy to keep up with a winger on the edge of the field to help create a match-winning play. And he did this on an injured leg which had had him in doubt for the game. I do not want to harp on the importance of support play, but it is the sort of thing Rocky simply does not receive enough credit for.

As he linked arms with his teammates, Rocky kept a close eye on the ice-cool O'Connor, the Wallabies' third kicker. Giteau and Beale had missed earlier attempts, but O'Connor raised the flags with a wide-angled conversion. The monkey, which had grown to the size of King Kong, was off the Wallabies' backs. As the rest of the Wallabies piled on top of O'Connor in a jubilant pile, Rocky dragged himself over to join his teammates in celebration. Rocky was happy. The broad smile on his face was testament to that. But the tour had just begun and there was a long way to go yet.

The Wallabies had won two of their last three Tests after the fulltime siren on foreign soil. Winning close matches was a hallmark of John Eales' golden Wallabies of 1998–2001. Rocky's Wallabies seemed to be rediscovering a lost art.

'It definitely stung him, as it did all of us, to get stung by [the All Blacks],' Stephen Moore said. 'To lose the Tri Nations and the Bledisloe Cup again, from a captain's perspective, I know [Rocky] takes it very personally. Throughout it all he maintained his composure and belief that we could get there. By no means have we achieved anything yet, but I guess that win in Hong Kong put a huge amount of belief in the guys' minds. The fact that it could be done, you know.

'[There was] an overwhelming sense of relief because a lot of us have been in the same boat. It was pretty special to be able to sit down after that game and say there it is, we've done it, finally. You could say it doesn't really mean too much and it was a dead rubber and all that, but the belief we took out of it is going to be beneficial to us, that's for sure. It was certainly better to win than to lose. Psychologically, it gives belief to the boys that we can do it. The group knows it can beat anyone now.'

But the win in Hong Kong would lose some of its meaning if the Wallabies could not back it up. I wrote at the time that the Wallabies' opening Test in Europe against Wales in Cardiff was their most important of the year. It was not that Wales was the strongest opponent the Wallabies would face, but it was time to break that alarming trend that had developed over the past three years, perhaps longer, which exposed a fatal flaw in the Australians' psychological make-up – the apparent incapacity to back up a good performance with another.

Although they did not play particularly well against Wales, the Wallabies' hard-fought 25–16 win was so important because they did not suffer their usual psychological drop-off. While Wales dominated the Wallabies' scrum after Stephen Moore withdrew with a back injury just before the kick-off, the Welsh could not suppress the sheer exuberance of the Australians, particularly the back three of Kurtley Beale, James O'Connor and Drew Mitchell, who tore Wales' defence to shreds. It probably started in South Africa, but the Wallabies back three was quickly becoming the most dangerous trio in world rugby. On the back of an early try to David Pocock, the Wallabies held a narrow lead at halftime, but could not gain any real ascendancy. The Wallabies cleverly changed tactics in the second half. After noticing that Wales did not pose any attacking threat from long range, Deans told the Wallabies to play for field position. The trick was to introduce a seemingly conservative element to the strategy and yet maintain an attacking mindset. It worked beautifully.

It was a pity the Wallabies could not maintain their momentum against England at Twickenham. After their poor scrummaging performance against Wales, the Wallabies expected England to target their Achilles heel in the set piece. England had inflicted more pain on the Australian scrum than any other team in the last decade so it was a reasonable assumption that the English would be salivating at the chance of enjoying another slice of Wallabies pie. But the scrum was not the decisive factor in the game. England beat Australia 35–18 by playing an attacking style of game. England had finally figured out how to play total rugby and that was scary.

England outplayed and out-enthused the Wallabies. Yet, the Wallabies dominated the first quarter of the game, playing their high-tempo, expansive style. They just could not translate pressure into points. It is a common occurrence in rugby that if a team dominates possession and territory for any length of time early in the game and fails to score, it has a detrimental effect on the side's performance. Conversely, the English grew in confidence as the match wore on. Stephen Moore was again strong for the Wallabies at Twickenham, a ground where he seems to thrive, but Rocky was a stand-out. His defence was superb, shooting up and hitting the Englishmen deep behind the advantage line, picking up and dumping, among others, much vaunted tighthead prop Andrew Cole, and forcing turnovers. If there was one Wallaby who was running at a pace ahead of the English, it was Rocky, but it was not enough and Australia was well beaten.

Deans made five changes to the Wallabies' starting 15 for the Test against Italy in Florence. Berrick Barnes, Luke Burgess, Lachie Turner, James Slipper and Rob Simmons were selected in the starting line-up, while Matt Giteau, Will Genia, Benn Robinson and Mark Chisholm reverted to the bench, with James O'Connor returning to Australia to attend a funeral. Without intending any disrespect to Italy, coaches often rest players against the Azzurri, but Deans had chosen what he thought was his best available team. Genia was on the bench because of a rib cartilage injury, but Giteau and Robinson had been dropped for the first time since Deans took over. I thought Rocky might get a rest in Florence, but after what happened at Twickenham, Deans was taking no chances.

Historically, the Wallabies struggle to beat the Azzurri on Italian soil and this game was no different, Australia labouring to a 32–14 win. If anything, the Wallabies were probably guilty of trying too hard to make things happen, and instead just made errors. One of the best scrummaging forward packs in Europe, the Italians targeted the Australian set piece and demolished it, but that was all they had. The Wallabies were always in control of the game and would have thrashed the Italians if they could have held onto the ball.

You could see Rocky was fired up, although he denied it when I put it to him in a conversation we had in Paris the following week. At one stage, Italian prop Andrea Lo Cicero pushed Ben Alexander over after a scrum, further asserting his authority. Rocky immediately challenged Lo Cicero, shoving him backwards. In an instant Rocky was surrounded by four burly Italian forwards, but he did not back down. When I questioned him about it he just said it was not a good look for a Wallabies forward to be treated like that. Ironically, in a match in which Rocky was pretty successful in breaking the defensive line, his only real reward was by way of an opportunist try at the end of the game when he seized on a ball which squirted out of an Italian scrum five metres from their line.

The success of the tour now rested on the result of the final Test against Six Nations champions France in Paris. I caught up with Rocky one morning at the team's hotel. I called his room from the reception desk.

'Hello.'

'Hi Rock. It's Bret. I'm in the foyer.'

'Did we have an appointment?'

'No, I've come to Paris to interview Michael Cheika. You are going to help arrange it. Remember?'

'Okay, I'll come down.'

An appointment! I had flown 10 000 kilometres and he was asking me if I had an appointment. Perhaps I was a victim of Rocky's dry sense of humour or maybe he was buried in Wallabies work. Either way, I was unsettled by his almost Gallic nonchalance. We sat down in the lobby. I had come a long way and I was anxious to have my interview with Cheika sorted out, but Rocky was more interested in talking about the Wallabies' scrum, at least the perception of it.

'What's the word on the street?' Rocky asked me.

'The word on the street?' I said. 'I'm in Paris. I can barely speak schoolboy French and I'm staying in a one-star hotel in the Latin Quarter without a TV. I've got no idea what the word on the street is about anything.'

'Hmm,' Rocky said.

After giving Rocky some unsolicited, and unqualified, advice on scrummaging — which he politely listened to, I must say — I then steered the conversation back to the main topic, at least as far as I was concerned, which was my interview with Michael Cheika. Rocky said he would text me with a time and place and asked me to text him back to confirm I had received the message.

'There's just one problem,' I said sheepishly. 'I don't know how to text. I can receive, but I don't know how to send.'

Rocky looked at me as if I were from outer space, although space age is probably not the right metaphor, more like stone age as far as technology and I are concerned. Taking my mobile phone, Rocky patiently showed me how to send a text message.

'Just press five and I'll know it's you,' he said.

So if I got nothing else out of writing this book, I could always say Rocky Elsom taught me how to send a text message.

France had destroyed the powerful Argentine scrum the previous week and *Les Bleus* were looking to pulverise the Wallabies, who were somewhat less capable, at least that's what the French thought. The French prepared for the Test with a computer-driven scrum simulator, which was programmed to duplicate the Wallabies' scrummaging manoeuvres, including collapsing. But the French obsession with the scrum backfired. While it is true that France accumulated all of its 16 points from scrum penalties, including a penalty try for repeated collapsing, it was also true that the French failed to profit from any other area of the game. Once Benn Robinson replaced the sin-binned Ben Alexander at loosehead and James Slipper moved across to tighthead, the Wallabies scrum stabilised and was no longer a factor.

Surpassing Andrew Slack as fifth among Australian captains, Rocky, in his 20th Test in charge, led the Wallabies to an astonishing 59–16 win, their biggest ever against *Les Bleus*. In sub-zero temperatures the Wallabies lit up Paris like a bonfire, putting on one of the most dazzling displays of running rugby ever witnessed in the French capital or any other city for that matter. Remarkably, the score was locked at 13-all at halftime with the Wallabies scoring 46–3 in the second half as French faces went rouge with embarrassment. Rocky played very well, but then again, who did not in a game that looked to have nothing in it, but was blown open by relentless Wallabies motion?

In an embarrassing moment for Rocky he almost scored one of the Wallabies' seven tries, but failed to ground the ball after chasing a Quade Cooper chip. Rocky managed to pat the ball back for Drew Mitchell to put a hand on it for his hat-trick, but as the leading forward try-scorer in the team, I doubt Rocky would have been too impressed with his own execution. Still, only Mitchell, James O'Connor, Kurtley Beale and Quade Cooper scored more tries than Rocky, which was good company to be among.

'It was incredible,' Stephen Moore said. 'It was very even up until about 50 minutes into the game and then we scored a couple of tries almost against the run of play and they sort of packed it in, which is strange for a team like France at home. The floodgates really opened. It was almost a bit weird to be honest. On the flipside it was great to put a team like that away, particularly in front of a full house.

'Something we spoke about — and Rock was pretty big on this — was the fact that a tour is generally judged on your final game. That's what everyone talks about. The year before, it was the Welsh game. This time it's France and we said this is our last performance for a while and we want to make it count. It was great. Everything just came together.

'Rocky was very proud of the boys — the way we really dug in. That was it really. As you know he doesn't say a whole lot. He just felt a big sense of pride. We all did. It was great to sit down and have a beer with the boys after the game. To finish like that was a real big positive for us. If we had gone down in that game, it would leave a bit of doubt in everyone's mind. But I think everyone left that tour under no illusions that we can get the job done against any team.

'I guess as the captain he would have felt a bit more comfortable than he did at the start of the year. But you can't rest on your laurels. You have to keep pushing on, I guess. He would love nothing more than to be involved in a World Cup victory. That goes for everyone in the Wallabies who will be lucky enough to be involved in the whole thing. There's no better bloke at the moment to be steering the ship than Rock.'

For Robbie Deans, the win against France was the culmination of the work the Wallabies had done over the last three years. 'The best thing was the accumulative effect was starting to kick in,' Deans said. 'When you are on the inside you see the growth of these blokes, Rocky being one of them. You saw the accumulative effect of all the work and all of the deposits that have been made, not only by individuals, working with what they do and their combinations, but also the accumulative effect of dialogue and just coming together on one page and understanding each person's part in that, including Rocky.

'That's the benefit of touring because you get a lot of time to work on the detail and get the clarity around the understandings and to grow those qualities. What you saw in the last outing – we were running out of time because the end of the season was coming – was the culmination of that. We saw the potential of the group. A lot of these blokes are young men, but they are now starting to look … they are establishing themselves to the extent they are now looking outside of themselves and looking at what they can do and what they can offer and how they can make a difference to the people around them as opposed to just doing their thing and coping.

'Rocky is in that same space as a leader. He is now looking at how to make a difference to the people around him. The whole group is in a similar space. He obviously enjoyed the work of his team. What a captain needs more than anything is people lining up alongside him and he got the response from the group that he had been seeking.'

Rocky was the only player in the world to play every minute of every Test in 2010, a testament to his toughness, durability and indefatigability. If he was not already so, Deans was satisfied he had found the right man to lead the Wallabies into the 2011 World Cup in New Zealand. 'Just his growth,' Deans said. 'He has broadened in terms of his understanding. He had broadened in terms of his preparedness to get outside his comfort zone and take those steps.

'I've already alluded to the physical challenges he has had. If he can overcome those inhibiting physical factors he has had and hits the ground running, I think you'll see a revelation. And you saw it start to come on this tour. He played every minute of every Test this season. He earned it. It comes back to what I said earlier. If you are going to rely on someone, you need to choose wisely who you rely on.'

# 9

## ROCK OF AGES

*When you look at Rocky you can see a player that you can count on to be at his best when you really need him to be his best.*

Former Leinster coach, Michael Cheika

The night before the 15th Heineken Cup final, at a lavish dinner in the Hotel de Ville in Paris, the European Dream Team was named. It was the best XV from across European club competitions from 1995 to 2010. As you could imagine it was a star-studded line-up, including all-time greats of the game like Brian O'Driscoll (53 caps), Martin Johnson (67 caps) and Fabien Pelous (59 caps). In recognition of his one sensational season with Leinster, Rocky, with just nine caps, was named at blindside flanker, the only southern hemisphere player honoured.

'The extraordinary thing was Rocky had only played one season in the Heineken Cup,' Mick Dawson said. 'The rest were all kind of lifers — Brian O'Driscoll, Anthony Foley, Ronan O'Gara — it actually epitomised the extraordinary contribution he made to the competition that they actually put him in the team. Lawrence Dallaglio [former England captain] didn't get into the team, for example, and Rocky got in ahead of Lawrence. Lawrence could easily have been picked at 6. And he's a former Heineken Cup winner himself you know. It just shows you the contribution Rocky made. That was his legacy, you know.'

Michael Cheika believed Rocky deserved his place in the Dream Team, regardless of how long he played in Europe. 'If I was to reflect on years past and I was to pick a [Dream Team] team from it, I'd probably have to pick him in it,' Cheika said. 'So even though he only played one year, that was the only year he was in it, so he's got a 100 per cent record, hasn't he? There's something to be said for that; impact and all those types of things. I don't think it has to be based on longevity, not that I'm into those types of things to be honest.

'When you look at Rocky, you can see a player that you can count on to be at his best when you really need him to be at his best. He is definitely a player who you can count on to be at his best when you need him. You can't ask any more from a player.'

Most sports fans love nothing more than to sit down in a bar over a beer and debate questions such as would Muhammad Ali out-box Rocky Marciano or would Marciano knock out the Greatest? It is difficult to compare sportsmen and -women of different eras, some would say impossible. But it does not stop people from trying. Rocky's selection in the European Dream Team was a good point to consider where he ranks in the pantheon of Australia's, and the world's, great blindside flankers, keeping in mind his career is not over yet.

I know Rocky would not like to be compared to other blindside flankers either in Australia or internationally, contemporary or historically. Whether someone thinks Rocky was a better number 6 than so and so or what's his name would probably embarrass him or, more importantly, not really mean anything. I had a conversation with Rocky once about where he stands in the pantheon of blindside flankers so he knows my opinion, which I will share with you for what it is worth.

I attended my first rugby Test in 1975 when the Wallabies beat England 16–9 at the Sydney Cricket Ground, featuring a long-haired breakaway named Ray Price, who flung the English forwards around with his Cumberland Throw. Since then I have had the pleasure of watching some great Australian blindside flankers such as Tony Shaw, David Codey, Willie Ofahengaue, Matt Cockbain and Owen Finegan and others who played on both sides of the scrum, including Greg Cornelsen, Simon Poidevin and George Smith. In this same period there have been some great international flankers, who did not necessarily specialise on the blindside, such as Ian Kirkpatrick, Jean-Pierre Rives, John Jeffries, Michael Jones, Alan Whetton, Richard Hill, Jerry Collins, Juan Smith, Schalk Burger, Jerome Kaino and Thierry Dusautoir, but to name a few.

You could argue that any of these flankers were better than Rocky in certain aspects of play, but most of these players were really only outstanding in maybe one or two, maybe three, areas whereas Rocky can do it all — ball-running, tackling, rucking and mauling, cleaning out, lineout jumping, scrummaging, passing, ball-scavenging and ultimately leading. Rocky is a unique forward with the size and strength of a second-rower, the athleticism of a number 8, the speed and tenacity of an openside flanker and the vision of a playmaker. I will not embarrass Rocky by describing him as the best blindside flanker in modern rugby, but I think it is fair to say he is the most complete number 6 the game has ever seen, which distinguishes him from the rest, and makes him a legitimate all-time great.

Of course, Rocky still has years of top-class rugby ahead of him, whether it is with the Wallabies or back in Europe, and may not even have reached his peak yet. Who knows what new chapters of his story remain to be written? For Rocky, in many ways, the journey has just begun because he has the potential to achieve so much beyond rugby. When I think about Rocky and what he has already accomplished and what he is yet to do both on and off the field, I am reminded of Weary Dunlop, the Australian surgeon who was renowned for his leadership while being held prisoner by the Japanese in World War Two. Dunlop was the first Victorian-born player to play for the Wallabies, making his Test debut against the All Blacks in Sydney in 1932 as a number 8. You often hear people say, did you know Weary Dunlop played for the Wallabies? I wonder if people one day will ask the same question about Rocky Elsom.

# ACKNOWLEDGEMENTS

When I submitted this manuscript to my editor Kylie Mason at HarperCollins*Publishers* she gave me the wonderful feedback that I had managed to get inside Rocky's world. Anyone who knows Rocky would appreciate that this is not an easy thing to do. In fact, Rocky's world is like an impenetrable fortress: you have to find the secret door to enter. Even when you locate the door it is usually locked. That magical door was opened to me by Rocky's mother, Vicki. It is a cliché to say this book could not have been written without her, but it is true. Vicki in turn became my ally, co-conspirator, collaborator, muse and, ultimately, my friend. In many ways this is her book as much as it is mine. Of course, Rocky could have blocked my path to the door at any time but he didn't and I thank him for that.

Without the insights and observations of the people who know Rocky best I could not have captured this rare picture of him. Along with Vicki, I am indebted to Kelly and Sam Elsom, Russell Clarke, Sam McGregor, Robbie Martin, Stephen Moore, Tony McGahan, Peter Gledhill, Greg Hose, Richard Brown, Ricky Stuart, Mark Hughes, Gary Carden, Les Kiss, Bob Dwyer, Al Kanaar, Simon Poidevin, Nathan Sharpe, John Connolly, Michael Foley, Michael

Cheika, Mick Dawson, Felim O'Rourke, Robbie Deans, Evian Gordon and Angus Bathgate.

Special thanks to my publisher Jeanne Ryckmans for her continuing support and faith in me as a writer as well as her unwavering belief in Rocky's story. Kylie Mason told me she could not wait to get her teeth into the manuscript. I am happy to say she did not leave any teeth marks in a well-edited text. If a picture tells a thousand words, I was very fortunate indeed to have photographer Adam Knott's brilliant portrait of Rocky on the cover. I also received valuable assistance from Dave Gibson, Matt Green, Tom Walsh, Matt McIlraith, John Fordham, Tony Sim and Lurline Campbell.

Last, but certainly not least, I thank my wife Jenny and our daughters, Sophie and Rachel, for their love and patience.

www.ingramcontent.com/pod-product-compliance
Lightning Source LLC
Chambersburg PA
CBHW032335300426
44109CB00041B/859